Computer Science with C++

Padmaja Bhaskar

Published by

BONFRING®
Intellectual Integrity

Computer Science with C++

ISBN 978-93-86638-43-4

Author

Padmaja Bhaskar

Bonfring

309, 2nd Floor, 5th Street Extension, Gandhipuram,

Coimbatore - 641 012.

Tamilnadu, India.

E-mail: info@bonfring.org

Website: www.bonfring.org

Phone: 0422 4213231

Preface

I am pleased to place before the students the thoroughly revised copy of this book.

This book covers the entire syllabus for Computer Science with C++. Each chapter of this book contains a detailed description of the basic terminology and the conventions used in programming.

A variety of questions both solved and unsolved has been included in each of the chapter. This book includes 5 Practice papers as per the board.

I hope that the warm response of the students will continue to inspire to bring out the revised version with improved quality and examination oriented study material.

I would like to convey my heartfelt thanks to my parents, family, friends, publisher and their staff for their constant support and efforts in bringing out this book.

I am sure that after practicing this book, the level of confidence and morale of the students will help them to take the Board Exams more confidently.

The readers are requested to give their valuable suggestions.

Best of Luck to all the students!

Padmaja Bhaskar

Unit	Contents	Page No

Unit Wise Marks Distribution in QP for Last Six Years

S. No	Unit Name	Marks
1	**UNIT 1 Programming in C++**	30
2	**UNIT 2 Data Structures**	14
3	**UNIT 3 Database and SQL**	08
4	**UNIT 4 Boolean Logic**	08
5	**UNIT 5 Communication and Network Concepts**	10
	Total Marks	**70**

Weightage to different topics/content units

S.No	Topics	Marks
1	Review of C++ covered in Class XI	12
2	Object Oriented Programming in C++	12
3	Data Structure & Pointers	14
4	Data File Handling in C++	06
5	Databases and SQL	08
6	Boolean Algebra	08
7	Communication and Open Source Concepts	10
	Total	70

Weightage to different forms of questions

S.No	Forms of Questions	Marks for each question	No. of Questions	Total Marks
1	Very Short Answer questions (VSA)	01	09	09
2	Short answer questions - Type I (SA I)	02	13	26
3	Short answer questions - Type II (SA II)	03	05	15
4	Long answer questions (LA)	04	05	20
		Total	32	70

Difficulty level of questions

S.No.	Estimated difficulty level	Percentage of marks
1	Easy	15%
2	Average	70%
3	Difficult	15%

UNIT 1

PROGRAMMING IN C++

Introduction

- C++ programming language was developed by AT&T Bell Laboratories in 1979 by Bjarne Stroustrup.
- C++ is fully based on Object Oriented Technology i.e. C++ is ultimate paradigm for the modeling of information.
- C++ is the successor of C language.
- It is a case sensitive language.

Character Set- Set of valid characters which are recognized by C++compiler.

i.e Digits (0-9),

Alphabets (A-Z & a-z) and special characters + - * ,. " ' < > = { ( ]) space etc.,

i.e 256 ASCII characters.

Tokens–The Smallest individual unit of a program are known as tokens. Following are the tokens.

- **Keyword**-Reserved words having special meaning that the language cannot use as identifier.
- **Identifiers-** Names given to any variable, function, class, union etc. Naming convention (rule) for writing identifier is as under:
    1. It can contain Alphabets, digits or underscore
    2. It must be started with alphabet or underscore (_).
    3. It must not contain special characters.
    4. It cannot be a reserved word.
- **Literals-**Value of specific data type assigned to a variable or constant. Four type of Literals:
    1. Integer Literal i.e int x =10
    2. Floating point Literal i.e float x=123.45.
    3. Character Literal i.e char x= 'a', single character enclosed in single quotes.
    4. String Literal i.e cout<< "Welcome", anything enclosed in double quotes.
- **Operator** – performs some action on data.

- Arithmetic (+,-,*,/,%)
- Assignment operator (=)
- Increment / Decrement (++, --)
- Relational/comparison (<,>, <=,>=,==,!=).
- Logical (AND (&&), OR (||), NOT (!).
- Conditional (? :)

Precedence of Operators

++(post increment),--(post decrement)	High
++(pre increment),--(pre decrement),sizeof !(not),-(unary),+unary plus)	
*(multiply), / (divide), %(modulus)	
+(add),-(subtract)	
<(less than), <=(less than or equal), >(greater than), >=(greater than or equal to) ==(equal), !=(not equal)	
&& (logical AND) || (logical OR)	
?:(conditional expression)	
=(simple assignment) and other assignment operators(arithmetic assignment operator)	
, Comma operator	Low

- **Punctuation –** used as separators in c++ e.g. [{ ( ) }] , ; # = : etc

Data type- A specifier to create memory block of some specific size and type. C++offers two types of data types:

1. **Fundamental type :** Which are not composed of any other data type i.e. int, char, float and void
2. **Derived data type:** Which are made up of fundamental data type i.e array, function, class, union etc

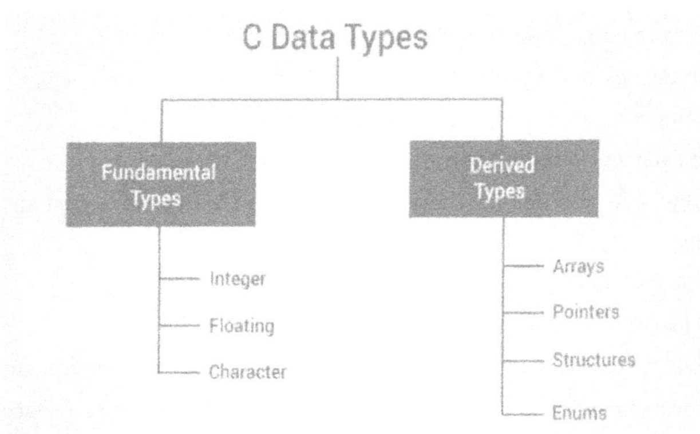

Data type conversion- Conversion of one data type into another data type. Two type of conversion.

Data Type	Memory (bytes)	Range	Format Specifier
short int	2	-32,768 to 32,767	%hd
unsigned short int	2	0 to 65,535	%hu
unsigned int	4	0 to 4,294,967,295	%u
int	4	-2,147,483,648 to 2,147,483,647	%d
long int	4	-2,147,483,648 to 2,147,483,647	%ld
unsigned long int	4	0 to 4,294,967,295	%lu
long long int	8	-(2^63) to (2^63)-1	%lld
unsigned long long int	8	0 to 18,446,744,073,709,551,615	%llu
signed char	1	-128 to 127	%c
unsigned char	1	0 to 255	%c
float	4		%f
double	8		%lf
long double	12		%Lf

1. **Implicit Conversion** – It is automatically taken care by complier in the case of lower range to higher range e.g. int x, char c='A' then x=c is valid i.e character value in c is automatically converted to integer.
2. **Explicit Conversion-** It is user-defined that forces an expression to be of specific type. E.g. double x1, x2 and int res then res=int (x1+x2).

Variable- Named storage location where value can be stored and changed during program execution. e.g. **int x, float y, float amount, char c.**

Constant- Memory block where value can be stored once but can't be changed later on during program execution. e.g. **const int pi =3.14.**

cout – It is an object of **ostream class** defined in **iostream.h** header file and used to display a value on monitor.

cin – It is an object of **istream** class defined in **iostream.h** header file and used to read value from keyboard for specific variable.

Comment - Used for better understanding of program statements and escaped by the compiler to compile. e.g. – single line (//) and multi- line (/*....*/)

Cascading – Repeatedly use of input or output operators (">>" or "<<") in one statement with cin or cout.

Control Structures

Sequence control statement(if)	conditional statement (if else)	Multiple Choice Statement If –else-if	Switch Statement (Alternate for ifelse-if) works for only exact match	loop control statement (while ,do... while, for)
Syntax	Syntax	Syntax	Syntax	Syntax

if(expression)
{
statements;
}
	If(expression)
	{
	statements;
	}
	else
	{
	statements;
	}
		If (expression)
		{
		statements
		}
		else if(expression)
		{
		statement
		}
		else
		{
		statement
		}
			switch(int / char variable)
			{ case literal1:
			[statements
			break;]
			case literal2:
			[statements,
			break;]
			default:statements;
			}
			Break is compulsory statement with every case because if it is not included then the controls executes next case statement until next break encountered or end of switch reached. Default is optional, it gets executed when no match is found
				while(expression)
				{
				statements;
				}
				Entry control loop works for true condition.
				
				do
				{
				statements;
				} while(expression);
				Exit Control Loop
				
				execute at least once if the condition is false at beginning.
				
				for loop
				for(expression1;expression2;expression3)
				{
				statement;}
				Entry control loop works for true condition and preferred for fixed no.of times.

Note: any non-zero value of an expression is treated as true and exactly 0 (i.e. all bits contain 0) is treated as false.

Nested loop -loop within loop.

exit()- Defined in process.h and used to terminate the program depending upon certain condition.

break- Exit from the current loop depending upon certain condition.

continue- to skip the remaining statements of the current loop and passes control to the next loop control statement.

goto- control is unconditionally transferred to the location of local label specified by<identifier>.

```
For example
A1:
cout<<"test";
goto A1;
```

Some Standard C++ libraries

Header File	Purpose
iostream.h	Defines stream classes for input/output streams
stdio.h	Standard input and output
ctype.h	Character tests
string.h	String operations
math.h	Mathematical functions such as sin() and cos()
stdlib.h	Utility functions such as malloc() and rand()

Some Functions

- isalpha(c) - check whether the argument is alphabetic or not.
- islower(c) - check whether the argument is lowecase or not.
- isupper(c) - check whether the argument is upercase or not.
- isdigit(c) - check whether the argument is digit or not.
- isalnum(c) - check whether the argument is alphanumeric or not.
- tolower () - converts argument in lowercase if its argument is a letter.
- toupper(c) - converts argument in uppercase if its argument is a letter.
- strcat() - concatenates two string.
- Strcmp - compare two string.
- pow(x,y) - return x raised to power y.
- sqrt(x) - return square root of x.
- random(num) - return a random number between 0 and (num-1)
- randomize( ) - initializes the random number generator with a random value.

Array- It is a collection of elements of same type that are referred by a common name.

One Dimensional Array

- An array is a continuous memory location holding similar type of data in single row or single column. Declaration in c++ is as under:

const int size =10;

int a[size] or int a[20]. The elements of array accessed with the help of an index.

For example: for (i=0;i<20;i++) cout<<a[i];

A	A[0]	A[1]	A[2]	A[3]	A[4]	A[5]	A[6]	A[7]	A[8]	A[9]

- **String (Array of characters)** –Defined in c++ as one dimensional array of characters as char s[80]= "R V Sai ram";

S	R	V		S	a	i	r	a	m	\0

Two Dimensional Array

A two dimensional array is a continuous memory location holding similar type of data arranged in a row and column format (like a matrix structure).

Declaration – int a[3][4], means 'a' is an array of integers that are arranged in 3 rows & 4 columns.

	0	1	2	3
0	A[0][0]	A[0][1]	A[0][2]	A[0][3]
1	A[1][0]	A[1][1]	A[1][2]	A[1][3]
2	A[2][0]	A[2][1]	A[2][2]	A[2][3]

Function –It is a name given to group of statements that does some specific task and may return a value. Function can be invoked (called) any no. of times and anywhere in the program.

Function prototype- Function declaration that specifies the function name, return type and parameter list of the function.

Syntax: **return_type** function_name (**type var1, type var2,...., type varn**).

Actual Parameters

Variables associated with function name during function call statement.

Formal Parameters

Variables which contains copy of actual parameters inside the function definition.

Local Variables

Declared inside the function and its scope and lifetime is within the function only and hence accessible only inside function.

Global Variables

Declared outside the function and its scope and lifetime is whole program and hence accessible to all function in the program from point declaration.

Example

```
#include <iostream.h>
int a=20; // global
void main()
{
        int b=10; // local
        cout<<a<<b;
}
```

Passing Value to Function

- **Passing by value (call by value)** - In this method separate memory is created for formal arguments and if any changes done on formal variables, it will not affect the actual variables. So actual variables are preserved in this case.
- **Passing by address/reference(call by reference)** - In this method no separate memory is created for formal variables i.e formal variables share the same location of actual variables and hence any change on formal variables automatically gets reflected back to actual variables.

Example

```
void sample( int a, int &b)
{       a=a+100;
        b=b+200;
   cout<<a<<b;
}
void main()
{       int a=50, b=40;
cout<<a<<b; // output 50 40
        sample(a,b) // output 150 240
        cout<<a<<b; // output 50 240
}
```

Function Overloading

Processing of two or more functions having same name but different list of parameters

Function Recursion

Function that calls itself either directly or indirectly.

Structure-Collection of logically related different data types (Primitive and Derived) referenced under one name.

```
e.g. struct employee
{       int empno;
        char name[30];
        char design[20];
        char department[20];
}
```

Declaration: employee e;

Input /Output: cin>>e.empno; // members are accessed using dot(.) operator.
cout<<e.empno;

Nested Structure

- A Structure definition within another structure.
- A structure containing object of another structure.

e.g.
```
struct address
{
    int houseno;
    char city[20];
    char area[20];
    long int pincode;
}
struct employee
{
    int empno;
    char name[30];
    char design[20];
    char department[20];
    address add; // nested structure
}
```

Declaration: employee e;

Input /Output: **cin>>e.add.houseno;** // members are accessed using dot(.) operator.

cout<<e.add.houseno;

#define Directives

- Use to define a constant number or macro or to replace an instruction.

1 Marks Questions

1. Which C++ header file(s) will be essentially required to be included to run /execute the following C++ code:

```
void main()
{
        char Msg[ ]="Sunset Gardens";
        for (int I=5;I<strlen(Msg);I++)     //String.h
        puts(Msg);                          // stdio.h
}
```

   Ans : stdio.h, string.h

2. Name the header files that shall be need for the following code: (CBSE 2012)

```
void main()
{
        char text[] ="Something"
        cout<<"Remaining SMS chars: "<<160-strlen(text)<<endl;  //string.h
}
```

   Ans: iostream.h, string.h

2 Marks Questions

1. Rewrite the following program after removing the syntactical error(s) if any.Underline each correction. (CBSE 2012).

```
#include<iostream.h>
Class Item
{
      long IId, Qty;
public:
      void Purchase { cin>>IId>>Qty;}
      void Sale()
      {
            cout<<setw(5)<<IId<<"Old:"<< Qty<<endl;
            cout<< "New :"<<Qty<<endl;
      } };
void main()
{
```

```
    Item I;
    Purchase();
    I.Sale()
}
```

Ans : #include<iostream.h>

```
class Item // C capital
{
long IId, Qty;
public:
void Purchase ( ) { cin>>IId>>Qty;} // ( ) after function name
void Sale( )
{
cout<<setw(5)<<IId<<"Old:"<< Qty<<endl;
cout<< "New :"<<Qty<<endl;
}};
void main()
{
Item I;
I. Purchase( ); // object missing
I.Sale( ) ; // ; is missing
}
```

2. Find the output of the following program: (CBSE 2012).

```
#include<iostream.h>
#include<ctype.h>
typedef char Str80[80];
void main()
{
    char *Notes;
    Str80 str= " vR2GooD";
    int L=6;
    Notes =Str;
    while(L>=3)
    {
        Str[L]=(isupper(Str[L])? tolower(Str[L]) : toupper(Str[L]));
```

```
                cout<<Notes<<endl;
                L--;
                Notes++; }  }
```

* consider that all required header file are included

Note (index)	L	str	Output
		vR2GooD	
0	6	vR2Good	vR2Good
1	5	vR2GoOd	R2GoOd
2	4	vR2GOOd	2GOOd
3	3	vR2gOOd	gOOd

Ans : vR2Good

R2GoOd

2GOOd

gOOd

3. Observe the following program and find out, which output(s) out id (i) to (iv) will not be expected from program? What will be the minimum and maximum value assigned to the variable Chance?

```
#include<iostream.h> CBSE 2012
#include<stdlib.h>
void main()
{
    randomize();
    int Arr[] = {9,6};, N;
    int Chance = random(2)+10;
    for(int c=0;c<2;c++)
    {
            N= random(2);
            cout<<Arr[N];
    }
}
```

i) 9#6#

ii) 19#17#

iii) 19#16#

iv) 20#16#

Ans:

The output not expected from program are (i),(ii) and (iv)

Minimum value of Chance =10

Maximum value of Chance = 11

3 Marks Questions

1. Find the output of the following program: (CBSE 2012).

```
#include<iostream.h>
class METRO
{
      int Mno, TripNo, PassengerCount;
public:
      METRO ( int Tmno=1)
      { Mno =Tmno; PassengerCount=0;}
      void Trip(int PC=20)
      { TripNo++, PassengerCount+=PC};
      void StatusShow()
      { cout<<Mno<< “:”<<TripNo<< “ :”<<PassengerCount<<endl;}
};
void main()
{
```

M			
	5	0	0
	5	**1**	**20**

```
      METRO M(5),T;
      M.Trip();
```

T			
	1	0	0
	1	**1**	**0**

```
      M.StatusShow();
      T.StatusShow();
      M.StatusShow();
}
```

Ans : 5: 1: 20

1: 1: 0

5: 1: 20

2 & 3 Marks Practice Questions

1. Rewrite the following program after removing the syntactical error(s) if any. Underline each correction.

```
#include<iostream.h>
void main( )
{
F = 10, S = 20;
test(F;S);
test(S);
}
void test(int x, int y = 20)
{ x=x+y;
count<<x>>y;
}
```

2. Rewrite the following program after removing syntactical error(s) if any. Underline each correction.

```
#include "iostream.h"
Class MEMBER
{
int Mno;
float Fees;
PUBLIC:
void Register ( ) {cin>>Mno>>Fees;}
void Display( ) {cout<<Mno<<" : "<<Fees<<endl;}
};
void main()
{ MEMBER delete;
Register();
delete.Display();
}
```

3. Find the output for the following program

```
#include<iostream.h>
#include<ctype.h>
void Encript ( char T[ ])
```

```
{
for( int i=0 ; T[i] != ' \0' ; i += 2)
if( T[i] = = 'A' || T[i] = = 'E' )
T[i] = '#' ;
else if (islower (T[i] ))
T[i] = toupper(T[i]);
else
T[i] = '@';}
void main()
{ char text [ ] = "SaVE EArTh in 2012";
encrypt(text);
cout<<text<<endl;
}
```

4. Find the output of the following program:

```
#include<iostream.h>
void main( )
{ int U=10,V=20;
for(int I=1;I<=2;I++)
{ cout<<"[1]"<<U++<<"&"<<V 5 <<endl;
cout<<"[2]"<<++V<<"&"<<U + 2 <<endl; } }
```

5. Rewrite the following C++ program after removing the syntax error(s) if any. Underline each correction. [CBSE 2010]

```
include<iostream.h>
class FLIGHT
{ Long FlightCode;
Char Description[25];
public
void addInfo()
{ cin>>FlightCode; gets(Description);}
void showInfo()
{ cout<<FlightCode<<":"<<Description<<endl;}
};
void main( )
{ FLIGHT F; addInfo.F();   showInfo.F;        }
```

6. In the following program, find the correct possible output(s)from the options

```
#include<stdlib.h>
#include<iostream.h>
void main( )
{
randomize( );
char City[ ][10]={"DEL", "CHN", "KOL", "BOM", "BNG"};
int Fly;
for(int I=0; I<3;I++)
{Fly=random(2) + 1;
cout<<City[Fly]<< ":";
}
}
```

Outputs

1. DEL : CHN : KOL: (ii) CHN: KOL : CHN:
2. KOL : BOM : BNG: (iv) KOL : CHN : KOL:

7. In the following C++ program what is the expected value of Myscore from options (i) to (iv) given below. Justify your answer.

```
#include<stdlib.h>
#include<iostream.h>
void main( )
{
 randomize( );
int Score[ ] = {25,20,34,56,72,63},Myscore;
cout<<Myscore<<endl;
}
```

(i) 25

(ii) 34

(iii) 20

(iv) Garbage Value.

Function Overloading in C++

- A function name having several definitions that are differentiable by the number or types of their arguments is known as function overloading.

Example

A same function **print()** is being used to print different data types:

```
#include <iostream.h>
class printData
{
public:
void print(int i)
{
    cout << "Printing int: " << i << endl;
}
void print(double f)
{
    cout << "Printing float: " << f << endl;
}
void print(char* c)
{
    cout << "Printing character: " << c << endl;
}
};
int main(void)
{
    printData pd;          // Call print to print integer
    pd.print(5);           // Call print to print float
    pd.print(500.263);     //// Call print to print character
    pd.print("Hello C++"); return 0;
}
```

When the above code is compiled and executed, it produces following result:

Printing int: 5

Printing float: 500.263

Printing character: Hello C++

Object Oriented Programming Concepts

Object Oriented Programming follows bottom up approach in program design and emphasizes on safety and security of data..

Features of Object Oriented Programming

Inheritance

- Inheritance is the process of forming a new class from an existing class or base class. The base class is also known as parent class or super class.
- Derived class is also known as a child class or sub class. Inheritance helps in reusability of code, thus reducing the overall size of the program.

Data Abstraction

- It refers to the act of representing essential features without including the background details. Example: For driving, only accelerator, clutch and brake controls need to be learnt rather than working of engine and other details.

Data Encapsulation

- It means wrapping up data and associated functions into one single unit called class.
- A class groups its members into three sections: public, private and protected, where private and protected members remain hidden from outside world and thereby helps in implementing data hiding.

Modularity

- The act of partitioning a complex program into simpler fragments called modules is called as modularity.
- It reduces the complexity to some degree.
- It creates a number of well-defined boundaries within the program.

Polymorphism

- Poly means many and morphs mean form, so polymorphism means one name multiple forms.
- It is the ability for a message or data to be processed in more than one form.
- C++ implements Polymorhism through Function Overloading, Operator overloading and Virtual functions.

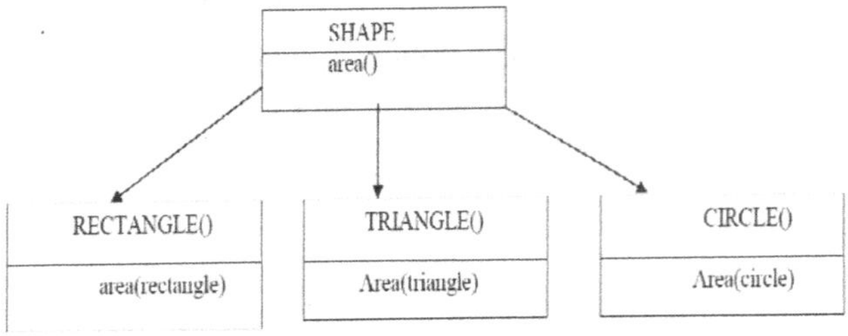

Objects and Classes

The major components of Object Oriented Programming are. **Classes & Objects**

A **Class is** a group of similar objects. **Objects** share two characteristics *state* and *behavior (data members and member functions)*

Classes in Programming

- It is a collection of variables, often of different types and its associated functions.
- Class just binds data and its associated functions under one unit there by enforcing encapsulation.
- Classes define types of data structures and the functions that operate on those data structures.
- A class defines a blueprint for a data type.

Declaration/Definition

A class definition starts with the keyword **class** followed by the class name; and the class body, enclosed by a pair of curly braces.

A class definition must be followed either by a semicolon or a list of declarations.

```
class class_name
{
access_specifier_1:
        member1;
access_specifier_2:
        member2;
...
} object_names;
```

[Note: the default access specifier is private.]

Example

```
class Box
{
        int a;
public:
        double length;      // Length of a box
        double breadth;     // Breadth of a box
        double height;      // Height of a box
} container;            // container is an object of class Box
```

Access Specifiers in Classes

Access specifiers are used to identify access rights for the data and member functions of the class. There are three main types of access specifiers in C++ programming language:

- Private.
- Public.
- Protected.

Member-Access Control

Type of Access	Meaning
Private	Class members declared as **private** can be used only by member functions and friends (classes or functions) of the class.
Protected	Class members declared as **protected** can be used by member functions and friends (classes or functions) of the class. Additionally, they can be used by classes derived from the class.
Public	Class members declared as **public** can be used by any function.

Importance of Access Specifiers

Access control helps prevent you from using objects in ways they were not intended to be used. Thus it helps in implementing data hiding and data abstraction.

Objects in C++

Objects represent instances of a class. Objects are basic run time entities in an object oriented System.

Creating Object/Defining the Object of a Class

The general syntax of defining the object of a class is:

Class_name object_name;

In C++, a class variable is known as an object. The declaration of an object is similar to that of a variable of any data type. The members of a class are accessed or referenced using object of a class.

```
Box Box1; // Declare Box1 of type Box
Box Box2; // Declare Box2 of type Box
```

Both of the objects Box1 and Box2 will have their own copy of data members.

Accessing/calling members of a class. All member of a class are private by default.

- Private member can be accessed only by the function of the class itself.
- Public member of a class can be accessed through any object of the class. They are accessed or called using object of that class with the help of dot operator (.).

The general syntax for accessing data member of a class is:-

Object_name.Data_member = value;

The general syntax for accessing member function of a class is:-

Object_name. Function_name (actual arguments);

Class methods definitions (Defining the member functions)

Member functions can be defined in two places:-

- **Outside the class definition**

The member functions of a class can be defined outside the class definitions. It is only **declared inside** the class but **defined outside** the class. The general form of member function definition outside the class definition is:

```
Return_type Class_name:: function_name (argument list)
{
        Function body
}
```

Where symbol :: is a scope resolution operator.

```
class sum
{
        int A, B, Total;
public:
        void getdata ();
        void display ();
};
```

```
void sum:: getdata () // Function definition outside class definition Use of :: operator
{
        cout<<" \ n enter the value of Aand B";
        cin>>A>>B;
}
void sum:: display () // Function definition outside class definition Use of :: operator
{
        Total =A+B;
        cout<<"\n the sum of A and B="<<Total;
}
```

- **Inside the class definition**

  The member function of a class can be declared and defined inside the class definition.

```
class sum
{
        int A, B, Total;
public:
        void getdata ()
        {
                cout< "\n enter the value of A and B";
                cin>>A>>B;
        }
        void display ()
        {
                total = A+B;
                cout<<"\n the sum of A and B="<<total;
        }
};
```

Differences between Structure and Classes in C++

Structure	Class
• Defined using struct keyword	• Defined using class keyword
• Members are public by default	• Members are private by default
• It cannot be inherited	• It can be inherited

Inline Functions

- Inline functions definition starts with keyword inline.
- The compiler replaces the function call statement with the function code. Itself (expansion) and then compiles the entire code.
- They run little faster than normal functions as function calling overheads are saved.
- A function can be declared inline by placing the keyword inline before it.

Example

```
inline void Square (int a)
{
```

In place of function call , function body is substituted because Square () is inline function

```
        cout<<a*a;
}
void main()
{.
        Square(4); { cout <<4*4;}           // { cout <<4*4;}
        Square(8) ; { cout <<8*8; }         // { cout <<8*8; }
}
```

Pass Object as an Argument

/*C++ PROGRAM TO PASS OBJECT AS AN ARGUMEMT. The program adds the two heights given in feet and inches. */

```
#include< iostream.h>
#include< conio.h>
class height
{
        int feet,inches;
public:
        void getht(int f,int i)
        {
                feet=f;
                inches=i;
        }
        void putheight()
```

```
	{
		cout< < "\nHeight is:"< < feet< < "feet\t"< < inches< < "inches"< < endl;
	}
	void sum(height a,height b)
	{
		height n;
		n.feet = a.feet + b.feet;
		n.inches = a.inches + b.inches;
		if(n.inches ==12)
		{
			n.feet++;
			n.inches = n.inches -12;
		}
		cout< < endl< < "Height is "< < n.feet< < " feet and "< < n.inches< < endl;
	}
};
void main()
{
	height h,d,a;
	clrscr();
	h.getht(6,5);
	a.getht(2,7);
	h.putheight();
	a.putheight();
	d.sum(h,a);
	getch();
}
/**********OUTPUT***********/
Height is 6feet 5inches
Height is 2feet 7inches
Height is 9 feet and 0
```

4 Marks Solved Problems

1. Define a class TAXPAYER in C++ with following description:

Private Members

- Name of type string.
- PanNo of type string.
- Taxabincm (Taxable income) of type float.
- TotTax of type double.
- A function CompTax ( ) to calculate tax according to the following slab.

Taxable Income	**Tax%**
Up to 160000	0
>160000 and <=300000	5
>300000 and <=500000	10
>500000	15

Public Members

- A parameterized constructor to initialize all the members.
- A function INTAX ( ) to enter data for the tax payer and call function CompTax ( ) to assign TotTax.
- A function OUTAX ( ) to allow user to view the content of all the data members.

Ans

```
class TAXPAYER
{
        char Name[30],PanNo[30];
        float Taxabincm;
        double TotTax;
        void CompTax()
        {
                if(Taxabincm >500000)
                        TotTax= Taxabincm*0.15;
                else if(Taxabincm>300000)
                        TotTax= Taxabincm*0.1;
                else if(Taxabincm>160000)
                        TotTax= Taxabincm*0.05;
                else
                        TotTax=0.0;
        }
```

```
public
        TAXPAYER(char nm[], char pan[], float tax, double tax) //parameterized constructor
        {
                strcpy(Name,nm);
                strcpy(PanNo,pan);
                Taxabincm=tax;
                TotTax=ttax;
        }
        void INTAX()
        {
                gets(Name);
                cin>>PanNo>>Taxabincm;
                CompTax();
        }
        void OUTAX()
        { cout<<Name<<'\n'<<PanNo<<'\n'<<Taxabincm<<'\n'<<TotTax<<endl; }
};
```

2. Define a class HOTEL in C++ with the following description

Private Members

- Rno //Data Member to store Room No
- Name //Data Member to store customer Name
- Tariff //Data Member to store per day charge
- NOD //Data Member to store Number of days
- CALC //A function to calculate and return amount as NOD*Tariff and if the value of NOD*Tariff is more than 10000 then as 1.05*NOD*Tariff

Public Members

- Checkin( ) //A function to enter the content RNo,Name, Tariff and NOD
- Checkout() //A function to display Rno, Name, Tariff, NOD and Amount (Amount to be displayed by calling function CALC( )

Solution:

```
#include<iostream.h>
class HOTEL
{
        unsigned int Rno;
        char Name[25];
```

```
        unsigned int Tariff;
        unsigned int NOD;
        int CALC( )
        {
                int x;
                x=NOD*Tariff;
                if( x>10000)
                        return(1.05*NOD*Tariff);
                else
                        return(NOD*Tariff);
        }
public:
        void Checkin()
        {
                cin>>Rno>>Name>>Tariff>>NOD;
        }
        void Checkout()
        {
                cout<<Rno<<Name<<Tariff<<NOD<<CALC();
        }
};
```

3. Define a class Applicant in C++ with following description

Private Members

- A data member ANo (Admission Number) of type long.
- A data member Name of type string.
- A data member Agg (Aggregate Marks) of type float.
- A data member Grade of type char.
- A member function GradeMe ( ) to find the Grade as per the Aggregate Marks obtained by a student. Equivalent Aggregate marks range and the respective Grades are shown as follows.

Aggregate Marks	**Grade**
> = 80	A
Less than 80 and > = 65	B
Less than 65 and > = 50	C
Less than 50	D

Public Members

- A function Enter ( ) to allow user to enter values for ANo, Name, Agg & call function GradeMe ( ) to find the Grade.
- A function Result ( ) to allow user to view the content of all the data members.

Ans

```
class Applicant
{
        long ANo;
        char Name[25];
        float Agg;
        char Grade;
        void GradeMe( )
        {
                if (Agg > = 80)
                        Grade = 'A';
               else if (Agg >= 65 && Agg < 80 )
                        Grade = 'B';
               else if (Agg >= 50 && Agg < 65 )
                        Grade = 'C';
               else
                        Grade = 'D';
        }
public:
        void Enter ( )
        {
               cout <<"\n Enter Admission No. "; cin>>ANo;
               cout <<"\n Enter Name of the Applicant "; cin.getline(Name,25);
               cout <<"\n Enter Aggregate Marks obtained by the Candidate :"; cin>>Agg;
               GradeMe( );
        }
        void Result( )
        {
               cout <<"\n Admission No. "<<ANo;
               cout <<"\n Name of the Applicant ";<<Name;
               cout<<"\n Aggregate Marks obtained by the Candidate. " << Agg;
               cout<<\n Grade Obtained is " << Grade ;
        }
};
```

4. Define a class ITEM in C++ with following description

Private Members

- Icode of type integer (Item Code).
- Item of type string (Item Name).
- Price of type Float (Price of each item).

- Qty of type integer (Quantity in stock).
- Discount of type float (Discount percentage on the item).
- A find function finddisc ( ) to calculate discount as per the following rule.

If Qty <=50	discount is 0%
If 50 < Qty <=100	discount is 5%
If Qty>100	discount is 10%

Public Members

- A function Buy ( ) to allow user to enter values for Icode, Item,Price, Qty and call function Finddisc ( ) to calculate the discount.
- A function showall ( ) to allow user to view the content of all the data members.

Ans

```
class ITEM
{       int Icode,Qty;
        char item[20];
        float price,discount;
        void finddisc();
public:
        void buy();
        void showall();
};
void stock::finddisc( )
{       if (qty<=50)
                Discount=0;
        else if (qty> 50 && qty <=100)
                Discount=0.05*price;
        else if (qty>100)
                Discount=0.10*price;
}
void stock::buy( )
{       cout<<"Item Code :";cin>>Icode;
        cout<<"Name :";gets(Item);
        cout<<"Price :";cin>>Price;
        cout<<"Quantity :";cin>>Qty;
        finddisc();
}
void TEST::DISPTEST()
{       cout<<"Item Code :";cout<<Icode;
        cout<<"Name :";cout<<Item;
        cout<<"Price :";cout<<Price;
        cout<<"Quantity :";cout<<Qty;
        cout<<"Discount :";cout<<discount; }
```

4 Marks Practice Problem

1. Q 1 Define a class employee with the following specifications (4)

Private members of class employee:

- empno integer.
- ename 20 characters.
- basic, hra, da float.
- netpay float.
- calculate() A function to calculate basic + hra + da with float return type Public member function of class employee.
- Havedata () function to accept values for empno, sname, basic, hra, da and invoke calculate () to calculate netpay.
- Dispdata () function to display all the data members on the screen.

2. Define a class Student with the following specifications : (4)

Private members:

- roll_no integer
- name 20 characters
- class 8 characters
- marks[5] integer
- percentage float
- Calculate () a function that calculates overall percentage of marks and return the percentage of marks.

public members:

- Readmarks () a function that reads marks and invoke the Calculate function.
- Displaymarks () a function that prints the marks.

3. Define a class report with the following specification : (4)

Private members:

- adno 4 digit admission number
- name 20 characters
- marks an array of 5 floating point values
- average average marks obtained
- getavg() to compute the average obtained in five subjects

Public members:

- readinfo() function to accept values for adno, name, marks, and invoke the function getavg().
- displayinfo() function to display all data members on the screen you should give function definitions.

4. Declare a class myfolder with the following specification : (4)

Private members of the class:

- Filenames – an array of strings of size [10] [25](to represent all the names of files inside myfolder).
- Availspace – long (to represent total number of bytes available in myfolder).
- Usedspace – long (to represent total number of bytes used in myfolder).

public members of the class:

- Newfileentry() – A function to accept values of Filenames, Availspace and Usedspace fromuser.
- Retavailspace() – A Fucntion that returns the value of total Kilobytes available (1 Kilobytes = 1024 bytes).
- Showfiles() – a function that displays the names of all the files in myfolder.

2 Marks Practice Problems

1. What is relation between class and object?
2. What are inline functions? Give example
3. Difference between private & public access specifiers.
4. How class implements data-hiding & encapsulation?
5. What is the difference between structure and a class?
6. How is inline function different from a normal function?

Constructors and Destructors

Constructors

A member function with the same as its class is called Constructor and it is used to initialize the object of that class with a legal initial value.

Example

```
class Student
{
        int rollno;
        float marks;
public:
        student( )                      //Constructor
        {
                rollno = 0 ;
                marks = 0.0 ;
        }
//other public members
};
```

Types of Consructors

1. *Default Constructor*

A constructor that accepts no parameter is called the Default Constructor. If you don't declare a constructor or a destructor, the compiler makes one for you. The default constructor and destructor take no arguments and do nothing.

2. *Parameterized Constructors*

A constructor that accepts parameters for its invocation is known as parameterized Constructors. It is also known as Regular Constructors.

Destructors

A destructor is also a member function whose name is the same as the class name but is preceded by tilde("~"). It is automatically executed by the compiler when an object is destroyed. Destructors are usually used to deallocate memory and do other cleanup tasks for a class object and its class members when the object is destroyed. A destructor is called for a class object when that object passes out of scope or is explicitly deleted.

Example

```
class TEST
{
        int Regno,Max,Min,Score;
Public:
        TEST( ) // Default Constructor
        {                       }
        TEST (int Pregno,int Pscore)            // Parameterized Constructor
        {
                Regno = Pregno ;Max=100;Max=100;Min=40;Score=Pscore;
        }
        ~ TEST ( )              // Destructor
        {
        Cout<<"TEST Over"<<endl;
        }
};
```

The Following Points Apply to Constructors and Destructors

- Constructors and destructors do not have return type, not even void nor can they return values.
- References and pointers cannot be used on constructors and destructors because their addresses cannot be taken.
- Constructors cannot be declared with the keyword virtual.
- Constructors and destructors cannot be declared static, const, or volatile.
- Unions cannot contain class objects that have constructors or destructors.
- The compiler automatically calls constructors when defining class objects and calls destructors when class objects go out of scope.
- Derived classes do not inherit constructors or destructors from their base classes, but they do call the constructor and destructor of base classes.
- The default destructor calls the destructors of the base class and members of the derived class.
- The destructors of base classes and members are called in the reverse order of the completion of their constructor:
- The destructor for a class object is called before destructors for members and bases are called.

Copy Constructor

A copy constructor is a special constructor in the C++ programming language used to create a new object as a copy of an existing object.

A copy constructor is a constructor of the form **classname (classname &).** The compiler will use the copy constructors whenever you initialize an instance using values of another instance of the same type. Copying of objects is achieved by the use of a copy constructor and assignment operator.

Example

```
class Sample{ int i, j;}
public:
        Sample(int a, int b) // constructor
        {  i=a;   j=b; }
        Sample (Sample & s) //copy constructor
        {
                j=s.j ; i=s.j;
                Cout <<"\n Copy constructor working \n";
        }
        void print (void)
        {cout <<i<< j<< "\n";}
};
```

Note: The argument to a copy constructor is passed by reference, the reason being that when an argument is passed by value, a copy of it is constructed. But the copy constructor is creating a copy of the object for itself, thus, it calls itself. Again the called copy constructor requires another copy so again it is called.in fact it calls itself again and again until the compiler runs out of the memory .so, in the copy constructor, the argument must be passed by reference.

The Following Cases May Result in a Call to a Copy Constructor

- **When an object is passed by value to a function**

The pass by value method requires a copy of the passed argument to be created for the function to operate upon. Thus to create the copy of the passed object, copy constructor is invoked.

If a function with the following prototype:

void cpyfunc(Sample); // Sample is a class.

Then for the following function call

cpyfunc(obj1); // obj1 is an object of Sample type.

The copy constructor would be invoked to create a copy of the obj1 object for use by cpyfunc().

- **When a function returns an object**

When an object is returned by a function the copy constructor is invoked

Sample cpyfunc(); // Sample is a class and it is return type of cpyfunc()

If func cpyfunc() is called by the following statement

obj2 = cpyfunc();

Then the copy constructor would be invoked to create a copy of the value returned by cpyfunc() and its value would be assigned to obj2. The copy constructor creates a temporary object to hold the return value of a function returning an object.

1 & 2 Marks Solved Problems

1. Answer the questions after going through the following class

```
class Exam
{
    char Subject[20] ;
    int Marks ;
public :
    Exam() // Function 1
    {
        strcpy(Subject, "Computer" ) ; Marks = 0 ;}
        Exam(char P[ ]) // Function 2
    {
        strcpy(Subject, P) ;
        Marks=0 ;
    }
    Exam(int M) // Function 3
    {
        strcpy(Subject, "Computer") ; Marks = M ;
    }
    Exam(char P[ ], int M) // Function 4
    {
```

```
            strcpy(Subject, P) ; Marks = M ;
        }
    };
```

(a) Which feature of the Object Oriented Programming is demonstrated using Function 1, Function2, Function 3 and Function 4 in the above class Exam?
Ans: Function Overloading (Constructor overloading).

(b) Write statements in C++ that would execute Function 3 and Function 4 of class Exam.
Ans: Exam a(10); and Exam b("Comp", 10).

2. Consider the following declaration

```
class welcome
{
public:
        welcome (int x, char ch); // constructor with parameter
        welcome(); // constructor without parameter
        void compute();
private:
        int x; char ch;
};
```

Which of the following are valid statements?

```
welcome obj (33, 'a9');
welcome obj1(50, '9');
welcome obj3();
obj1= welcome (45, 'T');
obj3= welcome;
```

Ans. Valid and invalid statements are

```
welcome obj (33, 'a9');     valid
welcome obj1(50, '9');      valid
welcome obj3();             invalid
obj1= welcome (45, 'T');    valid
obj3= welcome;              invalid
```

2 Marks Practice Problems

1. What do you understand by constructor and destructor functions used in classes? How are these functions different from other member functions? (2)
2. What do you understand by default constructor and copy constructor functions used in classes? How are these functions different from normal constructors? (2)
3. Given the following C++ code, answer the questions (i) & (ii). (2)

```
class TestMeOut
{
public :
        ~TestMeOut() // Function 1
        {
        cout << "Leaving the examination hall " << endl;
        }
        TestMeOut() // Function 2
        {
        cout << "Appearing for examination " << endl;
        }
        void MyWork() // Function 3
        {
        cout << "Attempting Questions " << endl;
        }
};
```

1. In Object Oriented Programming, what is Function 1 referred as and when does it get invoked/called?
2. In Object Oriented Programming, what is Function 2 referred as and when does it get invoked/called?

Inheritance

- Inheritance is the process by which new classes called *derived* classes are created from existing classes called *base* classes.
- The derived classes have all the features of the base class and the programmer can choose to add new features specific to the newly created derived class.
- The idea of inheritance implements the **IS-A** relationship. For example, mammal IS-A animal, dog IS-A mammal hence dog IS-A animal as well and so on.

Example of Single Inheritance

Consider a base class **Shape** and its derived class **Rectangle** as follow:

```
// Base class
class Shape
{
public:
        void setWidth(int w)
        {
                width = w;
        }
        void setHeight(int h)
        {
                height = h;
        }
protected:
        int width;
        int height;
};
// Derived class
class Rectangle: public Shape
{
public:
        int getArea()
        {
                return (width * height);
        }
```

```
};
int main(void)
{Rectangle Rect;
        Rect.setWidth(5);
        Rect.setHeight(7);
        // Print the area of the object.
        cout << "Total area: " << Rect.getArea() << endl;
        return 0;
}
```

When the above code is compiled and executed, it produces following result:

Total area: 35

Access Control and Inheritance

A derived class can access all the non-private members of its base class. Thus base-class members that should not be accessible to the member functions of derived classes should be declared private in the base class. We can summarize the different access types according to who can access them in the following way:

Access	public	protected	private
Same class	yes	yes	yes
Derived classes	yes	yes	no
Outside classes	yes	no	no

A derived class inherits all base class methods with the following exceptions:

- Constructors, destructors and copy constructors of the base class.
- Overloaded operators of the base class.
- The friend functions of the base class.

When deriving a class from a base class, the base class may be inherited through **public, protected** or **private** inheritance. We hardly use **protected** or **private** inheritance but **public** inheritance is commonly used. While using different type of inheritance, following rules are applied:

1. Public Inheritance: When deriving a class from a public base class:
    - **public** members of the base class become **public** members of the derived class and
    - **protected** members of the base class become **protected** members of the derived class.

- A base class's **private** members are never accessible directly from a derived class, but can be accessed through calls to the **public** and **protected** members of the base class.

2. **Protected Inheritance:** When deriving from a **protected** base class, **public** and **protected** members of the base class become **protected** members of the derived class.
3. **Private Inheritance:** When deriving from a **private** base class, **public** and **protected** members of the base class become **private** members of the derived Class.

Types of Inheritance

1. **Single class Inheritance**
   - Single inheritance is the one where you have a single base class and a single derived class.

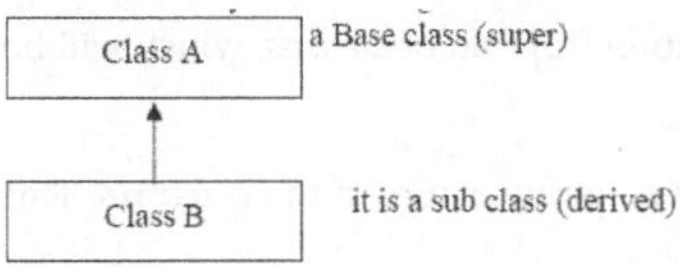

2. **Multilevel Inheritance**
   - In Multi level inheritance, a subclass inherits from a class that itself inherits from another class.

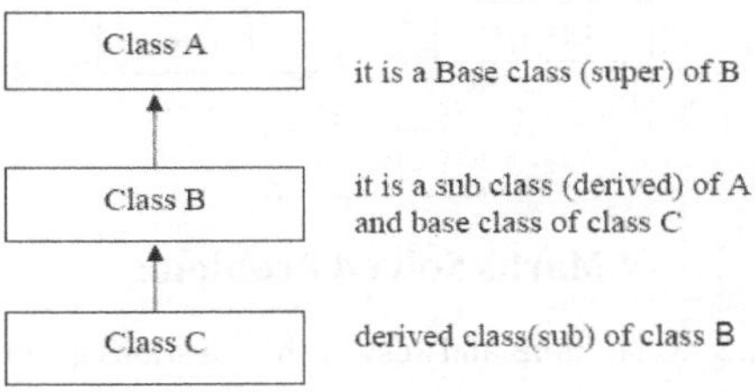

3. **Multiple Inheritance**
   - In Multiple inheritances, a derived class inherits from multiple base classes. It has properties of both the base classes.

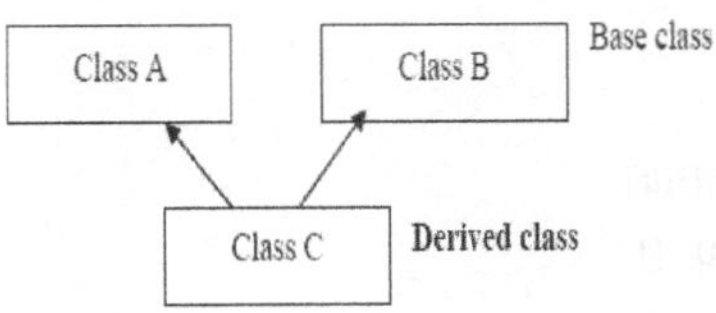

4. **Hierarchical Inheritance**

- In hierarchial Inheritance, it's like an inverted tree. So multiple classes inherit from a single base class.

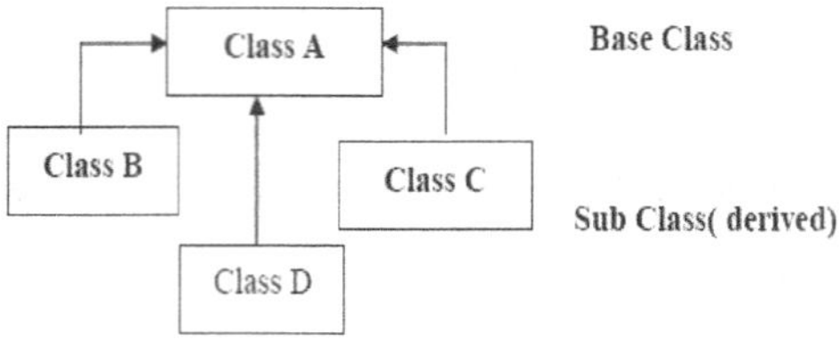

5. **Hybrid Inheritance**

- It combines two or more forms of inheritance .In this type of inheritance, we can have mixture of number of inheritances but this can generate an error of using same name function from no of classes, which will bother the compiler to how to use the functions.
- Therefore, it will generate errors in the program. This has known as ambiguity or duplicity.

Ambiguity problem can be solved by using **virtual base classes.**

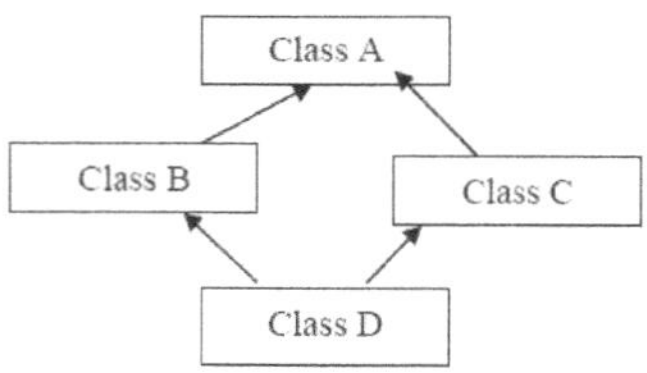

4 Marks Solved Problems

1. Consider the following declarations and answer the questions given below :

```
class WORLD
{
        int H;
protected :
        int S;
public :
        void INPUT(int);
        void OUTPUT();
```

```
};
class COUNTRY : private WORLD  // Base class WORLD & Sub class Contry
{
        int T;
protected :
        int U;
public :
        void INDATA( int, int)
        void OUTDATA();
};
class STATE : public COUNTRY   // Base Class COUNTRY & Sub Class STATE
{
        int M;
public :
        void DISPLAY (void);
};
```

1. Name the base class and derived class of the class COUNTRY.
2. Name the data member(s) that can be accessed from function DISPLAY().
3. Name the member function(s), which can be accessed from the objects of class STATE.
4. Is the member function OUTPUT() accessible by the objects of the class COUNTRY ?

Ans

1. Base class : WORLD
   Derived class: STATE
2. M.
3. DISPLAY(), INDATA() and OUTDATA()
4. No

2. Consider the following declarations and answer the questions given below :

```
class living_being
{
        char name[20];
protected:
        int jaws;
public:
```

```
        void inputdata(char, int);
        void outputdata();
}
class animal : protected living_being
{
        int tail;
protected:
        int legs;
public:
        void readdata(int, int);
        void writedata();
};
class cow : private animal
{       char horn_size;
public:
        void fetchdata(char);
        void displaydata();
};
```

1. Name the base class and derived class of the class animal.
2. Name the data member(s) that can be accessed from function displaydata.
3. Name the data member(s) that can be accessed by an object of cow class.
4. Is the member function outputdata accessible to the objects of animal class.

Ans

1. Base class : living_being

   Derived class: cow
2. horn_size, legs, jaws
3. etchdata() and displaydata()
4. No

3. Consider the following and answer the questions given below:

```
class MNC
{
        char Cname[25]; // Company name
protected :
        char Hoffice[25]; // Head office
```

```
public :
        MNC( );
        char Country[25];
        void EnterDate( );
        void DisplayData( );
};
class Branch : public MNC
{
        long NOE; // Number of employees
        char Ctry[25]; // Country
protected:
        void Association( );
public :
        Branch( );
        void Add( );
        void Show( );
};
class Outlet : public Branch
{
        char State[25];
public :
        Outlet();
        void Enter();
        void Output();
};
```

1. Which class's constructor will be called first at the time of declaration of an object of class Outlet?
2. How many bytes an object belonging to class Outlet require?
3. Name the member function(s), which are accessed from the object(s) of class Outlet.
4. Name the data member(s), which are accessible from the object(s) of class Branch.

Ans

1. class MNC
2. 129

3. void Enter(), void Output(), void Add(), void Show(), void EnterData(), void DisplayData().
4. char country[25]

4. Consider the following and answer the questions given below :

```
class CEO
{
        double Turnover;
protected :
        int Noofcomp;
public :
        CEO( );
        void INPUT( );
        void OUTPUT( );
};
class Director : public CEO
{
        int Noofemp;
public :
        Director( );
        void INDATA();
        void OUTDATA( );
protected:
        float Funda;
};
class Manager : public Director
{
        float Expense;
public :
        Manager();
        void DISPLAY(void);
};
```

1. Which constructor will be called first at the time of declaration of an object of class Manager?
2. How many bytes will an object belonging to class Manager require ?

3. Name the member function(s), which are directly accessible from the object(s) of class Manager.
4. Is the member function OUTPUT() accessible by the objects of the class Director ?

Ans

1. CEO()
2. 16
3. DISPLAY(), INDATA(), OUTDATA(), INPUT(), OUTPUT()
4. Yes

4 Marks Practice Problems

1. Consider the following declarations and answer the questions given below:

```
class vehicle
{
    int wheels;
protected:
    int passenger;
public:
    void inputdata( int, int);
    void outputdata();
};
class heavyvehicle : protected vehicle
{
    int dieselpetrol;
protected:
    int load;
public:
    void readdata( int, int);
    void writedata();
};
class bus:private heavyvehicle
{
    char marks[20];
public:
    void fetchdata(char);
    void displaydata();
```

```
};
```

1. Name the class and derived class of the class heavyvehicle.
2. Name the data members that can be accessed from function displaydata()
3. Name the data members that can be accessed by an object of bus class
4. Is the member function outputdata () accessible to the objects of heavyvehicle class.

2. Consider the following declarations and answer the questions given below:

```
class book
{
        char title[20];
        char author[20];
        int noof pages;
public:
        void read();
        void show();
};
class textbook: private textbook
{
        int noofchapters, noofassignments;
protected:
        int standard;
        void readtextbook();
        void showtextbook();
};
class physicsbook: public textbook
{
        char topic[20];
public:
        void readphysicsbook();
        void showphysicsbook();
};
```

1. Name the members, which can be accessed from the member functions of class physicsbook.
2. Name the members, which can be accessed by an object of Class textbook.
3. Name the members, which can be accessed by an object of Class physicsbook.
4. What will be the size of an object (in bytes) of class physicsbook.

3. Answer the questions (i) to (iv) based on the following

```
class CUSTOMER
{
        int Cust_no;
        char Cust_Name[20];
```

```
protected:
        void Register();
public:
        CUSTOMER( );
        void Status( );
};
class SALESMAN
{
        int Salesman_no;
        char Salesman_Name[20];
protected:
        float Salary;
public:
        SALESMAN( );
        void Enter( );
        void Show( );
};
class SHOP : private CUSTOMER, public SALESMAN
{
        char Voucher_No[10];
        char Sales_Date[8;
public :
        SHOP( );
        void Sales_Entry( );
        void Sales_Detail( );
    };
```

1. Write the names of data members, which are accessible from object belonging to class CUSTOMER.
2. Write the names of all the member functions which are accessible from object belonging to class SALESMAN.
3. Write the names of all the members which are accessible from member functions of class SHOP.
4. How many bytes will be required by an object belonging to class SHOP?

2 Marks Practice Problems

1. What is access specifier? What is its role?
2. What are the types of inheritance?
3. What is the significance of inheritance?
4. What is the difference between private and public visibility modes?

Data File Handling in C++

File: A file is a stream of bytes stored on some secondary storage devices.

- **Text file:** A text file stores information in readable and printable form. Each line of text is terminated with an **EOL** (End of Line) character.
- **Binary file:** A binary file contains information in the non-readable form i.e. in the same format in which it is held in memory.

File Stream

- **Stream:** A stream is a general term used to name flow of data. Different streams are used to represent different kinds of data flow.

There are three file I/O classes used for file read / write operations.

- **ifstream** - can be used for read operations.
- **ofstream** - can be used for write operations.
- **fstream** - can be used for both read & write operations.

- **fstream.h**:-This header file includes the definitions for the stream classes ifstream, ofstream and fstream. In C++ **file input output** facilities implemented through **fstream.h** header file.

It contain predefines set of operation for handling file related input and output, fstream class ties a file to the program for input and output operation.

A File Can Be Opened Using

- **By the constructor method**. This will use default streams for file input or output. This method is preferred when file is opened in input or output mode only.

Example: **ofstream file ("student.dat"); or ifstream file ("student.dat");**

- **By the open() member function** of the stream. It will preferred when file is opened in various modes i.e **ios::in, ios::out, ios::app, ios::ate** etc.

e.g **fstream file;**

file.open("book.dat", ios::in | ios::out | ios::binary);

File Modes

Open Mode	Description
ios::out	It open file in output mode (i.e write mode) and place the file pointer in beginning, if file already exist it will overwrite the file.
ios::in	It open file in input mode (read mode) and permit reading from the file.
ios::app	It opens the file in write mode, and place file pointer at the end of file
ios::ate	It open the file in write or read mode, and place file pointer at the end of file
ios::trunc	It truncates the existing file (empties the file).
ios::nocreate	If file does not exist this file mode ensures that no file is created and open() fails.
ios::noreplace	If file does not exist, a new file gets created but if the file already exists, the open() fails.
ios::binary	Opens a file in binary mode

eof( ): This function determines the end-of-file by returning true(non-zero) for end of file otherwise returning false(zero).

close(): This function terminates the connection between the file and stream associated with it.

Stream_object.close();

e.g file.close();

Text File Functions

Char I/O

- **get()** - read a single character from text file and store in a buffer. e.g **file.get(ch);**
- **put()** - writing a single character in textfile e.g. **file.put(ch);**
- **getline()** - read a line of text from text file store in a buffer. e.g **file.getline(s,80);**
- We can also use **file>>ch** for reading and **file<<ch** writing in text file.

Binary File Functions

- **read()**- reads a block of binary data or reads a fixed number of bytes from the specified stream and stores it in a buffer.

Syntax: Stream_object.read ((char *)& Object, sizeof (Object)) ;

e.g file.read ((char *)&s, sizeof(s)) ;

- **write()** - writes a block of binary data or writes fixed number of bytes from a specific memory location to the specified stream.

Syntax: Stream_object.write((char *)& Object, sizeof(Object));

e.g file.write ((char *)&s, sizeof(s));

Note: Both functions take two arguments, **Initial address** and **length of the variable**

File Pointer: The file pointer indicates the position in the file at which the next input/output is to occur. There **read pointer** and **write pointer** associated with a file.

Moving the file pointer in a file for various operations viz modification, deletion, searching etc. Following functions are used:

- **seekg():** It places the file pointer to the specified position in input mode of file.

e.g file.seekg(p,ios::beg); or file.seekg(-p,ios::end), or file.seekg(p,ios::cur)

i.e to move to **p** byte position from beginning, end or current position.

- **seekp():** It places the file pointer to the specified position in output mode of file.

e.g file.seekp(p,ios::beg); or file.seekp(-p,ios::end), or file.seekp(p,ios::cur)

i.e to move to **p** byte position from beginning, end or current position.

- **tellg():** This function returns the current working position of the file pointer in the input mode.

e.g int p=file.tellg( );

- **tellp():** This function returns the current working position of the file pointer in the output mode.

e.f int p=file.tellp( );

Steps To Create a File

- Declare an object of the desired file stream class (ifstream, ofstream, or fstream).
- Open the required file to be processed using constructor or open function.
- Process the file.
- Close the file stream using the object of file stream.

General Program Structure Used for Creating a Text File

To Create a Text File Using strings I/O

```
#include<fstream.h> //header file for file operations
	void main()
	{
	char s[80], ch;
	ofstream file("myfile.txt"); //open myfile.txt in default output mode
	do
	{
	cout<<"\n enter line of text";
	gets(s); //standard input
	file<<s; // write in a file myfile.txt
	cout<<"\n more input y/n";
	cin>>ch;
	}while( ch != 'n' || ch != 'N' ) ;
	file.close();
	} //end of main
```

To Create a Text File Using Characters I/O

```
	#include<fstream.h> //header file for file operations
	void main()
	{
	char ch;
```

```
ofstream file("myfile.txt"); //open myfile.txt in default output mode
do{
ch=getche();
if (ch==13) //check if character is enter key
cout<<'\n';
else
file<<ch; // write a character in text file 'myfile.txt '
} while(ch!=27); // check for escape key
file.close();
} //end of main
```

Text Files in Input Mode

To read content of 'myfile.txt' and display it on monitor.

```
#include<fstream.h> //header file for file operations
void main()
{
    char ch;
    ifstream file("myfile.txt"); //open myfile.txt in default input mode
    while(file)
    {
    file.get(ch) // read a character from text file ' myfile.txt'
    cout<<ch; // write a character in text file 'myfile.txt '
    }
    file.close();
} //end of main
```

2 Marks Questions

1. Write a function in a C++ to read the content of a text file "DELHI.TXT" and display all those lines on screen, which are either starting with 'D' or starting with 'M'. [CBSE 2012]

```
void DispDorM()
{
ifstream File("DELHI.TXT")
char str[80];
while(File.getline(str,80))
{
```

```
if(str[0] = ='D' || str[0] = ='M')
cout<<str<<endl;
}
File.close(); //Ignore
}
```

2. Write a function in a C++ to count the number of lowercase alphabets present in a text file "BOOK.txt".

```
int countalpha()
{
    ifstream Fin("BOOK.txt");
    char ch;
    int count=0;
    while(!Fin.eof())
    {
    Fin.get(ch);
    if (islower(ch))
    count++;
    }
    Fin.close();
    return count;
}
```

3. Function to calculate the average word size of a text file.

```
void calculate()
{
    fstream File;
    File.open("book.txt",ios::in);
    char a[20];
    char ch;
    int i=0,sum=0,n=0;
    while(File)
    {
```

```
        File.get(ch);
        a[i]=ch;
        i++;
        if((ch==' ') || ch(== '.')||(char==',')(ch=='\t')||(ch=='\n')
        {
        i --;
        sum=sum +i;
        i=0; N++;
        }
        }
        cout<<"average word size is "<<(sum/n);
    }
```

4. Assume a text file "coordinate.txt" is already created. Using this file create a C++ function to count the number of words having first character capital.

```
    int countword()
    {
        ifstream Fin("BOOK.txt");
        char ch[25];
        int count=0;
        while(!Fin.eof())
        {
        Fin>>ch;
        if (isupper(ch[0]))
        count++;
        }
        Fin.close();
        return count;
    }
```

5. Function to count number of lines from a text files (a line can have maximum 70 characters or ends at '.')

```
    int countword()
    {
```

```
ifstream Fin("BOOK.txt");
char ch[70];
int count=0;
if (!Fin)
{
cout<<"Error opening file!" ;
exit(0);
}
while(1)
{
Fin.getline(ch,70,'.');
if (Fin.eof())
break;
count++;
}
Fin.close();
return count;
}
```

2/3 Marks Practice Questions

1. Write a function in C++ to count the number of uppercase alphabets present in a text file "BOOK.txt"
2. Write a function in C++ to count the number of alphabets present in a text file "BOOK.txt"
3. Write a function in C++ to count the number of digits present in a text file "BOOK.txt"
4. Write a function in C++ to count the number of white spaces present in a text file "BOOK.txt"
5. Write a function in C++ to count the number of vowels present in a text file "BOOK.txt"
6. Assume a text file "Test.txt" is already created. Using this file, write a function to create three files "LOWER.TXT" which contains all the lowercase vowels and "UPPER.TXT" which contains all the uppercase vowels and "DIGIT.TXT" which contains all digits.

General Program Structure Used for Operating a Binary File

1. Program to create a binary file 'student.dat' using structure.

```
#include<fstream.h>

struct student

{

        char name[15];

        float percent;

};

void main()

{

        ofstream fout;  // f out is output file stream it will open file in write mode

        char ch;

        fout.open("student.dat", ios::out | ios:: binary); // student.dat will be opened in

                                                            // binary Mode

        clrscr();

        student s;      //s is a variable of type student that contains name & percent

        do

        {  // inputting data to record  s

        cout<<"\n enter name of student";

        gets(s);

        cout<<"\n enter persentage";

        cin>>percent;

        //Writing contents of s to file student.dat

        fout.write ( ( char * ) &s, sizeof ( s ) ) ;

        cout<<"\n more record y/n";

        cin>>ch;
```

```
}while(ch!='n' || ch!='N') ;

fout.close();

}
```

2. Program to read a binary file 'student.dat' display records on monitor.

```
#include<fstream.h>

struct student

{

char name[15];

float percent;

};

void main()

{

ifstream fin;        //fin is an input file stream that can open a file in read mode

student s;// s is a record of type student

fin.open("student.dat",ios::in | ios:: binary); // opening student.dat in binary mode

fin.read((char *) &s, sizeof(student)); //read a record from file 'student.dat' invariable s

while(file) // file will read until end of file does not come.

{

 //Displaying the content of s (reord) read from the student.dat

 cout<<s.name;

 cout<<"\n has the percent: "<<s.percent;

 fin.read((char *) &s, sizeof(student)); // reading the next record

}

fin.close();

}
```

Binary File Using Objects and other File Operations

1. Consider the following class declaration then write c++ function for following file operations viz create_file, read_file, add new records, modify record, delete a record, search for a record.

```
#include<iostream.h>
class student
{
int rno;
char name[30];
int age;
public:
void input( ) // function to input values for data member of current object
{
cout<<"\n enter roll no";
cin>>rno;
cout<<"\n enter name ";
gets(name);
cout<<"\n enter age";
cin>>age;
}
void output( )     // function to display contents of current object
{
cout<< "\n roll no:"<<rno;
cout<< "\n name :"<<name;
cout<< "\n age:"<<age;
}
int getrno( )      // function to get  the rno from current object
{
return rno;
}
};
```

```
void create_file( ) // function to create a blank file student.dat
{
ofstream fout;    // fout is output file stream object that will open a file in write mode
 fout.open("student", ios::out | ios:: binary); // opening file in binary mode
 fout.close();     // closing file student.dat
}
void read_file( )  //function to read records from student.dat one by into record s
{
 ifstream fin;
 student s;
 fin.open("student.dat",ios::in | ios:: binary); //opening the file
 fin.read((char *) &s,sizeof(student)); //reading first record from file to record s
 while(file)
  {
   s.output(); // displaying the content of object s (record)
   cout<< "\n";
   fin.read ( ( char * ) & s,sizeof ( student ) ) ; // reading next record
}
fin.close();
}
void modify_record()
{
student s;
fstream file;
file.open("student.dat",ios::in|ios::out|ios::ate|ios::binary); // opening student.dat in read & //write binary mode
 int r, pos = -1, f=0;
 cout<<"\n enter the rollo no of student whom data to be modified";
 cin>>r ;
 //Searching the record with rno = r
```

```
file.read( ( char * )&s, sizeof( s ) ) ;
while(file)
{
if (r == s.getrno( )) // will be true if required record found (rno = r)
{
f=1;      // f = 1 indicate record found
cout<<"\n record is ";
s.output();
pos =file.tellg()-size(s); //moving the write pointer one record back
break;
}
file.read((char *)&s,sizeof(s)); // writing the modified record to the file
}
if(f == 0 )        // f==0 indicate record did not found
cout<< "\n record not exist";
}
void delete_record()
{
fstream file("student.dat", ios::in|ios::binary);
fstream newfile("newstu.dat",ios::out|ios::binary);
student s;
cout<<"\n enter the rollno no of student whom record to be deleted";
cin>>r;
file.read ( (char *)&s, sizeof( s ) ) ;
while(file)
{
if (r!=s.getrno())
{
newfile.write((char *)&s,sizeof(s));
```

```
}
file.read((char *)&s,sizeof(s));
}
file.close();
newfile.close();
}
void search_record()
{
student s;
fstream file;
file.open("student.dat",ios::in|os::binary);
int r,flag = 0;
cout<<"\n enter the rollo no of student whom record to be searched";
cin>>r;
file.read( ( char * )&s, sizeof( s ) ) ;
while(file)
{
if (r==s.getrno())
{ cout<<"\n record is ";
s.output();
flag=1;
break;
}
file.read((char *)&s,sizeof(s));
}
if(flag==0)
cout<< "\n search unsuccessfull";
file.close();
}
```

1 Mark Questions

1. Observe the program segment carefully and answer the question that follows:

```
class stock
{
int Ino, Qty; Char Item[20];
public:
void Enter() { cin>>Ino; gets(Item); cin>>Qty;}
void issue(int Q) { Qty+=0;}
void Purchase(int Q) {Qty-=Q;}
int GetIno() { return Ino;}
};
void PurchaseItem(int Pino, int PQty)
{
fstream File;
47
File.open("stock.dat", ios::binary|ios::in|ios::out);
Stock s;
int success=0;
while(success= = 0 && File.read((char *)&s,sizeof(s)))
{
If(Pino= = ss.GetIno())
{
s.Purchase(PQty);
___________________ // statement 1
___________________ // statement 2
Success++;
}
}
if (success = =1)
cout<< "Purchase Updated"<<endl;
else
cout<< "Wrong Item No"<<endl;
File.close() ;
}
```

Ans.1.

i. Statement 1 to position the file pointer to the appropriate place so that the data updation is done for the required item.

```
File.seekp( File.tellg( ) - sizeof(stock);
                OR
File.seekp(-sizeof(stock),ios::cur);
```

ii. Staement 2 to perform write operation so that the updation is done in the binary file.

```
File.write((char *)&s, sizeof(s));
                OR
File.write((char *)&s, sizeof(stock));
```

3 Marks Question

1. Write a function in c++ to search for details (Phoneno and Calls) of those Phones which have more than 800 calls from binary file "phones.dat". Assuming that this binary file contains records/ objects of class Phone, which is defined below.

class Phone **CBSE 2012**

```
{
Char Phoneno[10]; int Calls;
public:
void Get() {gets(Phoneno); cin>>Calls;}
void Billing() { cout<<Phoneno<< "#"<<Calls<<endl;}
int GetCalls() {return Calls;}
};
```

Ans 1

```
void Search()
{
Phone P;
fstream fin;
fin.open( "Phone.dat", ios::binary| ios::in);
while(fin.read((char *)&P, sizeof(P)))
{
if(p.GetCalls() >800)
p.Billing();
}
Fin.close(); //ignore
}
};
```

2. Write a function in C++ to add new objects at the bottom of a binary file "STUDENT.DAT", assuming the binary file is containing the objects of the following class.

```
class STUD
{
int Rno;
char Name[20];
public:
void Enter()
{
cin>>Rno;gets(Name);
}
void Display()
{
cout<<Rno<<Name<<endl;
}
};
```

Ans 2

```
void searchbook(int bookno)
{
ifstream ifile("BOOK.DAT",ios::in|ios::binary);
if(!ifile)
{
cout<<"could not open BOOK.DAT file"; exit(-1);}
else
{
BOOK b; int found=0;
while(ifile.read((char *)&b, sizeof(b)))
{
if(b.RBno()==bookno)
{
b.Display(); found=1; break;
}
}
if(! found)
cout<<"record is not found ";
```

```
ifile.close();
}
}
```

3. Given a binary file PHONE.DAT, containing records of the following class type

```
class Phonlist
{
char name[20];
char address[30];
char areacode[5];
char Phoneno[15];
public:
void Register()
void Show();
void CheckCode(char AC[])
{
return(strcmp(areacode,AC);
}
};
```

Write a function TRANSFER( ) in C++, that would copy all those records which are having areacode as "DEL" from PHONE.DAT to PHONBACK.DAT.

Ans 3

```
void TRANSFER()
{
fstream File1,File2;
Phonelist P;
File1.open("PHONE.DAT", ios::binary|ios::in);
File2.open("PHONEBACK.DAT", ios::binary|ios::OUT)
while(File1.read((char *)&P, sizeof(P)))
{
if( p.CheckCode( "DEL"))
File2.write((char *)&P,sizeof(P));
}
File1.close();
File2.close();
}
```

Pointers

Pointer is a variable that holds a memory address of another variable of same type.

- It supports dynamic allocation routines.

C++Memory Map

- Program Code: It holds the compiled code of the program.
- Global Variables: They remain in the memory as long as program continues.
- Stack: It is used for holding return addresses at function calls, arguments passed to the functions, local variables for functions. It also stores the current state of the CPU.
- Heap: It is a region of free memory from which chunks of memory are allocated via DMA functions.

StaticMemory Allocation: Allocation of memory at compile time.

e.g. int a; // This will allocate 2 bytes for a during compilation.

Dynamic Memory Allocation: allocation of memory at run time using operator **new and delete**.

e.g int x =new int; **// dynamic allocation**

float y= new float;

delete x; **//dynamic deallocation**

delete y;

Free Store : It is a pool of unallocated heap memory given to a program that is used by the program for dynamic memory allocation during execution.

Declaration and Initialization of Pointers

Syntax : Datatype *variable_name;

```
int *p;       // p is an integer pointer contains address of an integer variable
float *p1;    // p1 is a float pointer contains address of a floating point variable
char *c;      // c is a character pointer contains address of a character variable
int a = 10;   // a is an integer variable hold value 10
int *p = &a;  //pointer initialization [ p is a integer pointer  holds address of a]
              // &a means address of a
```

Pointer Arithmetic

Two arithmetic operations, addition and subtraction, may be performed on pointers.

Adding 1 to a pointer actually adds the size of pointer's base type.

Base address: The address of the first byte is known as BASE ADDRESS.

Dynamic Allocation Operators

int * p = new int[10]; this will dynamically allocate 20 bytes (10*2) to integer pointer p.

Two Dimensional Arrays

```
int *arr, r, c;
r = 5; c = 5;
arr = new int [r * c];
```

Now to read the element of array, we can use the following loops :

```
For (int i = 0; i < r; i++)
{
        cout << "\n Enter element in row " << i + 1 << " : ";
        For (int j=0; j < c; j++)
                cin >> arr [ i * c + j];
}
```

Memory Released with Delete as below

```
delete arr;
```

Pointers and Arrays

Array of Pointers

To declare an array holding 5 int pointers

```
int * ip[5];
```

That would be allocated for 5 pointers that can point to integers.

ip[0] = &a;   ip[1] = &b;   ip[2] = &c;   ip[3] = &d;   ip[4] = &e;

ip	Address of a	Address of b	Address of c	Address of d	Address of e

Pointers and Strings

Pointer is very useful to handle the character array also. E.g :

```
void main()
{
        char str[ ] = "computer";
        char *cp;
        cp = str;           // cp will hold address of first element of array str
        cout<<str ;         //display string
        cout<<cp;           // display string
        for (cp =str; *cp != '\0'; cp++) // display character by character by character
        cout << "--"<<*cp;
}
```

Output

Computer

Computer

--c--o--m--p--u--t--e—r

Pointers and CONST

A **constant pointer** means that the pointer in consideration will always point to the same address. Its address cannot be modified.

Int n = 20;

int * const c = &n; // a constant pointer c to an integer n

A **pointer to a constant** refers to a pointer which is pointing to a symbolic constant.

const int b = 10; // a constant integer b

const int *pc = &b; // a pointer to a constant integer b

Pointers and Functions

Invoking Function by Passing the Pointers

When the pointers are passed to the function, the addresses of actual arguments in the calling function are copied into formal arguments of the called function.

```
#include<iostream.h>
void swap(int *m, int *n)
{
        int temp;
        temp = *m;
        *m = *n;
        *n = temp;
}
void main()
{
        void swap(int *m, int *n);
        int a = 5, b = 6;
        cout << "\n Value of a :" << a << " and b :" << b;
        swap(&a, &b);
        cout << "\n After swapping value of a :" << a << "and b :" << b;
}
```

Input: Value of a : 5 and b : 6

After swapping value of a : 6 and b : 5

Function Returning Pointers

A function can also returns a pointer.

Syntax: type * function-name (argument list);

```
#include <iostream.h>
int *min(int &x, int &y) // function returning int pointer
{
if (x < y )
        return (&x);
else
        return (&y)
}
void main()
{
        int a, b, *c;
        cout << "\nEnter a :"; cin >> a;
        cout << "\nEnter b :"; cint >> b;
        c = min(a, b); // pointer returned from the function min will be assigned to pointer
        variable c
        cout << "\n The minimum no is :" << *c;
}
```

Dynamic Structures

- **Dynamic allocation**

  The new operator can be used to create dynamic structures also.

  ```
  struct student
  {
          int rno;
          char name[20];
  };
  student *s = new student;
  ```

  To access structure member through structure pointer we use **arrow operator**(->).

  ```
  cout << s -> rno;
  cout << s -> name
  ```

- **Dynamic deallocation**

A dynamic structure can be released using the deallocation operator **delete** as shown below:

delete stu;

this Pointer : refers to the address of current object.

Solved Questions

1. How is *p different from **p?

Ans: *p means, it is a pointer pointing to a memory location storing a value in it. But **p means, it is a pointer pointing to another pointer which in turn points to a memory location storing a value in it.

2. How is &p different from *p?

Ans: &p gives us the address of variable p and *p. dereferences p and gives us the value stored in memory location pointed to by p.

3. Find the error in following code segment.

```
Float **p1, p2;

P2 = &p1;
```

Ans: In code segment, p1 is pointer to pointer, it means it can store the address of another pointer variable, whereas p2 is a simple pointer that can store the address of a normal variable. So here the statement p2 = &p1 has error.

4. What will be the output of the following code segment?

```
char C1 = 'A';

char C2 = 'D';

char *i, *j;

i = &C1;

j = &C2;

*i = j;

cout << C1;
```

Ans : It will print A.

5. How does C++ organize memory when a program is run?

   Ans: Once a program is compiled, C++ creates four logically distinct regions of memory:

   - area to hold the compiled program code.
   - area to hold global variables.
   - the stack area to hold the return addresses of function calls, arguments passed to the functions, local variables for functions, and the current state of the CPU.
   - The heap area from which the memory is dynamically allocated to the program.

6. Identify and explain the error(s) in the following code segment

```
float a[] = { 11.02, 12.13, 19.11, 17.41};

float *j, *k;

j = a;

k = a + 4;

j = j * 2;

k = k / 2;

cout << " *j = " << *j << ", *k = " << *k << "\n";
```

   Ans : The erroneous statements in the code are :

```
j = j * 2;
k = k / 2;
```

Because multiplication and division operations cannot be performed on pointer and j and k are pointers.

7. How does the functioning of a function differ when

   1. an object is passed by value ?
   2. an object is passed by reference ?

   Ans :

   1. When an object is passed by value, the called function creates its own copy of theobject by just copying the contents of the passed object. It invokes the object's copy constructor to create its copy of the object. However, the called function destroys its copy of the object by calling the destructor function of the object upon its termination.
   2. When an object is passed by reference, the called function does not create its own copy of the passed object. Rather it refers to the original object using its reference or alias name. Therefore, neither constructor nor destructor function of the object is invoked in such a case.

2 Marks Practice Questions

1. Differentiate between static and dynamic allocation of memory.
2. Identify and explain the error in the following program :

```
#include<iostream.h>
int main()
{
int x[] = { 1, 2, 3, 4, 5
};
for (int i = 0; i < 5; i++)
{
        cout << *x;
        x++;
} return 0;
}
```

3. Give the output of the following :

```
char *s = "computer";
for (int x = strlen(s) – 1; x >= 0; x--)
{
for(int y =0; y <= x; y++) cout << s[y];
cout << endl;
}
```

4. Identify the syntax error(s), if any, in the following program. Also give reason for errors.

```
void main()
{const int i = 20;
const int * const ptr = &i;
(
*ptr++; int j= 15; ptr= &j;
}
```

5. What is 'this' pointer? What is its significance?
6. What will be the output of following program ?

```
#include<iostream.h>
void main()
{
char name1[] = "ankur"; char
```

```
name2[] = "ankur"; if (name1 !=name2)
cout << "\n both the strings are not equal";
else
cout << "\n the strings are equal"; }
```

7. Give and explain the output of the following code:

```
void junk (int, int *);
int main()
{
int i = 6, j = -4;
junk (i, &j);
cout << "i = " << i << ", j = " << j << "\n";
return 0;
}
void junk(int a, int *b)
{
a = a* a;
*b = *b * *b;
}
```

UNIT 2

DATA STRUCTURES

A **data structure** is a particular way of storing and organizing data in a computer so that it can be used efficiently. The data structure can be classified into following two types:

- **Simple Data Structure:** These data structures are normally built from primitive data types like integers, floats, characters. For example arrays and structure.
- **Compound Data Structure:** simple data structures can be combined in various ways to form more complex structure called compound structures. Linked Lists, Stack, Queues and Trees are examples of compound data structure.

Data Structure Arrays

Data structure array is defined as linear sequence of finite number of objects of same type with following set of operation:

- Creating: defining an array of required size.
- Insertion: addition of a new data element in the in the array.
- Deletion: removal of a data element from the array.
- Searching: searching for the specified data from the array.
- Traversing: processing all the data elements of the array.
- Sorting: arranging data elements of the array in increasing or decreasing order
- Merging: combining elements of two similar types of arrays to form a new array of same type.

In C++ an array can be defined as

Datatype arrayname [size];

Where size defines the maximum number of elements can be hold in the array.

For example

```
float b[10]; //b is an array which can store maximum 10 float values
int c[5]; //c is an array which can store maximum 5 integer values
```

Array Initialization

```
void main()
{
int b[10]={3,5,7,8,9};                // array initialization
cout<<b[4]<<endl;
cout<<b[5]<<endl;
```

```
}
```

Output is

```
9
0
```

Searching

We can use two different search algorithms for searching a specific data from an array

- Linear search algorithm.
- Binary search algorithm.

Linear Search Algorithm

In Linear search, each element of the array is compared with the given item to be searched for. This method continues until the searched item is found or the last item is compared.

```
#include<iostream.h>
int linear_search(int a[], int size, int item)
{
        int i=0;
        while(( i<size) && (a[i] !=item))
                i++;
        if(i<size)
                return ( i); //returns the index number of the item in the array
        else
                return (-1);  //given item is not present in the array so it returns -1
                              //since -1 is not a legal index number
}
void main()
{
        int b[8]={2,4,5,7,8,9,12,15},size=8;
        int item;
        cout<<"enter a number to be searched for";
        cin>>item;
        int p = linear_search(b, size, item); //search item in the array b
        if(p == -1)
                cout<<item<<" is not present in the array"<<endl;
        else
                cout<<item <<" is present in the array at index no "<<p;
}
```

Binary Search Algorithm

Binary search algorithm is applicable for already sorted array only. In this algorithm, to search for the given item from the sorted array (in ascending order)

- The item is compared with the middle element of the array. If the middle element is equal to the item then index of the middle element is returned
- If item is less than the middle item then the item will be searched in first half segment of the array for the next iteration.
- If the item is larger than the middle element then the item will be searched in second half of the array for the next iteration
- The same process continues until either the item is found or the segment is reduced to the single element and still the item is not found (search unsuccessful).

```
#include<iostream.h>
int binary_search(int a[ ], int size, int item)
{
int first = 0, last = size-1, middle;
while(first<=last)
{
        Middle = ( first + last ) / 2;
        if( item = = a[middle])
        return middle;      // item is found
        else if(item< a[middle])
        last=middle-1; //item is present in left side of the middle element
        else
        first=middle+1; // item is present in right side of the middle element
}
        return -1; //given item is not present in the array, here, -1 indicates
        unsuccessful search
}
void main()
{
        int b[8]={2,4,5,7,8,9,12,15},size=8;
        int item;
        cout<<"enter a number to be searched for";
        cin>>item;
```

```
            int p=binary_search(b, size, item); //search item in the array b
            if(p = = -1)
                        cout<<item<<" is not present in the array"<<endl;
            else
                        cout<<item <<" is present in the array at index no "<<p;
    }
```

Steps to find item 12 in the array b.

First	Last	middle	B[middle] = item	comment
Item 12 will be search in array b {2,4,5,7,9,12,15}				
0	6	6/2 = 3	b[3] = 7	Item not found , item 12 is greater than 7
Item 12 will be search in second segment array b {9,12,15}				
4	7	11/2 = 5	b[5] = 9	Item not found, 12 is greater than 9
Now Item will be searched 2nd half of previous segment b{12,15}				
6	7	13/2 = 6	B[6]=12	Item found & function will return 6 (position of item in array b
*if first > last, the function will return -1 (item not found)				

Output

12 is present in the array at index no 6

Inserting a New Element in an Array

We can insert a new element in an array in two ways.

- If the array is unordered, the new element is inserted at the end of the array
- If the array is sorted then the new element is added at appropriate position without altering the order.

  To achieve this, all elements greater than the new element are shifted. For example, to add 10 in the given array below:

a[0]	a[1]	[2]	a[3]	a[4]	a[5]	a[6]	a[7]	a[8]
2	4	5	7	8	11	12	15	

Original array

a[0]	a[1]	[2]	a[3]	a[4]	a[5]	a[6]	a[7]	a[8]
2	4	5	7	8		11	12	15

Elements greater than 10 shifted to create free place to insert 10

a[0]	a[1]	[2]	a[3]	a[4]	a[5]	a[6]	a[7]	a[8]
2	4	5	7	8	10	11	12	15

Array after insertion

Following program implement insertion operation for sorted array.

```
#include<iostream.h>
void insert(int a[ ], int &n, int item) //n is the number of elements already present in
the array
{
int i=n-1;
while ((i>=0) &&(a[i]>item))
{
 a[i+1]=a[i]; // shift the ith element one position towards right
 i--;
}
a[i+1]=item; //insertion of item at appropriate place
n++; //after insertion, number of elements present in the array is increased by 1
}
void main()
{
int a[10]={2,4,5,7,8,11,12,15},n=8;
int i=0;

cout<<"Original array is:\n";      // displaying original array
for(i=0;i<n;i++)
 cout<<a[i]<<", ";
insert(a,n,10);                    // inserting new element
cout<<"\nArray after inserting 10 is:\n"; // displaying array after insertion
for(i=0; i<n; i++)
 cout<<a[i]<<", ";
```

```
}
Output is
Original array is:
2, 4, 5, 7, 8, 11, 12, 15
Array after inserting 10 is:
2, 4, 5, 7, 8, 10, 11, 12, 15
```

Deletion of an Item from a Sorted Array

In this algorithm the item to be deleted from the sorted array is searched and if the item is found in the array then the element is removed and the rest of the elements are shifted one position toward left in the array to keep the ordered array undisturbed. Deletion operation reduces the number of elements present in the array by1. For example, to remove 11 from the given array below:

a[0]	a[1]	[2]	a[3]	a[4]	a[5]	a[6]	a[7]
2	4	5	7	8	11	12	15

Original array

a[0]	a[1]	[2]	a[3]	a[4]	a[5]	a[6]	a[7]
2	4	5	7	8		12	15

Element removed

a[0]	a[1]	[2]	a[3]	a[4]	a[5]	a[6]	a[7]
2	4	5	7	8	12	15	

Following program implement deletion operation for sorted array.

```
#include<iostream.h>
void delete_item(int a[ ], int &n, int item) //n is the number of elements already present in the array
{
int i=0;
while(i<n && a[i]<item)
 i++;
if (a[i]==item) // given item is found
{
while (i<n)
{
```

```
a[i]=a[i+1]; // shift the (i+1)th element one position towards left
i++;
}
cout<<"\n Given item is successfully deleted";
}
else
cout<<"\n Given item is not found in the array";
n--;
}
void main()
{
int a[10]={2,4,5,7,8,11,12,15},n=8;
int i=0;
cout<<"Original array is :\n";                // displaying original arrary
for(i=0;i<n;i++)
 cout<<a[i]<<", ";
delete_item(a,n,11);                          //deleting an item from array
cout<<"\nArray after deleting 11 is:\n";      // displaying array after deletion
for(i=0; i<n; i++)
 cout<<a[i]<<", ";
}
```

Output is

Original array is:

2, 4, 5, 7, 8, 11, 12, 15

Given item is successfully deleted

Array after deleting 11 is:

2, 4, 5, 7, 8, 12, 15

Traversal

Processing of all elements (i.e. from first element to the last element) present in one-dimensional array is called traversal.

For example, printing all elements of an array, finding sum of all elements present in an array.

```
#include<iostream.h>
void print_array(int a[ ], int n) //n is the number of elements present in the array
{
int i;
cout<<"\n Given array is :\n";
for(i=0; i<n; i++)
 cout<<a[i]<<", ";
}
int sum(int a[ ], int n)
{
int i,s=0;
for(i=0; i<n; i++)
 s=s+a[i];
return s;
}
void main()
{
int b[10]={3,5,6,2,8,4,1,12,25,13},n=10;
int i, s;
print_array(b,n);
s = sum(b,n);
cout<<"\n Sum of all elements of the given array is : "<<s;
}
Output:
Given array is
3, 5, 6, 2, 8, 4, 1, 12, 25, 13
Sum of all elements of the given array is : 79
```

Sorting

The process of arranging the array elements in increasing (ascending) or decreasing (descending) order is known as sorting. There are several sorting techniques are available e.g. selection sort, insertion sort, bubble sort, quick sort, heap short etc.

Selection Sort

The basic idea of a selection sort is to repeatedly select the smallest element in the remaining unsorted array and exchange the selected smallest element with the first element of the unsorted array. For example, consider the following unsorted array to be sorted using selection sort

	A[0]	A[1]	A[2]	A[3]	A[4]
Original array	**10**	**2**	**20**	**5**	**9**
1st iteration	Find the smallest element & swap with 1st element				
Array after 1st iteration	2	**10**	**20**	**5**	**9**
2nd iteration		Find smallest element & swap with 2nd element			
Array after 2nd iteration	2	5	**20**	**10**	**9**
3rd iteration			Find smallest element & swap with 3rd element		
Array after 3rd iteration	2	5	9	**10**	**20**
4th iteration				Find smallest element & swap with 4th element	
Array after 4th iteration	2	5	9	10	**20**

```
#include<iostream.h>
void select_sort(int a[ ], int n)  //n is the number of elements present in the array
{
int i, j, p, small;
for(i=0;i<n-1;i++)
{
small=a[i]; // initialize small with the first element of unsorted part of the array
p=i; // keep index of the smallest number of unsorted part of the array in p
for(j=i+1; j<n; j++) //loop for selecting the smallest element form unsorted array
{
 if(a[j]<small)
{
 small=a[j];
 p=j;
}
}// end of inner loop----------
```

```
//----------exchange the smallest element with ith element-------------
a[p]=a[i];
a[i]=small;
//-----------end of exchange-------------
}
}           //end of function
void main( )
{
int a[7] = {8,5,9,3,16,4,7}, n = 7, i;
cout<<"\n Original array is :\n";
for(i=0;i<n;i++)
 cout<<a[i]<<", ";
select_sort(a,n);
cout<<"\nThe sorted array is:\n";
for(i=0; i<n; i++)
 cout<<a[i]<<", ";
}
```

Output is

Original array is

8, 5, 9, 3, 16, 4, 7

The sorted array is

3, 4, 5, 7, 8, 9, 16

Insertion Sort

Insertion sort algorithm divides the array of n elements in to two subparts, the first subpart contain a[0] to a[k] elements in sorted order and the second subpart contain a[k+1] to a[n] which are to be sorted. The algorithm starts with only first element in the sorted subpart because array of one element is itself in sorted order. In each pass, the first element of the unsorted subpart is removed and is inserted at the appropriate position in the sorted array so that the sorted array remain in sorted order and hence in each pass the size of the sorted subpart is increased by 1 and size of unsorted subpart is decreased by 1. This process continues until all n-1 elements of the unsorted arrays are inserted at their appropriate position in the sorted array.

For example, consider the following unsorted array to be sorted using selection sort

Original array

0	1	2	3	4	5	6
8	5	9	3	16	4	7
Sorted	unsorted					

Original array	S[0]	S[1]	S[2]	S[3]	S[4]	S[5]	S[6]
	8	5	9	3	16	4	7
After 1st iteration	5	8	9	3	16	4	7
After 2nd iteration	5	8	9	3	16	4	7
After 3rd iteration	3	5	8	9	16	4	7
After 4th iteration	3	5	8	9	16	4	7
After 5th iteration	3	4	5	8	9	16	7
After 6th iteration	3	4	5	7	8	9	16

```
#include<iostream.h>
void insert_sort(int a[ ],int n) //n is the no of elements present in the array
{
int i, j,p;
for (i=1; i<n; i++)
{
p = a[i];
j = i-1;
//inner loop to shift all elements of sorted subpart one position towards right
while( j >= 0 & &a [ j ] > p)
{
a[j+1] = a[j];
j--;
}                //---------end of inner loop
a[j+1] = p; //insert p in the sorted subpart
}
}
void main( )
{
int a[7]={8,5,9,3,16,4,7},n=7,i;
cout<<"\n Original array is :\n";
for(i=0;i<n;i++)
cout<<a[i]<<", ";
```

```
insert_sort(a,n);
cout<<"\nThe sorted array is:\n";
for(i=0; i<n; i++)
 cout<<a[i]<<", ";
}
```

Output is

Original array is

8, 5, 9, 3, 16, 4, 7

The sorted array is

3, 4, 5, 7, 8, 9, 16

Bubble Sort

Bubble sort compares a[i] with a[i+1] for all i=0..n-2,. If a[i] and a[i+1] are not in ascending order then exchange a[i] with a[i+1] immediately. After each iteration, all elements which are not at their proper position move at least one position towards their right place in the array. The process continues until all elements get their proper place in the array (i.e. algorithm terminates if no exchange occurs in the last iteration)

For example, consider the following unsorted array to be sorted using selection sort

Original array	S[0]	S[1]	S[2]	S[3]	S[4]	S[5]	S[6]
	8	**5**	**9**	**3**	**16**	**4**	**7**
After 1st iteration	**5**	**8**	**3**	**9**	**4**	**7**	16
After 2nd iteration	**5**	**3**	**8**	**4**	**7**	9	16
After 3rd iteration	**3**	**5**	**4**	**7**	8	9	16
After 4th iteration	**3**	**4**	**5**	7	8	9	16
After 5th iteration	**3**	**4**	5	7	8	9	16
After 6th iteration	3	4	5	7	8	9	16

```
#include<iostream.h>
void insert_sort(int s[ ],int n) //n is the no of elements present in the array
{
int i, j,p;
for (i=0;  i < n;  i++)
{
for( j=1; j < n-1; j++)
{
        if( s[j] > s[j+1)   // consecutive elements are being checked
```

```
            {           // swapping the consecutive elements if first value is > next value
                            p = s[j] ;
                            s[j]= s[j+1] ;
                            s[j+1] = p ;
            }
    }
    }
    void main( )
    {
    int a[7]={8,5,9,3,16,4,7},n=7,i;
    cout<<"\n Original array is :\n";
    for(i=0;i<n;i++)
     cout<<a[i]<<", ";
    insert_sort(a,n);
    cout<<"\nThe sorted array is:\n";
    for(i=0; i<n; i++)
     cout<<a[i]<<", ";
    }
```

Output is

Original array is

8, 5, 9, 3, 16, 4, 7

The sorted array is

3, 4, 5, 7, 8, 9, 16

Merging of Two Sorted Arrays into Third Array in Sorted Order

Algorithm to merge arrays a[m](sorted in ascending order) and b[n](sorted in descending order) into third array C[n+m] in ascending order.

```
#include<iostream.h>
Merge(int a[ ], int m, int b[n], int c[ ]) // m is size of array a and n is the size of array b
{
int i=0;            // i points to the smallest element of the array a which is at index 0
int j=m-1;          // j points to the smallest element of the array b which is at the index
m-1 since b
// is sorted in descending order
int k=0; //k points to the first element of the array c
```

```
while(i<m && j>=0)
{
 if(a[i] < b[j])
 c[k++]=a[i++]; // copy from array a into array c and then increment i and k
else
c[k++]=b[j--];                // copy from array b into array c and then decrement j and
                              //increment k
}
while(i<m)                    //copy all remaining elements of array a
 c[k++]=a[i++];
while(j>=0)                   //copy all remaining elements of array b
 c[k++]=b[j--];
}
void main()
{
int a[5]={2,4,5,6,7},m=5;          //a is in ascending order
int b[6]={15,12,4,3,2,1},n=6;      //b is in descending order
int c[11];
merge(a, m, b, n, c);
cout<<"The merged array is :\n";
for(int i=0; i<m+n; i++)
  cout<<c[i]<", ";
}
Output is
The merged array is:
1, 2, 2, 3, 4, 4, 5, 6, 7, 12, 15
```

Two Dimensional Arrays

1	2	3
4	5	6

Row-Major Order (used in C++ to Store Matrix)

In row-major storage, a multidimensional array in linear memory is accessed such that rows are stored one after the other. Memory allocation for above matrix will be,

1	2	3	4	5	6

offset = row * Numcols + column

Example 1

For a given array A[10][20] is stored in the memory along the row with each of its elements occupying 4 bytes. Calculate address of A[3][5] if the base address of array A is 5000.

Solution

For given array A[M][N] where M=Number of rows, N =Number of Columns present in the array.

address of A[I][J] = base address + sizeof (type)* offset

address of A[I][J] = base address + sizeof (type)* (I * N + J)

Where M=10, N=20, I=3, J=5, sizeof(type) = 4 bytes

address of A[3][5] = 5000 + 4 * (3 * 20 + 5)

= 5000 + 4*65 = 5000+260 = 5260

Example 2

An array A[50][20] is stored in the memory along the row with each of its elements occupying 8 bytes. Find out the location of A[5][10], if A[4][5] is stored at 4000.

Solution

Calculate base address of A i.e. address of A[0][0]

For given array A[M][N] where M=Number of rows, N =Number of Columns present in the array.

address of A[I][J] = base address + sizeof (type) * (I * N + J)

here M=50, N=20, sizeof(type)=8, I=4, J=5

address of A[4][5] = base address + 8 * (4*20 +5)

4000 = base address + 8 *85

Base address = 4000 – 85 * 8 = 4000 – 680 = 3320

Now to find address of A[5][10]

here M=50, N=20, sizeof(type)=8, I=5, J=10

Address of A[5][10] = base address + 8* (5*20 + 10)

= 3320 + 8*110 = 3320 + 880 = 4200

Column Major Order

In column-major storage, a multidimensional array in linear memory is accessed such that columns are stored one after the other. Memory allocation for above matrix will be

1	4	2	5	3	6

offset = row + column*NUMROWS

Address of element A[row][column]

Example1

For a given array A[10][20] is stored in the memory along the column with each of its elements occupying 4 bytes. Calculate address of A[3][5] if the base address of array A is 5000.

Solution

For given array A[M][N] where M=Number of rows, N =Number of Columns present in the array.

Address of A[I][J]= base address + sizeof(type) * (J * M + I)

here M=10, N=20, I=3, J=5, sizeof(type)=4 bytes

Address of A[3][5] = 5000 + 4 * (5 * 10 + 3)

= 5000 + 4*53 = 5000 + 215 = 5215

Example2

An array A[50][20] is stored in the memory along the column with each of its elements occupying 8 bytes. Find out the location of A[5][10], if A[4][5] is stored at 4000.

Solution

Calculate base address of A i.e. address of A[0][0]

For given array A[M][N] where M=Number of rows, N =Number of Columns present in the array.

address of A[I][J]= base address+ sizeof(type) * (J * M + I)

here M=50, N=20, sizeof (type) = 8, I = 4, J = 5

address of A[4][5] = base address +8* (5 * 50 +4)

4000 = base address + 8*254

Base address = 4000-8*55

= 4000 – 2032

= 1968

Now to find address of A[5][10]

here M=50, N=20, sizeof(type)=8, I =5, J=10

Address of A[5][10] = base address + 8 * (10*50 + 10)

=1968 + 8*510

= 1968+4080 = 6048

4 Marks Questions

1. Write a function in C++ which accepts an integer array and its size as arguments and replaces elements having even values with its half and elements having odd values with twice its value.
2. Write a function in C++ which accepts an integer array and its size as argument and exchanges the value of first half side elements with the second half side elements of the array.

   Example: If an array of eight elements has initial content as 2,4,1,6,7,9,23,10. The function should rearrange the array as 7,9,23,10,2,4,1,6.
3. Write a function in c++ to find and display the sum of each row and each column of 2 dimensional array. Use the array and its size as parameters with int as the data type of the array.
4. Write a function in C++, which accepts an integer array and its size as parameters and rearrange the array in reverse. Example if an array of five members initially contains the elements as 6,7,8,13,9,19 Then the function should rearrange the array as 19,9,13,8,7,6
5. Write a function in C++, which accept an integer array and its size as arguments and swap the elements of every even location with its following odd location. Example : if an array of nine elements initially contains the elements as 2,4,1,6,5,7,9,23,10 Then the function should rearrange the array as 4,2,6,1,7,5,23,9,10.
6. Write a function in C++ which accepts an integer array and its size as arguments and replaces elements having odd values with thrice and elements having even values with twice its value. Example: If an array of five elements initially contains the elements 3,4,5,16,9 Then the function should rearrange the content of the array as 9,8,15,32,27.

Stacks, Queues and Linked List

Stack

In computer science, a stack is a last in, first out (LIFO) *data structure*. A stack can be characterized by only two fundamental operations: *push* and *pop*. The push operation adds an item to the top of the stack. The pop operation removes an item from the top of the stack, and returns this value to the caller.

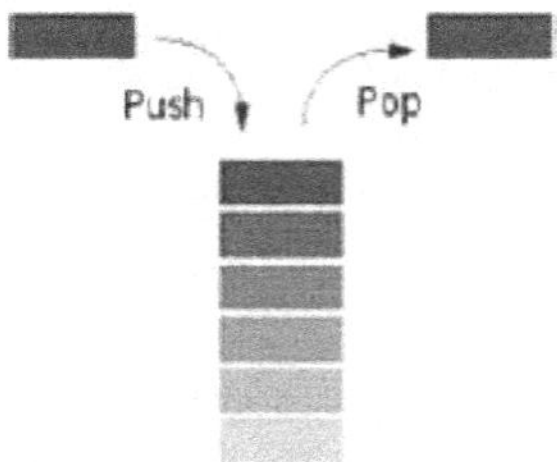

Stack Using Array

```
#include<iostream.h>
const int size = 5
class stack
{
int a[size]; //array a can store maximum 5 item of type int of the stack
int top;      //top will point to the last item pushed onto the stack
public:
stack( )      //constructor to create an empty stack, top=-1 indicate that no item is
{top = -1 ;} //present in the array
void push(int item)
{
If(top==size-1)
cout<<"stack is full, given item cannot be added";
else
a[++top]=item; //increment top by 1 then item at new position of the top in //the array a
}
int pop()
{
If (top==-1)
```

```
{
 out<<"Stack is empty ";
return -1; //-1 indicates empty stack
}
else
return a[top--];//return the item present at the top of the stack then decrement top by 1
}
};
void main()
{
stack s1;
s1.push(3);
s1.push(5);
cout<<s1.pop()<<endl;
cout<<s1.pop()<<endl;
cout<<s1.pop();
}
```

Output is

5

3

Stack is empty -1

Linked List

In Computer Science, a **linked list** (or more clearly, "singly-linked list") is a data structure that consists of a sequence of nodes each of which contains data and a pointer which points (i.e., a *link*) to the next node in the sequence.

Stack Implementation Using Linked List

```
#include<iostream.h>

struct node

{

        int item;     //data that will be stored in each node

        node * next; //pointer which contains address of another node
```

```
}; //node is a self-referential structure which contains reference of another object type node
class stack
{
        node *top;
public:
        stack() //constructor to create an empty stack by initializing top with NULL
        {
        top=NULL;
        }
        void push(int item);
        int pop();
        ~stack();
};
void stack::push(int item) //to insert a new node at the top of the stack
{
        node *t=new node; //dynamic memory allocation for a new object of node type
        if(t==NULL)
        cout<<"Memory not available, stack is full";
        else
        {
        t->item = item;
        t->next = top; //newly created node will point to the last inserted node or NULL if
                        //stack is empty
        top=t;          //top will point to the newly created node
        }
```

```
}
int stack::pop() //to delete the last inserted node(which is currently pointed by the top)
{
        if(top==NULL)
        {
        cout<<"Stack is empty \n";
        return 0;               // 0 indicating that stack is empty
        }
        else
        {
        node *t=top;            //save the address of top in t
        int r=top->item;        //store item of the node currently pointed by top
        top=top->next;          // move top from last node to the second last node
        delete t;               //remove last node of the stack from memory
        return r;
        }
}
stack::~stack()     //de-allocated all undeleted nodes of the stack when stack goes out of scope
{
        node *t;
        while(top!=NULL)
        {
        t=top;
        top=top->next;
        delete t;
```

```
        }
};
void main()
{
        stack s1;
        s1.push(3);
        s1.push(5);
        s1.push(7);
        cout<<s1.pop()<<endl;
        cout<<s1.pop()<<endl;
        cout<<s1.pop()<<endl;
        cout<<s1.pop()<<endl;
}
```

Output is

7

5

3

Stack is empty 0

Application of stacks in infix expression to postfix expression conversion

Infix expression	operand1 operator operand2	for example	a+b
Postfix expression	operand1 operand2 operator	for example	ab+
Prefix expression	operator operand1 operand2	for example	+ab

Some example of infix expression and their corresponding postfix expression

Infix expression	postfix expression
a*(b-c)/e	abc-*e/
(a+b)*(c-d)/e	ab+cd-*e/
(a+b*c)/(d-e)+f	abc*+de-/f+

Algorithm to Convert Infix Expression to Postfix Expression Using Stack

Suppose x is an infix expression and find postfix expression Y

1. Push "("to the STACK, and add ")" to the end of X.
2. Scan X from left to right and REPEAT Steps 3 to 6 for each element of X UNTIL the STACK is empty.
3. If an operand is encountered, add it to Y.
4. If a left parenthesis is encountered, push it on to STACK.
5. If an operator is encountered then:
   (a) Repeatedly pop from STACK and add to Y each operator which has the same precedence as or higher precedence than operator.
   (b) Add operator to STACK.
6. If a right parenthesis is encountered. Then:
   (a) Repeatedly pop from the STACK and add to Y each operator until a left parenthesis is encountered.
   (b) Remove the left parenthesis.
7. End.

For example convert the infix expression (A+B)*(C-D)/E into postfix expression showing stack status after every step.

Symbol scanned from infix	Stack status	Postfix expression
	(	
(	((	
A	((	A
+	((+	A
B	((+	AB
)	(	AB+
*	(*	AB+
(	(*(	AB+
C	(*(	AB+C
-	(*(-	AB+C
D	(*(-	AB+CD
)	(*	AB+CD-
/	(/	AB+CD-*
E	(/	AB+CD-*E
)		AB+CD-*E/

Answer: Postfix expression of **(A+B)*(C-D)/E** is **AB+CD-*E/**

Evaluation of Postfix Expression Using Stack

Algorithm to evaluate a postfix expression P.

/*Reading of expression takes place from left to right*/

1. Read the next element //First element for the first time
2. If element is an operator then push the element in the Stack
3. If the element is an operator then

   {

4. Pop two operands from the stack //pop one operator in case of unary operator
5. Evaluate the expression formed by the two operands and the operator
6. Push the result of the expression in the stack.

   }

7. If no-more-elements then

   Pop the result

   Else

   Go to step 1.

8. End.

Example 1: Evaluate the following postfix expression showing stack status after every step.

8, 2, +, 5, 3, -, *, 4 /

token scanned from postfix expression	Stack status after processing the scanned token	Operation performed
8	**8**	Push 8
2	8, **2**	Push 2
+	**10**	Op2=pop() i.e 2 Op1=pop() i.e 8 Push(op1+op2) i.e. 8+2
5	10, **5**	Push(5)
3	10, 5, **3**	Push(3)
-	10, **2**	Op2=pop() i.e. 3 Op1=pop() i.e. 5 Push(op1-op2) i.e. 5-3
*	**20**	Op2=pop() i.e. 2 Op1=pop() i.e. 10 Push(op1-op2) i.e. 10*2
4	20, **4**	Push 4
/	5	Op2=pop() i.e. 4 Op1=pop() i.e. 20 Push(op1/op2) i.e. 20/4
NULL	Final result 5	**Pop 5 and return 5**

Example 2: Evaluate the following Boolean postfix expression showing stack status after every step.

True, False, True, AND, OR, False, NOT, AND

token scanned from postfix expression	Stack status after processing the scanned token	Operation performed
True	**True**	Push True
False	True, **False**	Push False
True	True, False, **True**	Push True
AND	True, **False**	Op2=pop() i.e. True Op1=pop() i.e. False Push(Op2 AND Op1) i.e. False ANDTrue=False
OR	True	Op2=pop() i.e. False Op1=pop() i.e. True Push(Op2 OR Op1) i.e. True OR False=True
False	True, **False**	Push False
NOT	True, **True**	Op1=pop() i.e. False Push(NOT False) i.e. NOT False=True
AND	**True**	Op2=pop() i.e. True Op1=pop() i.e. True Push(Op2 AND Op1) i.e. True AND True=True
NULL	Final result **True**	Pop True and Return True

Queue

Queue is a linear data structure which follows First in First out (FIFO) rule in which a new item is added at the **rear** end and **deletion** of item is from the **front end** of the queue. In a FIFO data structure, the first element added to the queue will be the first one to be removed. Linear Queue implementation using Array

```
#include<iostream.h>
const int size=5;            // size of queue
class queue
{       int front , rear;
        int a[size];
public:
        queue()         //Constructor to create an empty queue
        {       front=0;
                rear=0;
        }

        void addQ( )            // insertion in array queue
        {       if(rear==size)
                        cout<<"queue is full<<endl;
                else
                        a[rear++]=item;
        }

        int delQ( )             // deletion from the array queue
        {       if(front==rear)
                {
                        cout<<"queue is empty"<<endl;
                        return 0;
                }
                else
                        return a[front++];
        }
};
void main()
```

```
{
        queue q1;
        q1.addQ(3);
        q1.addQ(5) ;
        q1.addQ(7) ;
        cout<<q1.delQ()<<endl ;
        cout<<q1.delQ()<<endl ;
        cout<<q1.delQ()<<endl;
        cout<<q1.delQ()<<endl;
}
```

Output is

3

5

7

Queue is empty 0

Queue Using Linked List

```
#include<iostream.h>
struct node
{       int item;
        node *next;
};
class queue
{       node *front, *rear;
public:
        queue( )                // constructor to create empty queue
        {       front=NULL;
                rear=NULL;
        }
        void addQ(int item);
        int delQ();
};
void queue::addQ(int item)
{       node * t=new node;
```

```
            t->item=item;
            t->next=NULL;
            if (rear==NULL) //if the queue is empty
            {           rear=t;
                        front=t; //rear and front both will point to the first node
            }
            else
            {           rear->next=t;
                        rear=t;
            }
}
int queue::delQ()
{           if(front==NULL)
                        cout<<"queue is empty"<<return 0;
            else
            {           node *t=front;
                        int r=t->item;
                        front=front->next; //move front to the next node of the queue
                        if(front==NULL)
                                    rear==NULL;
                        delete t;
                        return r;
            }}
void main()
{           queue q1;
            q1.addQ(3);
            q1.addQ(5) ;
            q1.addQ(7) ;
            cout<<q1.delQ()<<endl ;
            cout<<q1.delQ()<<endl ;
            cout<<q1.delQ()<<endl;
            cout<<q1.delQ()<<endl;
}
```

2, 3 & 4 Marks Practice Questions

1. Convert the following infix expressions to postfix expressions using stack (2)

   (i) A + (B * C) ^ D – (E / F – G)

   (ii) A * B / C * D ^ E * G / H

   (iii) ((A*B)-((C_D)*E/F)*G

2. Evaluate the following postfix expression E given below; show the contents of the stack during the evaluation

   (i) E= 5,9,+2,/,4,1,1,3,_,*,+ 2

   (ii) E= 80,35,20,-,25,5,+,-,*

   (iii) E= 30,5,2,^,12,6,/,+,-

   (iv) E=15, 3, 2, +, /, 7, + 2, *

3. An array A[40][10] is stored in the memory along the column with each element occupying 4 bytes. Find out the address of the location A[3][6] if the location A[30][10] is stored at the address 9000. (3)

4. Define functions in C++ to perform a PUSH and POP operation in a dynamically allocated stack considering the following: (4)

```
struct Node
{
        int X,Y;
        Node *Link;
};
class STACK
{
        Node * Top;
public:
        STACK( )
        {
        TOP=NULL;
        }
        void PUSH( );
        void POP( );
        ~STACK( );
};
```

5. Write a function in C++ to perform a Add and Delete operation in a dynamically allocated Queue considering the following: (4)

```
struct node
{
        int empno ;
        char name[20];
        float sal ;
        Node *Link;
};
```

UNIT 3

DATABASE AND SQL

Data: Raw facts and figures which are useful to an organization. We cannot take decisions on the basis of data.

Information: Well processed data is called information. We can take decisions on the basis of information

Field: Set of characters that represents specific data element.

Record: Collection of fields is called a record. A record can have fields of different data types.

File: Collection of similar types of records is called a file.

Table: Collection of rows and columns that contains useful data/information is called a table. A table generally refers to the passive entity which is kept in secondary storage device.

Relation: Relation (collection of rows and columns) generally refers to an active entity on which we can perform various operations.

Database: Collection of logically related data along with its description is termed as database.

Tuple: A row in a relation is called a tuple.

Attribute: A column in a relation is called an attribute. It is also termed as field or data item.

Degree: Number of attributes in a relation is called degree of a relation.

Cardinality: Number of tuples in a relation is called cardinality of a relation.

Primary Key: Primary key is a key that can uniquely identifies the records/tuples in a relation. This key can never be duplicated and NULL.

Foreign Key: Foreign Key is a key that is defined as a primary key in some other relation. This key is used to enforce referential integrity in RDBMS.

Candidate Key: Set of all attributes which can serve as a primary key in a relation.

Alternate Key: All the candidate keys other than the primary keys of a relation are alternate keys for a relation.

DBA: Data Base Administrator is a person (manager) that is responsible for defining the data base schema, setting security features in database, ensuring proper functioning of the data bases etc.

Relational Algebra: The relation algebra is the collection of operations on relations. Each operation takes one or more relations (tables) and produces another relation as its result. The operations defined in relational algebra are *select, project, Cartesian product, union, set difference, set interception, natural join, division etc.*

1. **Select operation(denoted by σ):-** select operation is used to select rows from a elation <"

   Let us consider the table **item**

ItemNo	Item_Name	Price
I1	Milk	10
I2	Bread	15
I3	Ice Cream	25
I4	Namkeen	20
I5	Cake	10

2. **Project Operation (denoted by π):-** Project operation select columns from a relation.

   Consider above table **Item.**

   To display item name & price of all items from Item table we can write.

   $\pi_{\text{Item\_Name, Price}}$ (Item).

   Result will be

Item_Name	Price
Milk	10
Bread	15
Ice Cream	25
Namkeen	20
Cake	10

3. **The Cartesian product operation (denoted by X):-** the Cartesian product of relation A and B is written as A X B. The Cartesian product yield a new relation having degree (Degree of A + Degree of B) and Cardinality (cardinality of A X Cardinality of B).

   Consider the following table **student** and **instructor.**

   The Cartesian product **Student X Instructor** result in following relation.

Adno	Stu_Name	Passed	**Id**	**Inst_name**	**Subject**
1023	Ajay	Y	101	Manoj	CS
1023	Ajay	Y	102	Subhash	ACC
6151	Sunil	N	101	Manoj	CS
6151	Sunil	N	102	Subhash	ACC
7575	Vinay	y	101	Manoj	CS
7575	Vinay	y	102	Subhash	ACC

4. **The Union Operation (denoted by U):-** it produces a relation that contains tuples from both operand relations.
Consider the following relations **science** and **commerce.**
The result of **Science U Commerce** will be as follows.

Adno	Name	Class
2190	Amit	XII
2345	Nihan	XII
5467	ajay	XI
5423	Sanjay	XII
7665	sumit	XI

5. **The Set Difference Operation (Denoted by -):-** allows to find tuples that are in one relation but not in another relation.
Consider above relation **science** and **commerce.**
The result of **Science - Commerce** will be as follows.

Adno	Name	Class
2190	Amit	XII
5467	ajay	XI

6. **The Set Interception Operation (denoted by ∩):-**Set Interception operation finds tuples that are common to the two operand relations.
Consider above relation **science** and **commerce.**
The result of **Science ∩ Commerce** will be as follows.

Adno	Name	Class
2345	Nihan	XII

Structured Query Language

SQL is a non-procedural language that is used to create, manipulate and process the databases (relations).

Characteristics of SQL

- It is very easy to learn and use.
- Large volume of databases can be handled quite easily.
- It is non-procedural language. It means that we do not need to specify the procedures to accomplish a task but just to give a command to perform the activity.
- SQL can be linked to most of other high level languages that makes it first choice for the database programmers.

Processing Capabilities of SQL

The following are the processing capabilities of SQL.

1. **Data Definition Language (DDL)**

DDL contains commands that are used to create the tables, databases, indexes, views, sequences and synonyms etc.

e.g: Create table, create view, create index, alter table etc.

2. **Data Manipulation Language (DML)**

DML contains command that can be used to manipulate the data base objects and to query the databases for information retrieval.

e.g Select, Insert, Delete, Update etc.

3. **Data Control Language**

This language is used for controlling the access to the data. Various commands like GRANT, REVOKE etc are available in DCL.

4. **Transaction Control Language (TCL)**

TCL include commands to control the transactions in a data base system. The commonly used commands in TCL are COMMIT, ROLLBACK etc.

Data Types of SQL

Support the Following Data Types

Data Type	Syntax	Description	Example
NUMBER	Number(n,d)	• Used to store a numeric value in a field/column • Where **n** specifies the number of digits and **d** specifies the number of digits after the decimal point.	**Amt Number(6,2)**
CHAR	Char (size)	Used to store fixed length string of length size	**Name Char(20)**
VARCHAR / VARCHAR2	varchar(size) / varchar2(size)	Used to store variable length string up to length size	**Address Varchar2(30)**
DATE	DATE	Used to store Date	**DOB Date**
LONG	LONG	This data type is used to store variable length strings of upto 2 GB size	**Accno** LONG
RAW/LONG RAW	RAW(bytes)/ LONG RAW(bytes)	Used to store binary data (images/pictures/ animation/clips etc.) up to the size **bytes**	**Address Raw(500)**

1&2 Mark Questions

1. Define the terms

    (i) Database Abstraction.

    (ii) Data inconsistency.

    (iii) Conceptual level of database implementation/abstraction.

    (iv) Primary Key.

    (v) Candidate Key.

    (vi) Relational Algebra.

    (vii) Domain.

Ans: Define the terms:

i. ***Database Abstraction***

Ans: Database system provides the users only that much information that is required by them, and hides certain details like, how the data is stored and maintained in database at hardware level. This concept/process is Database abstraction.

ii. ***Data Inconsistency***

Ans: When two or more entries about the same data do not agree i.e. when one of them stores the updated information and the other does not, it results in data inconsistency in the database.

iii. ***Conceptual Level of Database Implementation/Abstraction***

Ans: It describes what data are actually stored in the database. It also describes the relationships existing among data. At this level the database is described logically in terms of simple data-structures.

iv. ***Primary Key***

Ans: It is a key/attribute or a set of attributes that can uniquely identify tuples within the relation.

v. ***Candidate Key***

Ans: All attributes combinations inside a relation that can serve as primary key are candidate key as they are candidates for being as a primary key or a part of it.

vi. ***Relational Algebra***

Ans: It is the collections of rules and operations on relations (tables). The various operations are selection, projection, Cartesian product, union, set difference and intersection, and joining of relations.

vii. ***Domain***

Ans: It is the pool or collection of data from which the actual values appearing in a given column are drawn.

2 Marks Practice Questions

1. What is relation? What is the difference between a tuple and an attribute?
2. Define the following terminologies used in Relational Algebra:
   (i) Selection.
   (ii) Projection.
   (iii) Union.
   (iv) Cartesian product.
3. What are DDL and DML?
4. Differentiate between primary key and candidate key in a relation?
5. What do you understand by the terms **Cardinality** and **Degree** of a relation in relational database?
6. Differentiate between DDL and DML. Mention the 2 commands for each category.

Database and SQL: 6 Marks Questions

1. Write SQL Command for (a) to (d) and output of (g)

Graduate

S.NO	NAME	STIPEND	SUBJECT	AVERAGE	DIV
1	KARAN	400	PHYSICS	68	I
2	DIWAKAR	450	COMP Sc	68	I
3	DIVYA	300	CHEMISTRY	62	I
4	REKHA	350	PHYSICS	63	I
5	ARJUN	500	MATHS	70	I
6	SABINA	400	CHEMISTRY	55	II
7	JOHN	250	PHYSICS	64	I
8	ROBERT	450	MATHS	68	I
9	RUBINA	500	COMP Sc	62	I
10	VIKAS	400	MATHS	57	II

a. List the names of those students who have obtained DIV I sorted by NAME.
b. Display a report, listing NAME, STIPEND, SUBJECT and amount of stipend received in a year assuming that the STIPEND is paid every month.
c. To count the number of students who are either PHYSICS or COMPUTER SC graduates.
d. To insert a new row in the GRADUATE table: 11,"KAJOL", 300, "computer sc", 75, 1

e. Give the output of following sql statement based on table GRADUATE:

(i) Select MIN(AVERAGE) from GRADUATE where SUBJECT="PHYSICS";

(ii) Select SUM(STIPEND) from GRADUATE WHERE div=2;

(iii) Select AVG(STIPEND) from GRADUATE where AVERAGE>=65;

(iv) Select COUNT(distinct SUBJECT) from GRADUATE;

Sol:

a. SELECT NAME from GRADUATE where DIV = 'I' order by NAME;

b. SELECT NAME,STIPEND,SUBJECT, STIPEND*12 from GRADUATE;

c. SELECT SUBJECT,COUNT(*) from GRADUATE group by SUBJECT having SUBJECT='PHYISCS' or SUBJECT='COMPUTER SC';

d. INSERT INTO GRADUATE values(11,'KAJOL',300,'COMPUTER SC',75,1);

e. (i) 63

(ii) 800

(iii) 475

(iv) 4

2. Consider the following tables Sender and Recipient. Write SQL commands for the statements (i) to (iv) and give the outputs for SQL queries (v) to (viii).

Sender

SenderID	SenderName	SenderAddress	City
ND01	R Jain	2, ABC Appls	New Delhi
MU02	H Sinha	12 Newtown	Mumbai
MU15	S Jha	27/A, Park Street	Mumbai
ND50	T Prasad	122-K,SDA	New Delhi

Recipients

RecID	SenderID	RecName	RecAddress	recCity
KO05	ND01	R Bajpayee	5, Central Avenue	Kolkata
ND08	MU02	S Mahajan	116, A-Vihar	New Delhi
MU19	ND01	H Singh	2A, Andheri East	Mumbai
MU32	MU15	P K Swamy	B5, C S Terminals	Mumbai
ND48	ND50	S Tripathi	13, BI D Mayur Vihar	New delhi

(i) To display the names of all Senders from Mumbai.

Ans. SELECT sendername from Sender
where sendercity='Mumbai';

(ii) To display the RecIC, Sendername, SenderAddress, RecName, RecAddress for every Recipient.

Ans. Select R.RecIC, S.Sendername, S.SenderAddress, R.RecName, R.RecAddress from Sender S, Recepient R

where S.SenderID=R.SenderID;

(iii) To display Recipient details in ascending order of RecName

Ans. SELECT * from Recipent ORDER By RecName;

(iv) To display number of Recipients from each city

Ans. SELECT COUNT(*) from Recipient

Group By RecCity;

(v) SELECT DISTINCT SenderCity from Sender;

Ans.

SenderCity

Mumbai

New Delhi

(vi) SELECT A.SenderName, B.RecName From Sender A, Recipient B

Where A.SenderID = B.SenderID AND B.RecCity ='Mumbai';

Ans.

A.SenderName	**B.RecName**
R Jain	H Singh
S Jha	P K Swamy

(vii) SELECT RecName, RecAddress From Recipient.

Where RecCity NOT IN ('Mumbai', 'Kolkata') ;

Ans.

RecName	**RecAddress**
S Mahajan	116, A Vihar
S Tripathi	13, BID, Mayur Vihar

(viii) SELECT RecID, RecName FROM Recipent .

Where SenderID='MU02' or SenderID='ND50';

Ans.

RecID	RecName
ND08	S Mahajan
ND48	STripathi

3. Write SQL command for (a) to (f) on the basis of the table SPORTS

SPORTS

Student NO	Class	Name	Game1	Grade	Game2	Grade2
10	7	Sammer	Cricket	**B**	Swimming	**A**
11	8	Sujit	Tennis	**A**	Skating	**C**
12	7	Kamal	Swimming	**B**	Football	**B**
13	7	Venna	Tennis	**C**	Tennis	**A**
14	9	Archana	Basketball	**A**	Cricket	**A**
15	**10**	Arpit	Cricket	**A**	Atheletics	**C**

a. Display the names of the students who have grade 'C' in either Game1 or Game2 or both.

b. Display the number of students getting grade 'A' in Cricket.

c. Display the names of the students who have same game for both Game1 and Game2.

d. Display the games taken up by the students, whose name starts with 'A'.

e. Add a new column named 'Marks'.

f. Assign a value 200 for Marks for all those who are getting grade 'B' or grade 'A' in both Game1 and Game2.

Ans : a) SELECT Name from SPORTS where grade='C' or Grade2='C';

b) SELECT Count (*) from SPORTS where grade='A';

c) SELECT name from SPORTS where game1 = game2;

d) SELECT game, game2 from SPORTS where name like 'A%';

e) ALTER TABLE SPORTS add (marks int (4));

f) UPDATE SPORTS set marks=200 where grade='A';

4. Consider the following tables Stationary and Consumer. Write SQL commands for the statement (i) to (iv) and output for SQL queries (v) to (viii):

Stationary

S_ID	StationaryName	Company	Price
DP01	Dot Pen	ABC	10
PL02	Pencil	XYZ	6
ER05	Eraser	XYZ	7
PL01	Pencil	CAM	5
GP02	Gel Pen	ABC	15

Consumer

C_ID	ConsumerName	Address	S_ID
01	Good Learner	Delhi	PL01
06	Write Well	Mumbai	GP02
12	Topper	Delhi	DP01
15	Write & Draw	Delhi	PL02
16	Motivation	Banglore	PL01

(i) To display the details of those consumers whose Address is Delhi.

(ii) To display the details of Stationary whose Price is in the range of 8 to 15. (Both Value included)

(iii) To display the ConsumerName, Address from Table Consumer, and Company and Price from table Stationary, with their corresponding matching S_ID.

(iv) To increase the Price of all stationary by 2.

(v) SELECT DISTINCT Address FROM Consumer;

(vi) SELECT Company, MAX(Price), MIN(Price), COUNT(*) from Stationary GROUP BY Company;

(vii) SELECT Consumer.ConsumerName, Stationary.StationaryName, Stationary.Price FROM Strionary, Consumer WHERE Consumer.S_ID=Stationary.S_ID;

(viii) Select StationaryName, Price*3 From Stationary;

5. Consider the following tables GARMENT and FABRIC. Write SQL commands for the statements (i) to (iv) and give outputs for SQL queries (v) to (viii).

Garment

GCODE	DESCRIPTION	PRICE	FCODE	READYDATE
10023	PENCIL SKIRT	1150	F03	19-DEC-08
10001	FORMAL SHIRT	1250	F01	12-JAN-08
10012	INFORMAL SHIRT	1550	F02	06-JUN-08
10024	BABY TOP	750	F03	07-APR-07
10090	TULIP SKIRT	850	F02	31-MAR-07
10019	EVENING GOWN	850	F03	06-JUN-08
10009	INFORMAL PANT	1500	F02	20-OCT-08
10007	FORMAL PANT	1350	F01	09-MAR-08
10020	FROCK	850	F04	09-SEP-07
10089	SLACKS	750	F03	20-OCT-08

FABRIC

FCODE	TYPE
F04	POLYSTER
F02	COTTON
F03	SILK
F01	TERELENE

(i) To display GCODE and DESCRIPTION of a each dress in descending order of GCODE.

(ii) To display the details of all the GARMENTs, which have READYDATE in between 08–DEC–07 and 16–JUN–08 (inclusive of both the dates).

(iii) To display the average PRICE of all the GARMENTs, which are made up of FABRIC with FCODE as F03.

(iv) To display FABRIC wise highest and lowest price of GARMENTs from DRESS table. (Display FCODE of each GARMENT along with highest and lowest price)

(v) SELECT SUM (PRICE) FROM GARMENT WHERE FCODE= 'F01';

(vi) SELECT DESCRIPTION, TYPE FROM GARMENT, FABRIC WHERE GARMENT.FCODE = FABRIC. FCODE AND GARMENT. PRICE>=1260;

(vii) SELECT MAX (FCODE) FROM FABRIC;

(viii) SELECT COUNT (DISTINCT PRICE) FROM FABRIC;

UNIT 4

BOOLEAN LOGIC

Low Order Thinking Questions: (Boolean Algebra)

1. State and verify absorption law in Boolean algebra.

   Ans. Absorption Law states that:

   a. X+XY=X b. X(X+Y)=X

2. Verify X'.Y+X.Y'=(X'+Y').(X+Y) algebraically.

   Ans. LHS = X'Y + XY'

   = (X'+X) (X'+Y') (Y+X) (Y+Y')

   = 1.(X'+Y') (X+Y).1

   = (X'+Y') (X+Y)

   = RHS, hence proved

3. Write the equivalent Boolean Expression F for the following circuit diagram :

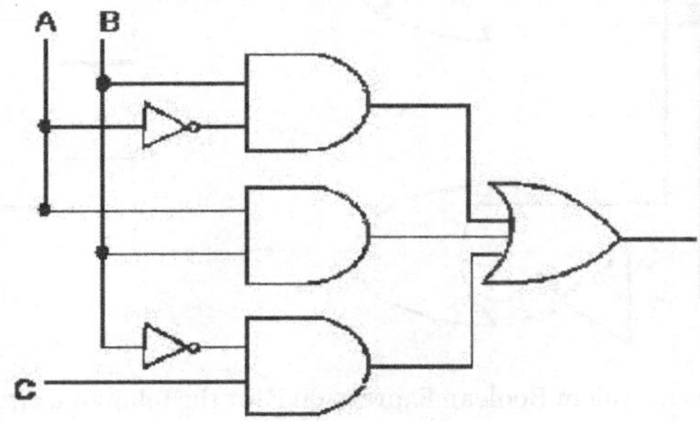

   Ans.: A'B+AB+B'C

4. If F(P,Q,R,S) = Π (3,4,5,6,7,13,15), obtain the simplified form using K-Map.

   Ans.:

	R+S	R+S'	R'+S'	R'+S
P+Q			0	
P+Q'	0	0	0	0
P'+Q'		0	0	
P'+Q				

   Reduction of groups following the reduction rule:

   Quad1 = M4.M5.M6.M7 = P+Q'

   Quad2 = M5.M7.M13.M15 = Q'+S'

   Pair = M3.M7 = P+R'+S'

   Therefore POS of F(P,Q,R,S) = (P+Q')(Q'+S')(P+R'+S')

5. F(a,b,c,d)=Σ(0,2,4,5,7,8,10,12,13,15)

F(a,b,c,d)	= B1 + B2 + B3		
B1	= m0+m4+m12+m8	=	c'd'
B2	= m5+m7+m13+m15	=	bd
B3	= m0+m2+m8+m10	=	b'd'
F(a,b,c,d)	= c'd' + bd + b'd'		

1/2 Marks Practice Questions

1. State and Prove DeMorgan Law using Truth Table.
2. State and prove Absorption Law algebraically.
3. State and Prove Distributive Law algebraically.
4. Write the equivalent Boolean Expression for the following Logic Circuit. (2)

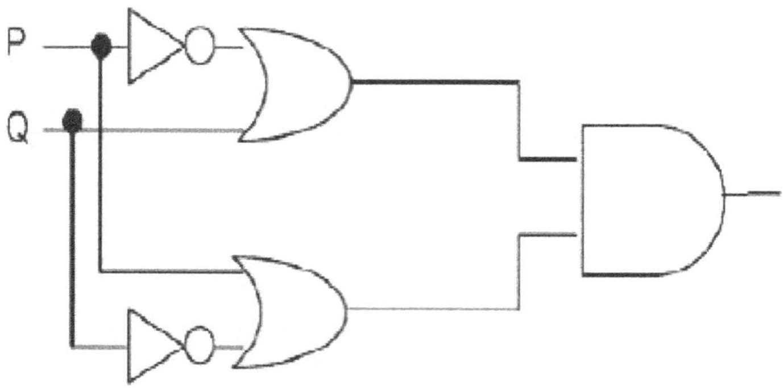

5. Write the equivalent Boolean Expression F for the following circuit diagram (2)

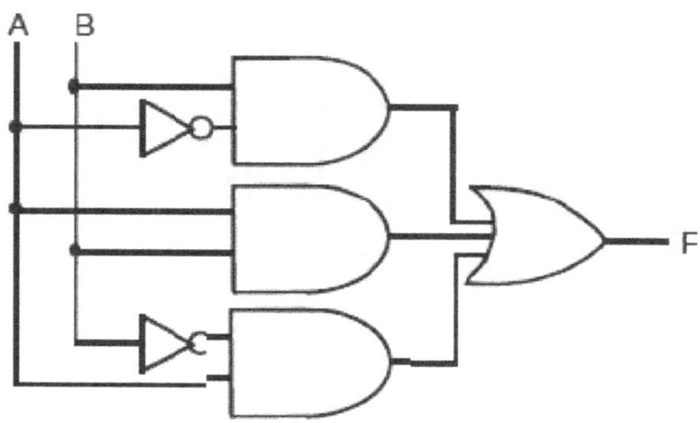

6. Write the equivalent Boolean Expression F for the following circuit diagram (2)

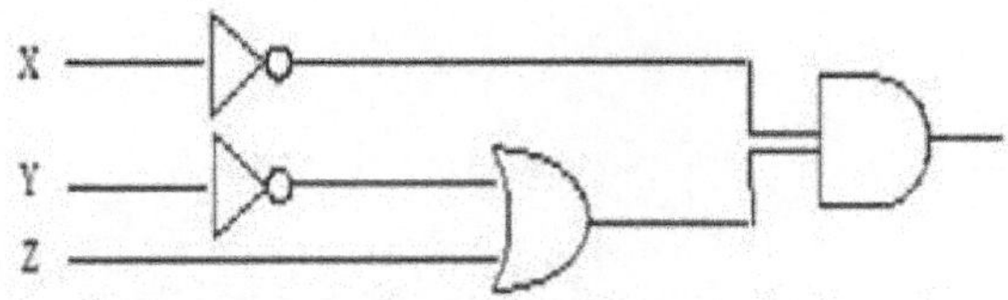

7. Convert the following Boolean expression into its equivalent Canonical Sum of Product Form((SOP)

(X'+Y+Z').(X'+Y+Z).(X'+Y'+Z).(X'+Y'+Z') 1

8. Convert the following Boolean expression into its equivalent Canonical Product of Sum form (POS):

A.B'.C + A'.B.C +A'.B.C' 1

9. Draw a Logical Circuit Diagram for the following Boolean expression:

10. A.(B+C') 2

11. Write the equivalent Boolean Expression F for the following circuit diagram: 2

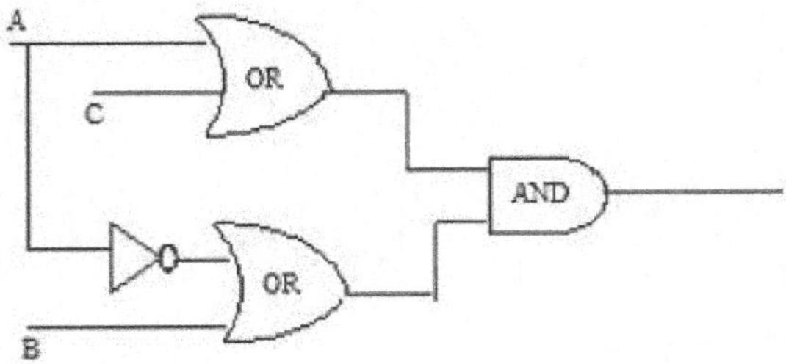

12. Prove that XY+YZ+YZ'=Y algebraically 2

13. Design (A+B).(C+D) using NOR Gate. 2

3 Marks Practice Questions

14. If F(a,b,c,d)=Σ(0,2,4,5,7,8,10,12,13,15), obtain the simplified form using K-Map.

15. If F(a,b,c,d) =Σ(0,3,4,5,7,8,9,11,12,13,15), obtain the simplified form using KMap

16. Obtain a simplified form for a boolean expression F(U,V,W,Z)= π (0,1,3,5,6,7,10,14,15)

17. Reduce the following boolean expression using K-Map

F(A,B,C,D) = Σ(5,6,7,8,9,12,13,14,15)

UNIT 5

COMMUNICATION AND NETWORK CONCEPTS

Network

The collection of interconnected computers is called a computer network.

Two computers are said to be interconnected if they are capable of sharing and exchanging information.

Need

- Resource Sharing.
- Reliability.
- Cost Factor.
- Communication Medium.

Resource Sharing means to make all programs, data and peripherals available to anyone on the network irrespective of the physical location of the resources and the user.

Reliability means to keep the copy of a file on two or more different machines, so if one of them is unavailable (due to some hardware crash or any other) then its other copy can be used.

Cost factor means it greatly reduces the cost since the resources can be shared

Communication Medium means one can send messages and whatever the changes at one end are done can be immediately noticed at another.

Evolution of Networking

1. **ARPANET**: In 1969, The US govt. formed an agency named ARPANET (Advanced Research Projects Agency NETwork) to connect computers at various universities and defense agencies. The main objective of ARPANET was to develop a network that could continue to function efficiently even in the event of a nuclear attack.
2. **Internet (INTERconnection NETwork)**: The Internet is a worldwide network of computer networks. It is not owned by anybody.
3. **Interspace**: Interspace is a client/server software program that allows multiple users to communicate online with real time audio, video and text chat in dynamic 3D environments.

Switching Techniques

Switching techniques are used for transmitting data across networks. Different types are:

1. **Circuit Switching**: In the Circuit Switching technique, first, the complete end-to-end transmission path between the source and the destination computers is established and then the message is transmitted through the path. The main advantage of this technique is guaranteed delivery of the message. Mostly used for voice communication.
2. **Message Switching**: In the Message switching technique, no physical path is established between sender and receiver in advance. This technique follows the store and forward mechanism.
3. **Packet Switching**: In this switching technique fixed size of packet can be transmitted across the network.

Comparison between the Various Switching Techniques: Criteria	Circuit Switching	Message Switching	Packet Switching
Path established in advance	Yes	No	No
Store and forward technique	No	Yes	Yes
Message follows multiple routes	No	Yes	Yes

Data Communication Terminologies

Data channel: The information/data carry from one end to another in the network by channel.

Baud & bits per second (bps): It's used to measurement for the information carry of a communication channel. Measurement Units: bit

1 Byte= 8 bits

1 KBPS (Kilo Byte Per Second)= 1024 Bytes

1 Kbps (kilobits Per Second) = 1024 bits

1 Mbps (Mega bits Per Second)=1024 Kbps

Bandwidth: It is amount of information transmitted or received per unit time.

Transmission Media

1. **Twisted pair cable**: It consists of two identical 1 mm thick copper wires insulated and twisted together. The twisted pair cables are twisted in order to reduce crosstalk and electromagnetic induction.

Advantages

1. It is easy to install and maintain.
2. It is very inexpensive.

Disadvantages

1. It is incapable to carry a signal over long distances without the use of repeaters.
2. Due to low bandwidth, these are unsuitable for broadband applications.

2. Co-axial Cables: It consists of a solid wire core surrounded by one or more foil or braided wire shields, each separated from the other by some kind of plastic insulator. It is mostly used in the cable wires.

Advantages

1. Data transmission rate is better than twisted pair cables.
2. It provides a cheap means of transporting multi-channel television signals around metropolitan areas.

Disadvantages

1. Expensive than twisted pair cables.
2. Difficult to manage and reconfigure.

3. Optical fiber: An optical fiber consists of thin glass fibers that can carry information in the form of visible light.

Advantages

1. Transmit data over long distance with high security.
2. Data transmission speed is high
3. Provide better noise immunity
4. Bandwidth is up to 10 Gbps.

Disadvantages

1. Expensive as compared to other guided media.
2. Need special care while installation.

4. Infrared: The infrared light transmits data through the air and can propagate throughout a room, but will not penetrate walls. It is a secure medium of signal transmission.The infrared transmission has become common in TV remotes, automotive garage doors, wireless speakers etc.

5. **Radio Wave**: Radio Wave an electromagnetic wave with a wavelength between 0.5 cm and 30,000m. The transmission making use of radio frequencies is termed as radio-wave transmission.

Advantages

1. Radio wave transmission offers mobility.
2. It is cheaper than laying cables and fibers.
3. It offers ease of communication over difficult terrain.

Disadvantages

1. Radio wave communication is insecure communication.
2. Radio wave propagation is susceptible to weather effects like rains, thunder storms etc.

6. **Microwave Wave**: The Microwave transmission is a line of sight transmission. Microwave signals travel at a higher frequency than radio waves and are popularly used for transmitting data over long distances.

Advantages

1. It is cheaper than laying cable or fiber.
2. It has the ability to communicate over oceans.

Disadvantages

1. Microwave communication is an insecure communication.
2. Signals from antenna may split up and transmitted in different way to different antenna which leads to reduce to signal strength.
3. Microwave propagation is susceptible to weather effects like rains, thunder storms etc.
4. Bandwidth allocation is extremely limited in case of microwaves.

7. **Satellite link**: The satellite transmission is also a kind of line of sight transmission that is used to transmit signals throughout the world.

Advantages

1. Area covered is quite large.
2. No line of sight restrictions such as natural mountains, tall building, towers etc.
3. Earth station which receives the signals can be fixed position or relatively mobile.

Disadvantages

1. Very expensive as compared to other transmission mediums.
2. Installation is extremely complex.

3. Signals sent to the stations can be tampered by external interference.

Network Devices

Modem: A MODEM (MOdulator DEModulator) is an electronic device that enables a computer to transmit data over telephone lines. There are two types of modems, namely, internal modem and external modem.

RJ45 connector: The RJ-45(Registered Jack) connectors are the plug-in devices used in the networking and telecommunications applications. They are used primarily for connecting LANs, particularly Ethernet.

Ethernet Card: It is a hardware device that helps in connection of nodes within a network.

Hub: A hub is a hardware device used to connect several computers together. Hubs can be either active or passive. Hubs usually can support 8, 12 or 24 RJ45 ports.

Switch: A switch (switching hub) is a network device which is used to interconnect computers or devices on a network. It filters and forwards data packets across a network. The main difference between hub and switch is that hub replicates what it receives on one port onto all the other ports while switch keeps a record of the MAC addresses of the devices attached to it.

Gateway: A gateway is a device that connects dissimilar networks.

Repeater: A repeater is a network device that amplifies and restores signals for long distance transmission.

Network Topologies and Types

Topology

- Topology refers to the way in which the workstations attached to the network are interconnected.

The BUS Topology: The bus topology uses a common single cable to connect all the workstations. Each computer performs its task of sending messages without the help of the central server. However, only one workstation can transmit a message at a particular time in the bus topology.

Advantages

1. Easy to connect and install.
2. Involves a low cost of installation time.
3. Can be easily extended.

Disadvantages

1. The entire network shuts down if there is a failure in the central cable.
2. Only a single message can travel at a particular time.
3. Difficult to troubleshoot an error.

The STAR Topology: A STAR topology is based on a central node which acts as a hub. A STAR topology is common in homes networks where all the computers connect to the single central computer using it as a hub.

Advantages

1. Easy to troubleshoot
2. A single node failure does not affect the entire network.
3. Fault detection and removal of faulty parts is easier.
4. In case a workstation fails, the network is not affected.

Disadvantages

1. Difficult to expand.
2. Longer cable is required.
3. The cost of the hub and the longer cables makes it expensive over others.
4. In case hub fails, the entire network fails.

The TREE Topology: The tree topology combines the characteristics of the linear bus and the star topologies. It consists of groups of star – configured workstations connected to a bus backbone cable.

Advantages

1. Eliminates network congestion.
2. The network can be easily extended.
3. Faulty nodes can easily be isolated from the rest of the network.

Disadvantages

1. Uses large cable length.
2. Requires a large amount of hardware components and hence is expensive.
3. Installation and reconfiguration is very difficult.

Types of Networks

LAN (Local Area Network): A Local Area Network (LAN) is a network that is confined to a relatively small area. It is generally limited to a geographic area such as writing lab, school or building. It is generally privately owned networks over a distance not more than 5 Km.

MAN (Metropolitan Area Network): MAN is the networks cover a group of nearby corporate offices or a city and might be either private or public.

WAN (Wide Area Network): These are the networks spread over large distances, say across countries or even continents through cabling or satellite uplinks are called WAN.

PAN (Personal Area Network): A Personal Area Network is computer network organized around an individual person. It generally covers a range of less than 10 meters. Personal Area Networks can be constructed with cables or wirelessly.

Network Protocols

- A protocol means the rules that are applicable for a network.
- It defines the standardized format for data packets, techniques for detecting and correcting errors and so on.
- A protocol is a formal description of message formats and the rules that two or more machines must follow to exchange those messages.
- E.g. using library books.

Types of Protocols are

1. HTTP.
2. FTP.
3. TCP/IP.
4. SLIP/PPP.

- **Hypertext Transfer Protocol (HTTP)** is a communications protocol for the transfer of information on the intranet and the World Wide Web. HTTP is a request/response standard between a client and a server. A client is the end-user; the server is the web site.
- **FTP (File Transfer Protocol)** is the simplest and most secure way to exchange files over the Internet. The objectives of FTP are:
- To promote sharing of files (computer programs and/or data).
- To encourage indirect or implicit use of remote computers.
- To shield a user from variations in file storage systems among different hosts.
- To transfer data reliably, and efficiently.
- TCP/IP (Transmission Control Protocol / Internet Protocol).

TCP - is responsible for verifying the correct delivery of data from client to server. Data can be lost in the intermediate network. TCP adds support to detect errors or lost data and to trigger retransmission until the data is correctly and completely received.

IP - is responsible for moving packet of data from node to node. IP forwards each packet based on a four byte destination address (the IP number). The Internet authorities assign ranges of numbers to different organizations. The organizations assign groups of their numbers to departments. IP operates on gateway machines that move data from department to organization to region and then around the world.

Telnet

It is an older internet utility that lets us log on to remote computer system. It also facilitates for terminal emulation purpose. Terminal emulation means using a pc like a mainframe computer through networking.

Wireless/Mobile Computing

Wireless communication is simply data communication without the use of landlines. Mobile computing means that the computing device is not continuously connected to the base or central network.

1. **GSM (Global System for Mobile communication):** it is leading digital cellular system. In covered areas, cell phone users can buy one phone that will work any where the standard is supported. It uses narrowband TDMA, which allows eight simultaneous calls on the same radio frequency.
2. **CDMA (Code Division Multiple Access)**: it is a digital cellular technology that uses spreadspectrum techniques. CDMA does not assign a specific frequency to each user. Instead, every channel uses the full available spectrum.
3. **WLL (Wireless in Local Loop):** WLL is a system that connects subscribers to the public switched telephone network using radio signals as a substitute for other connecting media.
4. **Email (Electronic Mail):** Email is sending and receiving messages by computer.
5. **Chat:** Online textual talk in real time, is called Chatting.
6. **Video Conferencing**: a two way videophone conversation among multiple participants is called video conferencing.
7. **SMS (Short Message Service):** SMS is the transmission of short text messages to and from a mobile pone, fax machine and or IP address.
8. **3G and EDGE:** 3G is a specification for the third generation of mobile communication of mobile communication technology. 3G promises increased bandwidth, up to 384 Kbps when a device is stationary.

EDGE (Enhanced Data rates for Global Evolution) is a radio based high speed mobile data standard.

Network Security Concepts

Viruses: Viruses are programs which replicate and attach to other programs in order to corrupt the executable codes. Virus enters the computer system through an external source and become destructive.

Worms: Worms are also self- replicating programs that do not create multiple copies of itself on one computer but propagate through the computer network. Worms log on to computer systems using the username and passwords and exploit the system.

Trojan horse: Though it is a useful program, however, a cracker can use it to intrude the computer system in order to exploit the resources. Such a program can also enter into the computer through an email or free programs downloaded through the Internet.

Spams: Unwanted e-mail (usually of a commercial nature sent out in bulk)

Cookies: Cookies are the text messages sent by a web server to the web browser primarily for identifying the user.

Firewall: A firewall is used to control the traffic between computer networks. It intercepts the packets between the computer networks and allows only authorized packets to pass.

Cyber Law: Cyber law refers to all the legal and regulatory aspects of Internet and the World Wide Web.

Cyber Crimes: Cyber crime involves the usage of the computer system and the computer network for criminal activity.

Hacking: Hacking is an unauthorized access to computer in order to exploit the resources.

Web Services

WWW: The World Wide Web or W3 or simply the Web is a collection of linked documents or pages, stored on millions of computers and distributed across the Internet.

HTML (Hyper Text Markup Language): HTML is a computer language that describes the structure and behavior of a web page. This language is used to create web pages.

XML (eXtensible Markup Language): Extensible Markup Language (XML) is a meta language that helps to describe the markup language.

HTTP (Hyper Text Transfer Protocol): A protocol to transfer hypertext requests and information between servers and browsers.

Domain Names: A domain name is a unique name that identifies a particular website and represents the name of the server where the web pages reside.

URL: The Uniform Resource Locator is a means to locate resources such as web pages on the Internet. URL is also a method to address the web pages on the Internet. There are two types of URL, namely, absolute URL and relative URL.

Website: A collection of related web pages stored on a web server is known as a website.

Web browser: A software application that enables to browse, search and collect information from the Web is known as Web browser.

Web Servers: The web pages on the Internet are stored on the computers that are connected to the Internet. These computers are known as web servers.

Web Hosting: Web Hosting or website hosting is the service to host, store and maintain the websites on the World Wide Web.

Web Scripting: The process of creating and embedding scripts in a web page is known as Web Scripting. Types of Scripts:

1. **Client Side Scripts**: - Client side scripts supports interaction within a webpage. E.g. VB Script, Java Script, PHP (**P**HP"S **H**ypertext **P**reprocessor).
2. **Server Side Scripts**: - Server side scripting supports execution at server – end. E.g. ASP, JSP, PHP

Open Source Terminologies

- **Free Software:** The S/W's is freely accessible and can be freely used changed improved copied and distributed by all and payments are needed to make for free S/W.
- **Open Source Software:** S/w whose source code is available to the customer and it can be modified and redistributed without any limitation .OSS may come free of cost but nominal charges has to pay nominal charges (Support of S/W and development of S/W).
- **FLOSS (Free Libre and Open Source Software):** S/w which is free as well as open source S/W. (Free S/W + Open Source S/W).
- **GNU (G**NU's **N**ot **U**nix**):** GNU project emphasize on the freedom and its objective is to create a system compatible to UNIX but not identical with it.
- **FSF (Free Software Foundation):** FSF is a non –profit organization created for the purpose of the free s/w movement. Organization funded many s/w developers to write free software.
- **OSI (Open Source Initiative)**: Open source software organization dedicated to cause of promoting open source software it specified the criteria of OSS and its source code is not freely available.

- **W3C (World Wide Web Consortium)**: W3C is responsible for producing the software standards for World Wide Web.
- **Proprietary Software:** Proprietary Software is the s/w that is neither open nor freely available, normally the source code of the Proprietary Software is not available but further distribution and modification is possible by special permission by the supplier.
- **Freeware:** Freeware are the software freely available, which permit redistribution but not modification (and their source code is not available). Freeware is distributed in *Binary Form* (ready to run) without any licensing fees.
- **Shareware:** Software for which license fee is payable after some time limit, its source code is not available and modification to the software are not allowed.
- **Localization:** localization refers to the adaptation of language, content and design to reflect local cultural sensitivities .e.g. Software Localization: where messages that a program presents to the user need to be translated into various languages.
- **Internationalization:** Opposite of localization.

Open Source/Free Software

- **Linux:** Linux is a famous computer operating system. popular Linux server set of program – LAMP(Linux, Apache, MySQL, PHP)
- **Mozilla:** Mozilla is a free internet software that includes.
    - A web browser.
    - An email client.
    - An HTML editor.
    - IRC client.
- **Apache server:** Apache web server is an open source web server available for many platforms such as BSD, Linux, and Microsoft Windows etc.
    - Apache Web server is maintained by open community of developers of Apache software foundation.
- **MYSQL:** MYSQL is one of the most popular open source database system. Features of MYSQl.
    - Multithreading.
    - Multi –User.
    - SQl Relational Database Server.
    - Works in many different platform.

- **PostgreSQL:** PostgresSQL is a free software object relational database server. PostgresSQL can be downloaded from **www.postgressql.org.**
- **Pango:** Pango project is to provide an open source framework for the layout and rendering of internationalized text into GTK + GNOME environment.Pango using Unicode for all of its encoding, and will eventually support output in all the worlds major languages.
- **OpenOffice:** OpenOffice is an office applications suite. It is intended to compatible and directly complete with Microsoft office.

OOo Version 1.1 includes:

  - Writer (word processor).
  - Calc (spreadsheet).
  - Draw (graphics program)etc.

- **Tomcat:** Tomcat functions as a servlet container. Tomcat implements the servlet and the JavaServer Pages .Tomcat comes with the jasper compiler that complies JSPs into servlets.
- **PHP (Hypertext Preprocessor):** PHP is a widely used open source programming language for server side application and developing web content.
- **Python: Python** is an interactive programming language originally as scripting language for Amoeba OS capable of making system calls.
- Cloud computing is the delivery of computing as a service rather than a product, whereby shared resources, software, and information are provided to computers and other devices as a utility (like the electricity grid) over a network (typically the Internet). Clouds can be classified as public, private or hybrid.

Tips to Solve Questions based on Networking

1. **Where Server should be placed**: Server should be placed in the building where the number of computers is **maximum**.
2. **Suggest a suitable cable layout of connection**: A suitable cable layout can be suggested in the following two ways:-
   i. **On the Basis of Server:** First the location of the Server is found out. Server is placed in that building where the number of computers are maximum (According to 80 – 20 rule). After finding the server position, each building distance is compared with the Server building directly or indirectly (taking other building in

between). The shortest distance is counted whether it is through directly or indirectly.

ii. **On the Basis of Distance from each building:** The distance between the each building is compared to all other buildings either directly or indirectly. The shortest distance is counted whether it is directly or through some other building.

3. **Where the following devices be placed**

   a) **MODEM**:

   b) **HUB / SWITCH:- In all the wings**

   c) **BRIDGE**:

   d) **REPEATER**: It is used if the distances higher than 70 m. It regenerates data and voice signals.

   e) **ROUTER**: When one LAN will be connected to the other LAN.

1 and 2 Marks Questions

1. What do you mean by a computer network?

   Ans: Computer network is an interconnection of autonomous computers connected together using transmission media.

2. What is the need for networking the computers?

   Ans: 1. Sharing of Information, 2. Reliability, 3. Reduces cost, 4. Time saving

3. What is the full form of ARPANET?

   Ans: Advanced Research Projects Agency Network

4. What are various data transmission modes?

   Ans: There are three modes of data transmission

   - Simplex.
   - Half-duplex.
   - Full-duplex.

5. What is the difference between Simplex and half duplex transmission?

   Ans: In simples transmission mode, the data can be transferred in only one direction where as in half duplex transmission mode, the data can be transmitted in both directions but one at a time.

6. What do you mean by MODEM?

   Ans: MODEM stands for MODulatorDEModuator. It is a device that can convert an analog signal into digital signal and vice versa.

7. Define the terms Bandwidth.

Ans: Bandwidth is the range of frequencies that is available for the transmission of data. Wider the bandwidth of a communication channel, the more data it can transmit in a given period of time.

8. What are various types of transmission media?

Ans: There are two broad categories of transmission media

- Guided media.
- Unguided Media.

9. Explain in brief the advantages and disadvantages of Twisted pair Cable.

Ans: Advantages

- Inexpensive.
- Often available in existing phone system.
- Well tested and east to get.

Disadvantages

- Susceptible to noise (sound, energy etc.).
- Not as durable as coaxial cable.
- Does not support high speed.
- What do you mean by communication protocol?.

Ans: A protocol is a set of rules to enable computers to connect with one another and to exchange information with minimum possible error.

10. List various functions of Communication protocol.

Ans: Data sequencing, Data Formatting, Flow control, Error Control,Connection Establishment and termination, Data Security.

11. List commonly used protocols.

Ans: HTTP, TCT/IP, FTP, SLIP, PPP, SMTP, POP, ICMP

12. What are the main functions of TCP

Ans: The TCP does the following activities.

- It breaks the data into packets that the network
- Verifies that all the packets arrived at the destination
- Reassembles the data

13. What do you mean by network topology?

Ans: Topology is how the nodes/computers are interconnected together.

14. List various types of Networks.

Ans: LAN, MAN, WAN

15. Give names of various networking topologies in LAN.

Ans: 1.Star Topology, 2.Ring topology, 3.Bus topology 4.Mesh Topology

16. Write two advantages and two disadvantages of STAR topology.

Ans: Advantages of STAR topology

- It is easy to modify and add new computers to a star network without disturbing the rest of the network.
- Troubleshooting a star topology network is easy.

Disadvantages

- All the nodes are dependent on the central system. Hub. Failure of hub result in shutting down of whole of the system.
- Long cable length is required.

17. What is NFS?

Ans: NFS stands for Network File System. NFS is a protocol that allows a set of computers to access each others files.

18. What are the characteristics of cloud computing?

Ans. Cloud computing exhibits the following key characteristics:

1. Agility: improves with users' ability to re-provision technological infrastructure resources.
2. Application programming interface (API) accessibility to software that enables machines to interact with cloud software in the same way that a traditional user interface (e.g., a computer desktop) facilitates interaction between humans and computers. Cloud computing systems typically use Representational State Transfer (REST)-based APIs.
3. Cost: cloud providers claim that computing costs reduce. A public-cloud delivery model converts capital expenditure to operational expenditure. This purportedly lowers barriers to entry, as infrastructure is typically provided by a third party and does not need to be purchased for one-time or infrequent intensive computing tasks
4. Device and location independence enable users to access systems using a web browser regardless of their location or what device they use (e.g., PC, mobile phone). As infrastructure is off-site (typically provided by a third-party) and accessed via the Internet, users can connect from anywhere.
5. Maintenance of cloud computing applications is easier, because they do not need to be installed on each user's computer and can be accessed from different places.

4 Marks Questions: Communication and Network Concepts

1. Knowledge Supplement Organization has set up its new centre at Manglore for its office and web based activities. It has four buildings as shown in the diagram below:

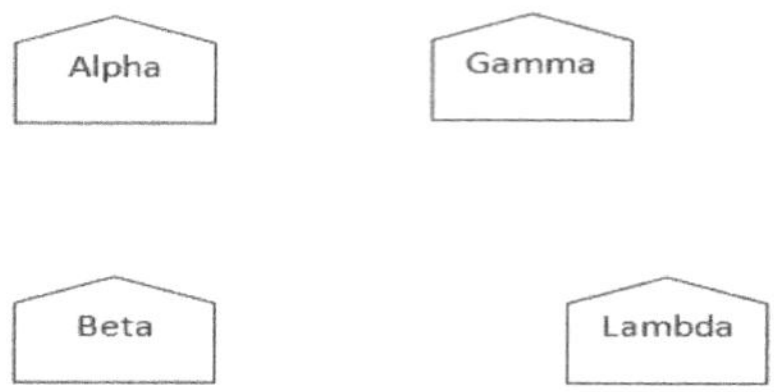

Center to center distance between various buildings Number of Computers.

Alpha to Beta	50m
Beta to Gamma	150m
Gamma to Lambda	25m
Alpha to Lambda	170m
Beta to Lambda	125m
Alpha to Gamma	90m

Alpha	25
Beta	50
Gamma	125
Lambda	10

   1. Suggest a cable layout of connections between the buildings
   2. Suggest the most suitable place (i.e building) to house the server of this organization with a suitable reason.
   3. Suggest the placement of the following devices with justification.
      i. Repeater.
      ii. Hub/Switch.
   4. The organization is planning to link its front office situated in the city in a hilly region where cable connection is not feasible, suggest an economic way to connect it with reasonably high speed?

2. BHARATH ELECTRONICS COMPANY in Coimbatore is setting up the network between its different departments located in different blocks. There are 4 blocks named as Meera (M), Tagore (T), Kalidas (K) and Bharathi (B).

   Distances between various blocks are given below:

Block B to Block K	100 m
Block B to Block M	200 m
Block B to Block T	400 m
Block K to Block M	300 m
Block M to Block P	100m
Block R to Block P	450 m

Number of Computers

Block M	15
Block R	100
Block A	50
Block P	150

1. Suggest a suitable Topology for networking the computers of all Blocks.
2. Name the Block where the Server is to be installed. Justify your answer.
3. Suggest the placement of Hub/Switch in the network.
4. Mention an economic technology to provide Internet accessibility to allBlocks.

3. If "Kanganalay Cosmetics" is planning to start their offices in four major cities in Uttar Pradesh to provide cosmetic product support in its retail fields. The company has planned to set up their offices in Lucknow at three different locations and have named them as "Head office", "Sales office", & "Prod office". The company's regional offices are located at Varanasi, Kanpur & Saharanpur. A rough layout of the same is as follows:

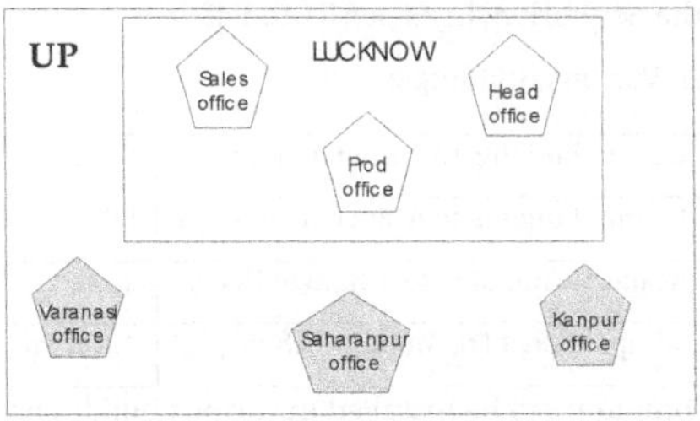

An approximate distance between these offices as per network survey team is as follows:

Place from	Place to	Distance
Head office	Sales office	15 KM
Head office	Prod office	8 KM
Head office	Varanasi Office	295 KM
Head office	Kanpur Office	195 KM
Head office	Saharanpur office	408 KM

Number of Computers

Head office	156
Sales office	25
Prod office	56
Varanasi Office	85
Kanpur Office	107
Saharanpur office	105

a) Suggest the placement of the ***repeater*** with justification. Name the branch where the ***server*** should be installed. Justify your answer.

b) Suggest the ***device*** to be procured by the company for connecting all the computers within each of its offices out of the following devices.

- Modem.
- Telephone.
- Switch/Hub.

c) The company is planning to link its head office situated in Lucknow with the office at Saharanpur. Suggest an economic way to connect it; the company is ready to compromise on the speed of connectivity. Justify your answer.

4. Dr. Rizvi Education Society of India is starting its new CBSE School in Mumbai (Maharashtra). The society is already running a School in Jaunpur (UP) named Dr. Rizvi Learners' Academy, having 3 major buildings in 2 km area campus. As a network expert you need to suggest the network plan as per E1 to E4:

Wire Distance Between Various Buildings:

Library building to Admin building	90m
Library building to Academic building	80m
Academic building to Admin building	15m
Jaunpur School to Mumbai School	1350km

Expected number of Computers to be installed in various buildings:

Library Building	20
Academic building	150
Admin building	35
Mumbai School	5

E1. Suggest the cable layout among various buildings inside school campus for connecting the buildings.

E2. Suggest the most suitable place to house the server of the school with a suitable reason.

E3. Suggest an efficient device from the following to be installed in each of the building to connect all the computers:

1. Bridge.
2. Repeater.
3. Switch.

E4. Suggest the most suitable service (very high speed) to provide data connectivity between Rizvi Learners' in Jaunpur and Mumbai CBSE School from the options.

Higher Order Thinking Questions

1. What is protocol? How many types of protocols are there?

Ans. When computers communicate each other, there needs to be a common set of rules and instructions that each computer follows. A specific set of communication rules is called a protocol. Some protocol: PPP, HTTP, SLIP, FTP, TCP/IP

2. What is the difference between Networking and Remote Networking?

Ans. The main difference between Networking and Remote Networking, is the network which we use in offices or other places locally such LAN or INTERNET and remote networking is one which we use TERMINAL Services to communicate with the remote users such WAN.

3. What is point-to-point protocol?

Ans. A communication protocol used to connect computer to remote networking services include Internet Service Providers. In networking, the Point-to-Point protocol is commonly used to establish a direct connection between two nodes. Its primary use has been to connect computers using a phone line.

4. How gateway is different from router?

Ans. A gateway operates at the upper levels of the OSI model and translates information between two completely different network architectures. Routers allow different networks to communicate with each other. They forward packets from one network to another based on network layer information. A gateway can interpret and translate the different protocols that are used on two distinct networks. Unlike routers that successfully connect networks with protocols that are similar, a gateway perform an application layer conversion of information from one protocol stack to another.

5. What is the role of network administrator?

Ans. Basic tasks for which a network administrator may be responsible:

- Setting up and configuring network hardware and software.
- Installing and configuring network media and connections.
- Connecting user nodes and peripherals of all kinds to the network.
- Adding users to and removing users from the network.
- Managing user account.
- Ensuring the security of the network.
- Provide training to the users to utilize the network's resources.

6. What is the difference between baseband and broadband transmission?

Ans. Baseband is a bi-directional transmission while broadband is a unidirectional transmission. No Frequency division multiplexing possible in base band but possible in broadband.

SNo	Baseband	Broadband
1	Entire bandwidth of the cable is consumed by a signal	Broadband transmission, signals are sent on multiple frequencies,allowing multiple signals to be sent simultaneously.
2	Digital signals	Analog signals
3	bi-directional transmission	unidirectional transmission
4	No Frequency division multiplexing possible	Frequency division multiplexing possible
5	Uses for short distance	Uses for long distance

7. What are the difference between domain and workgroup?

Ans.

SNo	Domain	Workgroup
1	One or more computers are servers	All Computers are peers.
2	If you have a user account on the domain, you can logon to any computer on the domain.	Each computer has a set of accounts.
3	There can be 100+ computers	Typically not more then 20-30 computers
4	The computers can be on different local network	All computers must be on the same local network.

8. What is the differences between POP3 and IMAP Mail Server?

Ans. IMAP is a standard protocol for accessing e-mail from a local server. A simpler e-mail protocol is Post Office Protocol 3 (POP3), which download mail to the computer and does not maintain the mail on the server. IMAP, e-mails are stored on the server, while in POP3, the messages are transferred to the client's computer when they are read.

9. Name different layer of the ISO OSI Model.

Ans. International Standard Orrganisation–Open Systems Interconnection has seven layers; Physical Layer, Data Link Layer, Network Layer, Transport Layer, Session Layer, Presentation Layer Application Layer.

10. What is client server architecture?

Ans. To designated a particular node which is well known and fixed address, to provide a service to the network as a whole. The node providing the service is known as the server and the nodes that use that services are called clients of that server. This type of network is called Client-Server Architecture.

11. What is FDM? Give example.

Ans. FDM-Frequency Division Multiplexing is used in analog transmission. It is often used in short distance. It is code transparent and any terminal of the same speed can use the same sub-channel after the sub-channel is established. The best example if FDM is the way we receive various stations in a radio.

12. Describe the following in brief:

a) MOSAIC.

b) USENET.

c) WAIS.

Ans.

1. MOSAIC: is the program for cruising the internet. The National centre wrote this program for Super Computer application at the university of Illinois. It has a simple window interface, which creates useful hypertext links that automatically perform some of the menu bar and button functions.
2. USENET: is the way to meet people and share information. Usenet newsgroup is a special group set up by people who want to share common interests ranging from current topic to cultural heritages.
3. WAIS: is a WIDE AREA INFORMATION SERVER.

COMPUTER SCIENCE (CODE 083)

SAMPLE PAPER SET - 1

Max. Marks: 70 **Duration : 3 Hours**

1.

a) What is the difference between Global Variable and Local Variable? 2

b) Write the names of the header files to which the following belong: 1

1. strcmp()
2. fabs()

c) Rewrite the following program after removing the syntactical errors (if any). 2

Underline each correction.

```
class PAYITNOW
{
    int Charge;
PUBLIC:
  void Raise(){cin>>Charge;}
  void Show{cout<<Charge;}
};
void main()
{
    PAYITNOW P;
    P.Raise();
    Show();
}
```

d) Find the output of the following program: 3

```
#include <iostream.h>
struct PLAY
{int Score, Bonus;};
void Calculate(PLAY &P, int N=10)
{
        P.Score++;P.Bonus+=N;
}
void main()
{
```

```
        PLAY PL={10,15};
        Calculate(PL,5);
        cout<<PL.Score<<":"<<PL.Bonus<<endl;
        Calculate(PL);
        cout<<PL.Score<<":"<<PL.Bonus<<endl;
        Calculate(PL,15);
        cout<<PL.Score<<":"<<PL.Bonus<<endl;
}
```

e) Find the output of the following program: 2

```
#include <iostream.h>
#include <ctype.h>
void Encrypt(char T[])
{
        for (int i=0;T[i]!='\0';i+=2)
                if (T[i]=='A' || T[i]=='E') T[i]='#';
        else if (islower(T[i])) T[i]=toupper(T[i]);
                else T[i]='@';
}
void main()
{
char Text[]="SaVE EArtH";//The two words in the string Text
                          //are separated by single space
        Encrypt(Text);
        cout<<Text<<endl;
}
```

f) In the following program, if the value of N given by the user is 15, what maximum and minimum values the program could possibly display? 2

```
#include <iostream.h>
#include <stdlib.h>
void main()
{
    int N,Guessme;
    randomize();
    cin>>N;
    Guessme=random(N)+10;
    cout<<Guessme<<endl;
}
```

2.

a) What do you understand by Data Encapsulation and Data Hiding? 2

b) Answer the questions (i) and (ii) after going through the following class: 2

```
class Seminar
{
        int Time;
public:
        Seminar()
        //Function 1
        {
        Time=30;cout<<"Seminar starts now"<<end1;
    }
    void Lecture()                                  //Function 2
        {
        cout<<"Lectures in the seminar on"<<end1;
    }
        Seminar(int Duration)                       //Function 3
        {
        Time=Duration;cout<<"Seminar starts now"<<end1;
    }
    ~Seminar()                                      //Function 4
    {
      cout<<"Vote of thanks"<<end1;
    }
};
```

i) In Object Oriented Programming, what is Function 4 referred as and when does it get invoked/called?

ii) In Object Oriented Programming, which concept is illustrated by Function 1 and Function 3 together? Write an example illustrating the calls for these functions.

c) Define a class TEST in C++ with following description: 4

Private Members

a. TestCode of type integer.

b. Description of type string.

c. NoCandidate of type integer.

d. CenterReqd (number of centers required) of type integer.

e. A member function CALCNTR () to calculate and return the number of centers as (NoCandidates/100+1).

Public Members

- A function SCHEDULE () to allow user to enter values for TestCode, Description, NoCandidate & call function CALCNTR() to calculate the number of Centres.
- A function DISPTEST () to allow user to view the content of all the data members.

d) Answer the questions (i) to (iv) based on the following: 4

```
class PUBLISHER
{
        char Pub[12];
        double Turnover;
protected:
        void Register();
public:
        PUBLISHER();
        void Enter();
        void Display();
};

class BRANCH
{
        char CITY[20];
protected:
        float Employees;
public:
        BRANCH();
        void Haveit();
        void Giveit();
};
class AUTHOR:private BRANCH,public PUBLISHER
{
        int Acode;
        char Aname[20];
```

```
        float Amount;
public:
        AUTHOR();
        void Start();
        void Show();
};
```

(i) Write the names of data members, which are accessible from objects belonging to class AUTHOR.

(ii) Write the names of all the member functions which are accessible from objects belonging to class BRANCH.

(iii) Write the names of all the members which are accessible from member functions of class AUTHOR.

(iv) How many bytes will be required by an object belonging to class AUTHOR?

3.

a) Write a function in C++ to merge the contents of two sorted arrays A & B into third array C. Assuming array A is sorted in ascending order, B is sorted in descending order, the resultant array is required to be in ascending order. 4

b) An array S[40][30] is stored in the memory along the row with each of the element occupying 2 bytes, find out the memory location for the element S[20][10], if an element S[15][5] is stored at the memory location 5500. 4

c) Write a function in C++ to perform Insert operation in a dynamically allocated Queue containing names of students. 4

d) Write a function in C++ to find the sum of both left and right diagonal elements from a two dimensional array (matrix). 2

e) Evaluate the following postfix notation of expression: 2

20,30,+,50,40,-,*

4.

a) Observe the program segment given below carefully and fill the blanks marked as Statement 1 and Statement 2 using seekp() and seekg() functions for performing the required task. 1

```
#include <fstream.h>
class Item
{
    int Ino;char Item[20];
```

```
public:
    //Function to search and display the content from a particular //record number
    void Search(int );
    //Function to modify the content of a particular record number
    void Modify(int);
};
void Item::Search(int RecNo)
{
        fstream File;
        File.open("STOCK.DAT",ios::binary|ios::in);
        ____________________
        //Statement 1
        File.read((char*)this,sizeof(Item));
        cout<<Ino<<"==>"<<Item<<endl;
        File.close();
}
void Item::Modify(int RecNo)
{
        fstream File;
        File.open("STOCK.DAT",ios::binary|ios::in|ios::out);
        cout>>Ino;cin.getline(Item,20);
                ____________________
//Statement 2
        File.write((char*)this,sizeof(Item));
        File.close();
}
```

b) Write a function in C++ to count the number of lines present in a text file "STORY.TXT". 2

c) Write a function in C++ to search for a BookNo from a binary file "BOOK.DAT", assuming the binary file is containing the objects of the following class. 3

```
class BOOK
{
        int Bno;
        char Title[20];
```

```
public:
int RBno(){return Bno;}
        void Enter(){cin>>Bno;gets(Title);}
        void Display(){cout<<Bno<<Title<<endl;}
};
```

5.

a) What do you understand by Degree and Cardinality of a table? 2

b) Consider the following tables ACTIVITY and COACH. Write SQL commands for the statements (i) to (iv) and give outputs for SQL queries (v) to (viii) 6

ACTIVITY

ACode	ActivityName	ParticipantsNum	PrizeMoney	ScheduleDate
1001	Relay 100x4	16	10000	23-Jan-2004
1002	High jump	10	12000	12-Dec-2003
1003	Shot Put	12	8000	14-Feb-2004
1005	Long Jump	12	9000	01-Jan-2004
1008	Discuss Throw	10	15000	19-Mar-2004

COACH

PCode	Name	ACode
1	Ahmad Hussain	1001
2	Ravinder	1008
3	Janila	1001
4	Naaz	1003

1. To display the name of all activities with their Acodes in descending order.
2. To display sum of PrizeMoney for each of the Number of participants groupings (as shown in column <u>ParticipantsNum</u> 10,12,16).
3. To display the coach's name and ACodes in ascending order of ACode from the table COACH.
4. To display the content of the GAMES table whose ScheduleDate earliar than 01/01/2004 in ascending order of ParticipantNum.
5. SELECT COUNT(DISTINCT ParticipantsNum) FROM ACTIVITY;
6. SELECT MAX(ScheduleDate),MIN(ScheduleDate) FROM ACTIVITY;
7. SELECT SUM(PrizeMoney) FROM ACTIVITY;

SELECT DISTINCT ParticipantNum FROM COACH;

6.

a) State and verify Demorgan's Laws. 2

b) Write the equivalent Boolean Expression for the following Logic Circuit 2

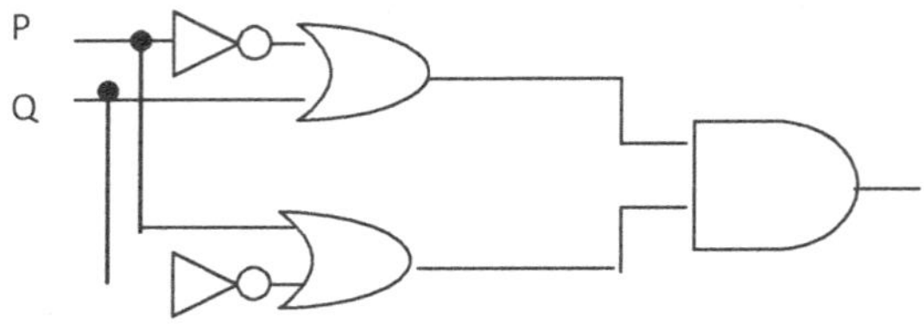

c) Write the POS form of a Boolean function F, which is represented in a truth table 1 as follows:

U	V	W	F
0	0	0	1
0	0	1	0
0	1	0	1
0	1	1	0
1	0	0	1
1	0	1	0
1	1	0	1
1	1	1	1

d) Reduce the following Boolean Expression using K-Map: 3

F(A,B,C,D)=Σ(0,1,2,4,5,6,8,10)

7.

a) What is the significance of ARPANET in the network? 1

b) Expand the following terminologies: 1

1. CDMA
2. GSM

c) Give two major reasons to have network security. 1

d) What is the purpose of using a Web Browser? Name any one commonly used Web Browser. 1

e) Knowledge Supplement Organisation has set up its new center at Mangalore for its office and web based activities. It has 4 blocks of buildings as shown in the diagram below:

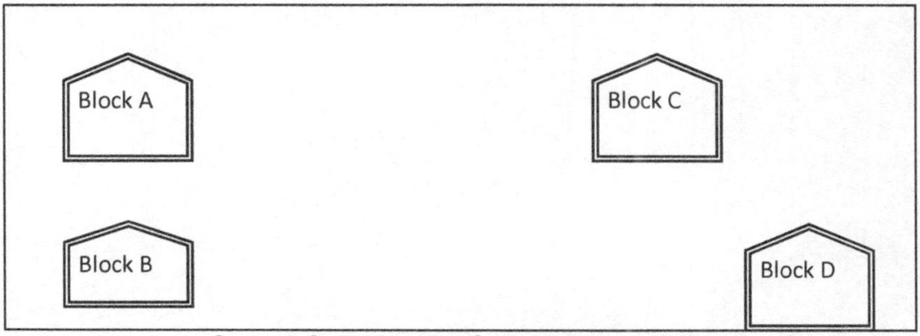

Center to Center Distances between Various Blocks

Black A to Block B	50 m
Block B to Block C	150 m
Block C to Block D	25 m
Block A to Block D	170 m
Block B to Block D	125 m
Block A to Block C	90 m

Number of Computers

Black A	25
Block B	50
Block C	125
Block D	10

e1) Suggest a cable layout of connections between the blocks. 1

e2) Suggest the most suitable place (i.e. block) to house the server of this organisation with a suitable reason. 1

e3) Suggest the placement of the following devices with justification 1

(i) Repeater.

(ii) Hub/Switch.

e4) The organization is planning to link its front office situated in the city in a hilly region where cable connection is not feasible, suggest an economic way to connect it with reasonably high speed? 1

CBSE Outside Delhi 2013-14

Series OSR **Code No. 91**

Roll No. | | | | | | | |

Candidates must write the Code on the title page of the answer-book.

- Please check that this question paper contains 16 printed pages.
- Code number given on the right hand side of the question paper should be written on the title page of the answer-book by the candidate.
- Please check that this question paper contains 7 questions.
- **Please write down the Serial Number of the question before attempting it.**
- 15 minutes time has been allotted to read this question paper. The question paper will be distributed at 10.15 a.m. From 10.15 a.m. to 10.30 a.m., the students will read the question paper only and will not write any answer on the answer-book during this period.

COMPUTER SCIENCE

Time allowed : 3 hours *Maximum Marks : 70*

Instructions :

(i) All questions are compulsory.

(ii) Programming Language : C++

1. (a) What is the difference between call by reference and call by value with respect to memory allocation ? Give a suitable example to illustrate using C++ code. 2

(b) Observe the following C++ code and write the name(s) of the header file(s), which will be essentially required to run it in a C++ compiler : *1*

```
void main()
{
  char CH,STR[20];
  cin>>STR;
  CH=toupper(STR[0]);
  cout<<STR<<"starts with"<<CH<<endl;
}
```

(c) Rewrite the following C++ code after removing all the syntax error(s), if present in the code. Make sure that you underline each correction done by you in the code. *2*

Important Note :

- Assume that all the required header files are already included, which are essential to run this code.
- The corrections made by you do not change the logic of the program.

```
typedef char[80] STR;
void main()
{
  Txt STR;
  gets(Txt);
  cout<<Txt[0]<<'\t<<Txt[2];
  cout<<Txt<<endline;
}
```

(d) Obtain the output from the following C++ program as expected to appear on the screen after its execution. 2

Important Note :

- All the desired header files are already included in the code, which are required to run the code.

```
void main()
{
  char *Text="AJANTA";
  int *P, Num[]={1,5,7,9};
  P=Num;
  cout<<*P<<Text<<endl;
  Text++;
  P++;
  cout<<*P<<Text<<endl;
}
```

(e) Obtain the output of the following C++ program, which will appear on the screen after its execution. 3

Important Note :

- All the desired header files are already included in the code, which are required to run the code.

```
class Game
{
  int Level, Score;
  char Type;
public:
  Game(char GType='P')
  {Level=1;Score=0;Type=GType;}
  void Play(int GS);
  void Change();
  void Show()
  {
    cout<<Type<<"@"<<Level<<endl;
    cout<<Score<<endl;
  }
};
```

```
void main()
{
  Game A('G'),B;
  B.Show();
  A.Play(11);
  A.Change();
  B.Play(25);
  A.Show();
  B.Show();
}
void Game::Change()
{
  Type=(Type=='P')?'G':'P';
}
void Game::Play(int GS)
{
  Score+=GS;
  if(Score>=30)
    Level=3;
  else if(Score>=20)
    Level=2;
  else
    Level=1;
}
```

) Read the following C++ code carefully and find out, which out of the given options (i) to (iv) are the expected correct output(s) of it. Also, write the maximum and minimum value that can be assigned to the variable **Taker** used in the code : 2

```
void main()
{
  int GuessMe[4]={100,50,200,20};
  int Taker=random(2)+2;
  for (int Chance=0;Chance<Taker;Chance++)
     cout<<GuessMe[Chance]<<"#";
}
```

(i) 100#

(ii) 50#200#

(iii) 100#50#200#

(iv) 100#50

2. (a) What is function overloading ? Write an example using C++ to illustrate the concept of function overloading. 2

(b) Answer the questions (i) and (ii) after going through the following class : 2

```
class Hospital
{
  int Pno, Dno;
public:
  Hospital(int PN);                //Function 1
  Hospital();                      //Function 2
  Hospital(Hospital &H);           //Function 3
  void In();                       //Function 4
  void Disp();                     //Function 5
};
void main()
{
  Hospital H(20);                  //Statement 1
}
```

(i) Which of the functions out of Function 1, 2, 3, 4 or 5 will get executed when the Statement 1 is executed in the above code ?

(ii) Write a statement to declare a new object G with reference to already existing object H using Function 3.

(c) Define a class Tourist in C++ with the following specification : 4

Data Members

- CNo - to store Cab No
- CType - to store a character 'A', 'B', or 'C' as City Type
- PerKM - to store per Kilo Meter charges
- Distance - to store Distance travelled (in KM)

Member Functions

- A constructor function to initialize CType as 'A' and CNo as '0000'
- A function CityCharges( ) to assign PerKM as per the following table :

CType	PerKM
A	20
B	18
C	15

- A function **RegisterCab()** to allow administrator to enter the values for CNo and CType. Also, this function should call **CityCharges()** to assign PerKM Charges.
- A function **Display()** to allow user to enter the value of Distance and display CNo, CType, PerKM, PerKM*Distance (as Amount) on screen.

(d) Consider the following C++ code and answer the questions from (i) to (iv) : *4*

```
class University
{
  long Id;
  char City[20];
protected:
  char Country[20];
public:
  University();
  void Register( );
  void Display( );
};
```

```
class Department: private University
{
  long DCode[10];
  char HOD[20];
protected:
  double Budget;
public:
  Department();
  void Enter();
  void Show();
};
class Student: public Department
{
  long RollNo;
  char Name[20];
public:
  Student();
  void Enroll();
  void View();
};
```

(i) **Which type of Inheritance is shown in the above example ?**

(ii) **Write the names of those member functions, which are directly accessed from the objects of class Student.**

(iii) **Write the names of those data members, which can be directly accessible from the member functions of class Student.**

(iv) **Is it possible to directly call function Display( ) of class University from an object of class Department ?**

(Answer as Yes or No).

3. (a) Write code for a function `void EvenOdd(int T[], int C)` in C++, to add 1 in all the odd values and 2 in all the even values of the array T. 3

Example : If the original content of the array T is

T[0]	T[1]	T[2]	T[3]	T[4]
35	12	16	69	26

The modified content will be :

T[0]	T[1]	T[2]	T[3]	T[4]
36	14	18	70	28

(b) An array A[20][30] is stored along the row in the memory with each element requiring 4 bytes of storage. If the base address of array A is 32000, find out the location of A[15][10]. Also, find the total number of elements present in this array. 3

(c) Write a user-defined function `AddEnd2(int A[][4],int N,int M)` in C++ to find and display the sum of all the values, which are ending with 2 (i.e., units place is 2). 2

For example if the content of array is :

22	16	12
19	5	2

The output should be

36

(d) Evaluate the following postfix expression. Show the status of stack after execution of each operation separately : 2

T, F, NOT, AND, T, OR, F, AND

(e) Write a function PUSHBOOK( ) in C++ to perform insert operation on a Dynamic Stack, which contains Book_no and Book_Title. Consider the following definition of NODE, while writing your C++ code. 4

```
struct NODE
{
  int Book_No;
  char Book_Title[20];
  NODE *Next;
};
```

4. (a) Fill in the blanks marked as Statement 1 and Statement 2, in the program segment given below with appropriate functions for the required task. *1*

```
class Agency
{
  int ANo;                              //Agent Code
  char AName[20];                       //Agent Name
  char Mobile[12];                      //Agent Mobile
public:
  void Enter();   //Function to enter details of agent
  void Disp();  //Function to display details of agent
  int RAno(){return ANo;}
  void UpdateMobile() //Function to update Mobile
  {
    cout<<"Updated Mobile:";
    gets(Mobile);
  }
};
void AgentUpdate()
{
  fstream F;
  F.open("AGENT.DAT",ios::binary|ios::in|ios::out);
  int Updt=0;
  int UAno;
  cout<<"Ano (Agent No - to update Mobile):";
  cin>>UAno;
  Agency A;
  while (!Updt && F.read((char*)&A,sizeof(A)))
  {
     if (A.RAno()==UAno)
     {
//Statement 1:To call the function to Update Mobile No.
         ________________________________ ;
```

```
//Statement 2:To reposition file pointer to re-write
              the updated object back in the file
        ______________________________________;
        F.write((char*)&A,sizeof(A));
        Updt++;
      }
  }

  if (Updt)
     cout<<"Mobile Updated for Agent"<<UAno<<endl;
  else
     cout<<"Agent not in the Agency"<<endl;
  F.close();
}
```

(b) Write a function **AECount()** in C++, which should read each character of a text file **NOTES.TXT**, should count and display the occurrence of alphabets **A** and **E** (including small cases **a** and **e** too). 2

Example :

If the file content is as follows :

```
CBSE enhanced its
CCE guidelines further.
```

The **AECount()** function should display the output as

```
A:1
E:7
```

(c) Assuming the class TOYS as declared below, write a function in C++ to read the objects of TOYS from binary file **TOYS.DAT** and display those details of those TOYS, which are meant for children of AgeRange "5 to 8". 3

```
class TOYS
{
  int ToyCode;
  char ToyName[10];
  char AgeRange;
public:
  void Enter()
  {
    cin>>ToyCode;
    gets(ToyName);
    gets(AgeRange);
  }
  void Display()
  {
    cout<<ToyCode<<":"<<ToyName<<endl;
    cout<<AgeRange<<endl;
  }
  char* WhatAge(){return AgeRange;}
};
```

5. (a) Explain the concept of Cartesian Product between two tables, with the help of appropriate example. 2

NOTE : Answer the questions (b) and (c) on the basis of the following tables **SHOPPE** and **ACCESSORIES**.

Table : SHOPPE

Id	SName	Area
S001	ABC Computronics	CP
S002	All Infotech Media	GK II
S003	Tech Shoppe	CP
S004	Geeks Tecno Soft	Nehru Place
S005	Hitech Tech Store	Nehru Place

Table : ACCESSORIES

No	Name	Price	Id
A01	Mother Board	12000	S01
A02	Hard Disk	5000	S01
A03	Keyboard	500	S02
A04	Mouse	300	S01
A05	Mother Board	13000	S02
A06	Keyboard	400	S03
A07	LCD	6000	S04
T08	LCD	5500	S05
T09	Mouse	350	S05
T10	Hard Disk	4500	S03

(b) Write the SQL queries : 4

(i) To display Name and Price of all the Accessories in ascending order of their Price.

(ii) To display Id and SName of all Shoppe located in Nehru Place.

(iii) To display Minimum and Maximum Price of each Name of Accessories.

(iv) To display Name, Price of all Accessories and their respective SName where they are available.

(c) Write the output of the following SQL commands : 2

(i) SELECT DISTINCT NAME FROM ACCESSORIES WHERE PRICE >= 5000;

(ii) SELECT AREA, COUNT(*) FROM SHOPPE GROUP BY AREA;

(iii) SELECT COUNT(DISTINCT AREA) FROM SHOPPE;

(iv) SELECT NAME, PRICE*0.05 DISCOUNT FROM ACCESSORIES WHERE SNO IN ('S02', 'S03');

6. (a) Name the law shown below and verify it using a truth table. 2

X+X'.Y=X+Y

(b) Obtain the Boolean Expression for the logic circuit shown below : 2

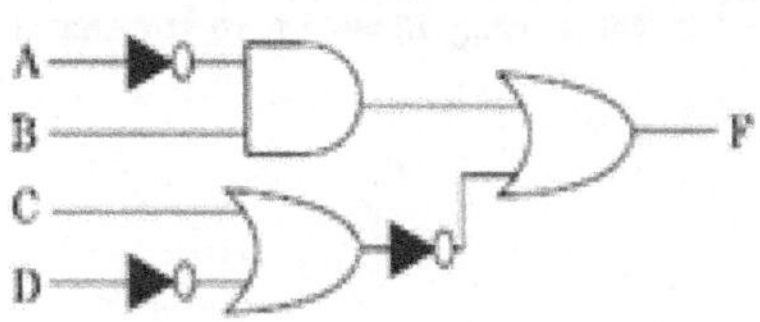

(c) Write the Product of Sum form of the function F(X, Y, Z) for the following truth table representation of F : *1*

X	Y	Z	F
0	0	0	1
0	0	1	0
0	1	0	0
0	1	1	1
1	0	0	0
1	0	1	0
1	1	0	1
1	1	1	1

(d) Obtain the minimal form for the following Boolean expression using Karnaugh's Map : *3*

$F(A,B,C,D) = \sum(1,3,4,5,6,7,12,13)$

7. (a) Write two characteristics of Wi-Fi. *1*

(b) What is the difference between E-mail and Chat ? *1*

(c) Expand the following : *1*

- GSM
- GPRS

(d) Which type of network (out of LAN, PAN and MAN) is formed, when you connect two mobiles using Bluetooth to transfer a video ? *1*

(e) Tech Up Corporation (TUC) is a professional consultancy company. The company is planning to set up their new offices in India with its hub at Hyderabad. As a network adviser, you have to understand their requirement and suggest to them the best available solutions. Their queries are mentioned as (i) to (iv) below.

Physical Locations of the blocks of TUC

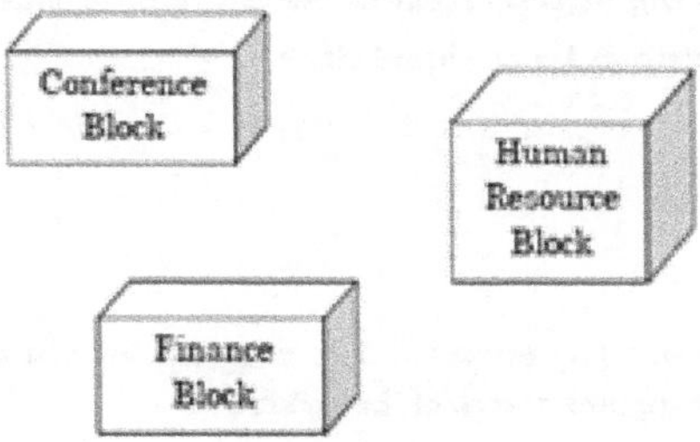

Block to Block distances (in Mtrs.)

Block (From)	Block (To)	Distance
Human Resource	Conference	60
Human Resource	Finance	120
Conference	Finance	80

Expected Number of Computers to be installed in each block

Block	Computers
Human Resource	125
Finance	25
Conference	60

(i) What will the most appropriate block, where TUC should plan to install their server ? *1*

(ii) Draw a block to block cable layout to connect all the buildings in the most appropriate manner for efficient communication. *1*

(iii) What will be the best possible connectivity out of the following, you will suggest to connect the new setup of offices in Bangalore with its London based office ? *1*

- Infrared
- Satellite Link
- Ethernet Cable

(iv) Which of the following devices will be suggested by you to connect each computer in each of the buildings ? *1*

- Gateway
- Switch
- Modem

(f) Write names of any two popular Open Source Software, which are used as Operating Systems. *1*

(g) Write any two important characteristics of Cloud Computing. *1*

COMPUTER SCIENCE

Time allowed: 3 hours **Maximum Marks: 70**

Instructions

1. All questions are compulsory.
2. Programming Language: C+ +

Question Paper Code 91/1

1.

a) What is the difference between Local Variable and Global Variable?

Also, give a suitable C++ code to illustrate both. 2

b) Write the names of the header files, which is/are essentially required to run/ execute the following C++ code:

```
void main ( )
{
        char C, String [ ] = "Excellence Overload";
        for (int I=0; String [ I ] ! = '\ 0'; I ++ )
        if (String [I] ==' ')
                cout<<end1;
        else
        {
                C=toupper(String[I]);
                cout<<C ;
        }
}
```

c) Rewrite the following program after removing the syntactical errors (if any). 2

Underline each correction.

```
#include[iostream.h]
typedef char Text(80) ;
void main ( )
{
        Text T= "Indian";
        int Count=strlen(T) ;
        cout<<T<<'has'<<Count<< 'characters' <<end1;
```

```
}
```

d) Find the output of the following program. **3**

```
#inc1ude<iostream.h>
        void ChangeArray(int Number, int ARR[ ], int Size)
        {
                for (int L =0; L<Size; L++)
                if (L<Number)
                        ARR [L] +=L;
                e1se
                        ARR [L] *=L;
        }
        void Show (int ARR [ ], int Size)
        {
                for (int L=0; L<Size; L++)
                        (L%2!=0) ?cout<<ARR[L] <<"#": cout<<ARR[L]<<end1 ;
        }
        void main ( )
        {
                int Array [ ] = {30, 20, 40, 10, 60, 50};
                ChangeArray (3, Array, 6) ;
                Show (Array, 6) ;
        }
```

e) Find the output of the following program. **2**

```
        #include<iostream.h>
        void main ( )
        {
                int Track [ ] = {10, 20, 30, 40}, *Striker ;
                Stxiker=Track :
                Track [1] += 30 ;
                cout<<"Striker>"<<*Striker<<end1 ;
                Striker - =10 ;
                Striker++ ;
                cout<<"Next@"<<*Striker<<end1 ;
                Striker+=2 ;
```

```
        cout<<"Last@"<<*Striker<<end1 ;
        cout<< "Reset To" <<Track[0] <<end1 ;
    }
```

f) Go through the C++ code shown below, and find out the possible output or outputs from the suggested Output Options (i) to (iv). Also, write the least value and highest value, which can be assigned to the variable Guess. **2**

```
#include <iostream.h>
#include <stdlib.h>
void main ( )
{
        randomize ( ) ;
        int Guess, High=4;
        Guess=random{High)+ 50 ;
        for{int C=Guess ; C<=55 ; C++)
        cout<<C<<"#" ;
}
```

(i) 50 # 51 # 52 # 53 # 54 # 55 #

(ii) 52 # 53 # 54 # 55

(iii) 53 # 54 #

(iv) 51 # 52 # 53 # 54 # 55

2.

a) Differentiate between members, which are present within the private visibility mode with those which are present within the public visibility modes. **2**

b) Write the output of the following C++ code. Also. Write the name of feature of Object Oriented Programming used in the following program jointly illustrated by the function [I] to [IV]. **2**

```
#include<iostream.h>
void Print ( )      // Function [I]
{
        for (int K=1 ; K<=60 ; K++) cout<< "-" ;
                cout<<end1 ;
}
void Print (int N)          // Function [II]
{
```

```
        for (int K=1 ; K<=N ; L++) cout<<"*" ;
              cout<<end1 ;
    }
    void Print (int A, int.B)       // Function [III]
    {
        for (int K=1. ;K<=B ;K++) cout <<A*K ;
              cout<<end1 ;
    }
        void Print (char T, int N) // Function [IV]
    {
    for (int K=1 ; K<=N ; K++) cout<<T ;
              cout<<end1;
    }
    void main ( )
    {
              int U=9, V=4, W=3;
              char C='@' ;
              Print (C,V) ;
              Print (U,W) ;
}
```

c) Define a class Candidate in C++ with following description. **4**

Private Members

A data member RNo (Registration Number) of type long

A data member Name of type string

A data member Score of type float

A data member Remarks of type string

A member function AssignRem( ) to assign Remarks as per the Score obtained by a candidate. Score range and the respective Remarks are shown as follows:

Score	**Remarks**
>=50	Selected
less than 50	Not selected

Public Members

A function ENTER ( ) to allow user to enter values for RNo, Name, Score & call function AssignRem( ) to assign the remarks.

A function DISPLAY ( ) to allow user to view the content of all the data members.

d) Answer the questions (i) to (iv) based on the following. **4**

```
class Strident
(
    int Rno;
    char Name [20] ;
    float Marks;
protected:
    void Result( ) ;
public:
    Student( ) ;
    void Register( ); void Display( ) ;
} ;
class Faculty
{
    long FCode;
    char FName[20];
protected:
    float Pay;
public :
    Faculty ( ) ;
    void Enter ( ) ;
    void Show ( ) ;
} ;
class Course : public Student, private Faculty
{
    long CCode [10]; char CourseName [50] ;
    char StartDate[8], EndDate[8] ;
public :
    Course ( ) ;
    void Commence ( ) ;
    void CDetail ( ) ;
} ;
```

(i) Which type of inheritance is illustrated in the above C++ code?

(ii) Write the names of the all data members, which is/are accessible from member function Commence of class Course.

(iii) Write the names of member functions, which are accessible from objects of class Course.

(iv) Write the name of all the members, which are accessible from objects of class Faculty.

3.

a) Write a Get1From2 ( ) function in C++ to transfer the content from two arrays FIRST [ ] and SECOND[ ] to array ALL[ ]. The even places (0, 2, 4, ...) of array ALL[ ] should get the content from the array FIRST[ ] and odd places (1, 3, 5,) of the array ALL[] should get the content from the array SECOND[ ]. 3

Example:

If the FIRST[ ] array contains

30, 60, 90

And the SECOND[ ] array contains

10, 50, 80

The ALL[ ] array should contain

30, 10, 60, 50, 90, 80

b) An array P[20] [50] is stored in the memory along the column with each of its element occupying 4 bytes, find out the 1ocation of P[15][10], if P[0][0] is stored at 5200. **3**

c) Write a function in C++ to perform Insert: operation on a dynamically allocated Queue containing Passenger details as given in the following definition of NODE. **4**

```
struct NODE
{
        long Pno;              //passenger Number
        char Pname[20] ; //passenger Name
        NODE *Link.;
};
```

d) Write a COLSUM( ) function in C++ to find sum of each column of a NxM Matrix. **2**

e) Evaluate the following postfix notation of expression. **2**

50, 60, + , 20, 10, -, *

4.

a) Observe the program segment given below carefully and fill the blanks marked as Statement 1 and Statement 2 using seekg( ), seekp( ), tellp( ) and tellg( ) functions for performing the required task. **1**

```
#include<fstream.h>
class PRODUCT
{
        int Pno; char Pname[20]; int Qty;
public :
        void ModifyQty( ) ;
        // The function is to modify quantity of a PRODUCT
} ;
void PRODUCT: :ModifyQty ( )
{
        fstream File ;
        Fil.open ("PRODUCT.DAT", ios::binary |ios : : in| ios: :out) ;
        int MPno;
        cout<<"Product No to modify quantity : ";
        cin>>MPNo; While (Fil.read ((char*) this, size of
        (PRODUCT)) {
                if (MPno == Pno)
                {
                Cout<<"Present Quantity:"<<Qty<<end1 ;
                cout<<"Changed Quantity:";cin>>Qty ;
                int Position = ____________; //Statement 1
                ____________________; // Statement 2
                Fil.write ((char*) this, sizeof (PRODUCT));
                                                    //Re-writing the record
                }
        }
        Fil.close ( ) ;
}
```

b) Write a function in C++ to count the no. of "Me" or "My" words present in a text file "DIARY. TXT". **2**

If the file "DIARY.TXT" content is as follows:

My first book was Me and My
family. It gave me chance to be
known to the world.

The output of the function should be

Count of Me/My in file: 4

c) Write a function in C++ to search for a laptop from a binary file "LAPTOP.DAT" containing the objects of class LAPTOP (as defined below). The user should enter the Model No and the function should search and display the details of the laptop. **3**

```
class LAPTOP
{
        long ModelNo ;
        float RAM, HDD ;
        char Details [120] ;
public:
        void StockEnter ( )
        {cin>>ModelNo>>RAM>>HDD; gets (Details);}
        void StockDisplay ( )
        {cout<<ModelNo<<RAM<<HDD<<Details<<endl;}
        long ReturnModelNo ( ) {return ModelNo ;} } ;
```

5.

a) What do you understand by Union & Cartesian Product operations in rela- tional algebra? **2**

Consider the following tables WORKER and PAYYLEVEL and answer (b) and (c) parts of this question. **4**

WORKER

ECODE	**NAME**	**DESIG**	**PLEVEL**	**DOJ**	**DOB**
11	Radhe Shyam	Supervisor	P001	13- Sep- 2004	23-Aug-1981
12	Chander Nath	Operator	P003	22-Feb-2010	12-Jul-1987
13	Fizza	Operator	P003	14-Jun-2009	14-Oct-1983
15	Ameen Ahmed	Mechanic	P002	21-Aug-2006	13-Mar-1984
18	Sanya	Clerk	P002	19-Dec-2005	09-Jun-1983

PAYLEVEL

PLEVEL	PAY	ALLOWANCE
P001	26000	12000
P002	22000	10000
P003	12000	6000

b) Write SQL commands for the following statements:

(i) To display the details of all WORKERs in descending order of DOB.

(ii) To display NAME and DESIG of those WORKERs, whose PLEVEL is either P001 or P002.

(iii) To display the content of all the WORKERs table, whose DOB is in between '19-JAN-1984' and '18-JAN-1987'.

(iv) To add a new row with the following:

19, 'Daya Kishore', 'Operator', 'P003', '19-Jun-2008', '11-Jun-1984'

c) Give the output of the following SQL queries. **2**

(i) SELECT COUNT (PLEVEL), PLEVEL FROM WORKER GROUP BY PLEVEL;

(ii) SELECT MAX (DOB), MIN (DOJ) FROM WORKER;

(iii) SELECT Name, Pay FROM WORKER W, PAYLEVEL P WHERE W. PLEVEL = S. PLEVEL AND P.ECODE<13 ;

(iv) SELECT PLEVEL, PAY+ALLOWANCE FROM PAYLEVEL WHERE PLEVEL= 'P003' ;

6.

a) Verify the following using Truth Table. **2**

U. (U' +V) = (U + V)

b) Write the equivalent Boolean Expression for the following logic Circuit. **2**

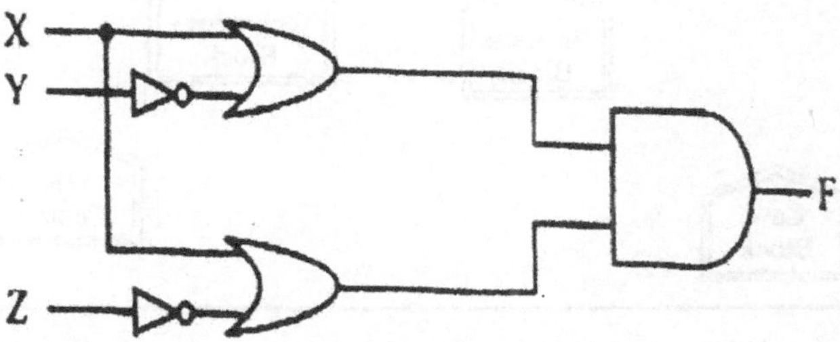

c) Write the POS form of a Boolean function F, which is represented in a truth table as follows. **1**

A	B	C	F
0	0	0	0
0	0	1	1
0	1	0	1
0	1	1	0
1	0	0	1
1	0	1	0
1	1	0	0
1	1	1	1

d) Reduce the following Boolean Expression using K-Map. **3**

F(P, Q, R, S) = Σ (0,1,2,4,5,6,8, 12)

7.

a) Differentiate between packet switching and message switching technique in network communication. **1**

b) Differentiate between BUS and STAR topology of networks. **1**

c) What is VoIP? **1**

d) Out of the following, identify client side script (s) and server side script(s). **1**

1. ASP.
2. Javascript.
3. VBScript.
4. JSP.

e) Quick learn University is setting up its Academic blocks at Prayag Nagar and planning to set up a network. The university has 3 academic blocks and one Human Resource Center as shown in the diagram below. **4**

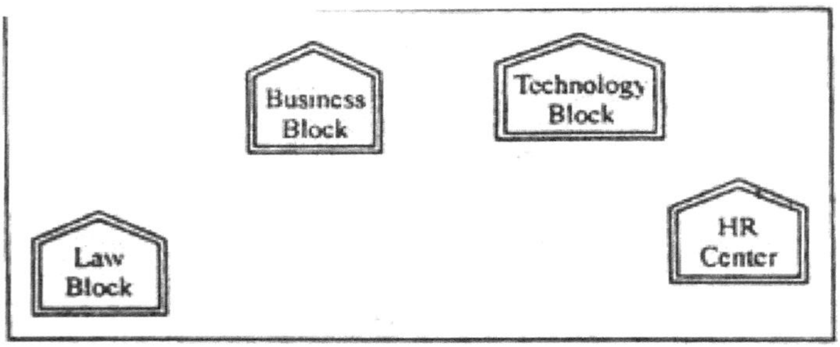

Center to center distance between various block/center is as follows:

Law Block to Business Block	40m
Law Block to Technology Block	80m
Law Block to HR Center	105m
Business Block to Technology Block	30m
Business Block to HR Center	35m
Technology Block to HR Center	15m

Number of Computers in each of the Blocks/Centre is follows:

Law Block	15
Technology Block	40
HR Center	115
Business Block	25

(e1). Suggest the most suitable place (i.e. Block/Center) to install the server of this university with a suitable reason.

(e2). Suggest an ideal layout for connecting these blocks/centers for a wired connectivity.

(e3). Which device you will suggest to be placed/installed in each of these blocks/ center to efficiently connect all the computers with in these blocks/center.

(e4). The university is planning to connect its admission office in the closest big city, which is more than 250 km from university, which type of network out of LAN, MAN or WAN will be formed? Justify your answer.

f) Which of the following will come under Cyber Crime? **1**

(i) Theft of a brand new sealed pack Laptop

(ii) Access to a bank account for getting unauthorized Money Transaction

(iii) Modification in a company data with unauthorized access

(iv) Photocopying a printed report.

g) Compare open source software and proprietary software. **1**

Computer Science

Question Paper Code 91

1.

a) What is the difference between Type Casting and Automatic Type conversion? Also, give a suitable C++ code to illustrate both. **2**

b) Write the names of the header files, which is/are essentially required to run/ execute the following c++ code. **1**

```
void main ( )
{
    char CH,Text[ ] ="+ve Attitude";
    for (int I=0 ; Text[I] ! ='\0' ;I++)
        if (Text[I]== ' ')
            cout<<end1;
        else
        {
            CH=toupper (Text [I]) ;
            cout<<CH;
        }
}
```

c) Rewrite the following program after removing the syntactical errors (if any). Underline each correction. **2**

```
include<iostream.h>
typedef char [80] String;
void main ( )
{
    String S= "Peace";
    int L=strlen(S) ;
    cout<<S<< 'has'<<L<< 'characters'<<end1;
}
```

d) Find the output of the following program. **3**

```
#include <iostream.h>
void SwitchOver(int A [ ], int N, int Split)
{
```

```
        for (int K=0 ; K<N; K++)
            if (K<Split)
                A(K]+ =K;
            else
                A [K]*=K;
}
void Display (int A [ ], int N)
{
    for (int K=0 ; K<N ; K++)
        (K%2==0)? cout<<A[K]<<"%":cout<<A(K]<<end1;
}
void main ( )
{
    int H[ ]= {30,40,50,20,10,5};
    SwitchOver (H, 6, 3);
    Display (H, 6);
}
```

e) Find the output of the following program. **2**

```
#include<iostream.h>
void main ( )
{
    int *Queen, Moves [ ] = {11, 22, 33, 44};
    Queen = Moves;
    Moves [2] + = 22;
    Cout<< "Queen @"<<*Queen<<end1;
    *Queen - = 11;
    Queen + = 2;
    cout<< "Now @"<<*Queen<<end1;
    Queen++;
    cout<< "Finally@"<<*Queen«end1;
    cout<< "New Origin @"<<Moves[0]<<end1;
}
```

f) Go through the C++ code shown below, and find out the possible output or outputs from the suggested Output Options (i) to (iv). Also, write the minimum and maximum values, which can be assigned to the variable MyNum. **2**

```
#include<iostream.h>
#include <stdlib.h>
void main ( )
{
randomize ( ) ;
int MyNum, Max=5;
MyNum = 20 + random (Max) ;
for (int N=MyNum; N<=25;N++)
cout<N<"*";
}
```

(i) 20*21*22*23*24*25

(ii) 22*23*24*25*

(iii) 23*24*

(iv) 21*22*23*24*25

2.

a) Differentiate between Constructor and Destructor function with respect to Object Oriented Programming. **2**

b) Write the output of the following C++ code. Also, write the .name of feature of Object Oriented Programming used in the following program jointly illustrated by the function [I] to [IV]. **2**

```
#include<iostream.h>
void Line ( )                                        //Function [I]
{
        for (int L=1;L<=80;L++)         cout<<"-";
        cout<<end1;
}
void Line (int N)                                    //Function[II]
{
        for (int L=l;L<=N;L++)          Cout<<"*";
        cout<<endl;
}
```

```
void Line (char C, int N)                                    //Function [III]
{
        for (int L=l;L<=N;L++)          cout<<C;
        cout<<end1;
}
void Line (int M, int, N)                                    //Function [IV]
{
        for (int L=1;L<=N;L++)          cout<<M*L;
        cout<<end1;
}
void main ( )
{
        int A=9, B=4, C=3;
        char K= '#' ;
        Line (K,B);
        Line (A,C);
}
```

c) Define a class Applicant in C++ with following description. **4**

Private Members

A data member ANo (Admission Number) of type long.

A data member Name of type string.

A data member Agg (Aggregate Marks) of type float.

A data member Grade of type char.

A member function GradeMe() to find the Grade as per the Aggregate Marks obtained by a student. Equivalent Aggregate Marks range and the respective Grades are shown as follows:

Aggregate Marks	**Grade**
>=80	A
less than 80 and >=65	B
less than 65 and >=50	C
less than 50	D

Public Members

A function ENTER() to allow user to enter values for ANo, Name, Agg & call function GradeMe() to find the Grade.

A function_RESULT( ) to allow user to view the content of all the data members.

(d) Answer the questions (i) to (iv) based on the following. **4**

```
class Student
{
        int Rollno:
        char SName[20];
        float Marksl;
protected:
        void Result ( ) ;
public:
        Student ( ) ;
        void Enroll ( ) ;void Display ( ) ;
} ;
class Teacher
{
        long TCode;
        char TName [20];
protected:
        float Salary;
public:
        Teacher ( );
        void Enter ( ) ;
        void Show ( ) ;
} ;
class Course: public Student, private Teacher
}
        long CCode [10]; char CourseName [50];
        char StartDate [8] , EndDate [8];
public:
        Course ( );
        void Commence ( );
        void CDetail ( ) ;
} ;
```

(i) Write the names of member functions, which are accessible from objects of class Course

(ii) Write the names of all the data members, which is/are accessible from member function Commence of class Course

(iii) Write the names of all the-members, which are accessible from objects of class Teacher.

(iv) Which type of Inheritance is illustrated in the above C++ code?

3.

a) Write a Get2From1() function in C++ to transfer the content from one array ALL[] to two different arrays Odd[] and Even[]. The Odd[] array should contain the values from odd positions (1,3,5,...) of ALL[] and Even [] array should contain the values from even positions (0, 2, 4,.....) of ALL []. **3**

Example

If the ALL[] array contains

12, 34, 56, 67, 89, 90

The Odd[] array should contain

34, 67, 90

And the Even [] array should contain

12, 56, 89

b) An array G[50][20] is stored in the memory along the row with each of its elements occupying 8 bytes. Find out the location of G[10][15], if G[0][0] is stored at 4200. **3**

c) Write a function in C++ to perform Delete operation on a dynamically allocated Queue containing Members details as given in the following definition of NODE. **4**

```
struct NODE
{
        long Mno                              //Member Number
        char Mname[20];                       //Member Name
        NODE *Link;
};
```

d) Write a DSUMO function in C++ to find sum of Diagonal Elements from a NxN Matrix. (Assuming that the N is a odd number). **2**

e) Evaluate the following postfix notation of expression.

True, False, NOT, AND, True, True, AND, OR **2**

4.

a) Observe the program segment given below carefully and fill the blanks marked as Statement 1 and Statement 2 using seekg( ), seekp( ) tellp( ) and tellg( ) functions for performing the required task. **1**

```
#include <fstream.h>
class ITEM
{
        int Ino;char Iname[20]; float Price;
        public:
        void ModifyPrice() ;//The function is to modify
                price of a particular ITEM
};
void item: :ModiyPrice()
{
        fstream File;
        File.open ("ITEM.DAT", ios::binary | ios::in | ios: :out) || ;
        int CIno;
        cout<<"Item No to modify price:";cin>>CIno;
        while (file.read ((char*) this, sizeof (ITEM)))
        {
                if (CIno==Ino)
                {
                        cout<<"Present Price:"<<Price<<end1;
                        cout<<"Changed price:"; cin>>Price;
                        int FilePos = ________ ; //Statement 1,
                        _________________; //Statement 2
                        File.write((char*)this,sizeof(ITEM)) ;
                                                // Re-writing the record
                }
        }
        File.close ( ) ;
}
```

b) Write a function in C++ to count the no. of "He" or "She" words present in a text file "STORY. TXT". **2**

If the file "STORY. TXT" content is as follows:

He is playing in the ground. She is
Playing with her dolls.

The output of the function should be Count of He/She in file: 2

c) Write a function in C++ to search for a camera from a binary file "CAMERA.DAT" containing the objects of class" CAMERA (as defined below). The user should enter the Model No and the function should search display the details of the camera. **3**

```
class CAMERA
    {
        long ModelNo;
        float MegaPixel;
        int Zoom;
        char Details[120];
public:
    void Enter ( ) {cin>>ModelNo>>MegaPixel>>Zoom;gets(Details);}
    void Display ( )
        {cout<<ModelNo<<MegaPixel<<Zoom<<Details<<endl;}
    long GetModelNo ( ) {return ModelNo;}
};
```

5.

(a) What do you understand by Selection & Projection operations in relational algebra? Consider the following tables EMPLOYEE and SALGRADE and answer (b) and (c) parts of this question. **2**

Table: Employee

ECODE	NAME	DESIG	SGRADE	DOJ	DOB
101	Abdul Ahmad	EXECUTIVE	S03	23-Mar-2003	13-Jan-1980
102	Rav:i. Chander	HEAD-IT	S02	12-Feb-2010	22-Jul-1987
103	John Ken	RECEPTIONIST	S03	24-June-2009	24-Feb-1983
105	Nazar Ameen	GM	S02	11-Aug-2006	03-Mar-1984
108	Priyam Sen	CEO	S01	29-Dec-2004	19-Jan-1982

Table: Salgrade

SGRADE	SALARY	HRA
S0l	56000	18000
S02	32000	12000
S03	24000	8000

(b) Write SQL commands for the following statements. **4**

(i) To display the details of all EMPLOYEEs, in descending order of DOJ.

(ii) To display NAME and DE51G of those EMPLOYEEs, whose SALGRADE is either 502 or 503

(iii) To display the content of all the EMPLOYEEs table, whose DOJ is in between'09-Feb-2006' and '08-Aug-2009'.

(iv) To add a new row with the following:

109, 'Harish Roy', 'HEAD-IT', 'S02', '09-Sep-2007, '21-Apr-1983'

(c) Give the output of the following SQL queries. **2**

(i) SELECT COUNT (SGRADE), SGRADE FROM EMPLOYEE GROUP BY SGRADE;

(ii) SELECT MIN(DOB), MAX (DOJ) FROM EMPLOYEE;

(iii) SELECT NAME, SALARY FROM EMPLOYEE E, SALGRADE S WHERE E.SGRADE= S.SGRADE AND E.ECODE<103;

(iv) SELECT SGRADE, SALARY+HRA ET:)M SALGRADE WHERE SGRADE='S02';

6.

a) Yerify the following using Truth Table. **2**

X+Y. Z=(X+Y).(X+Z)

b) Write the equivalent Boolean Expression for the following Logic Circuit. **2**

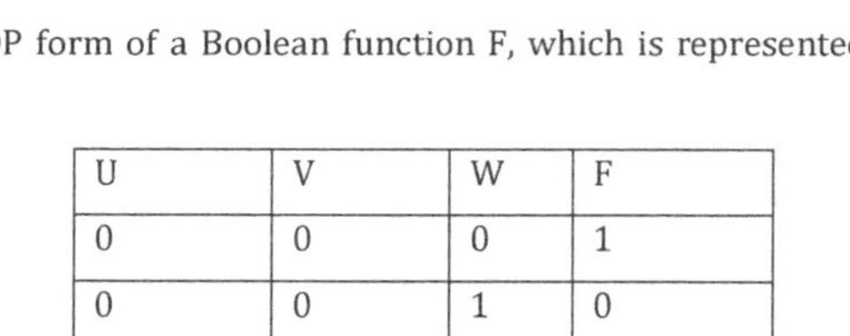

c) Write the SOP form of a Boolean function F, which is represented in a truth table as follows: 1

U	V	W	F
0	0	0	1
0	0	1	0
0	1	1	1
1	0	0	0
1	0	1	0
1	1	0	1
1	1	1	1

d) Reduce the following Boolean Expression using K-Map. **3**

$F(A, B, C, D) = \Sigma(0, 1, 2, 4, 5, 6, 7, 8, 10)$

7.

a) In networking, what-is WAN? How is it different from LAN? **1**

b) Differentiate between XML and HTML. **1**

c) What is WEB2.0? **1**

d) Out of the following, identify client side script (s) and server side script (s).

(i) Javascript.

(ii) ASP.

(iii) Vbscript.

(iv) JSP.

e) Great Studies University is setting up its Academic schools at Sunder Nagar and planning to set up a network. The university has 3 academic schools and one administration center as shown in the diagram below: **4**

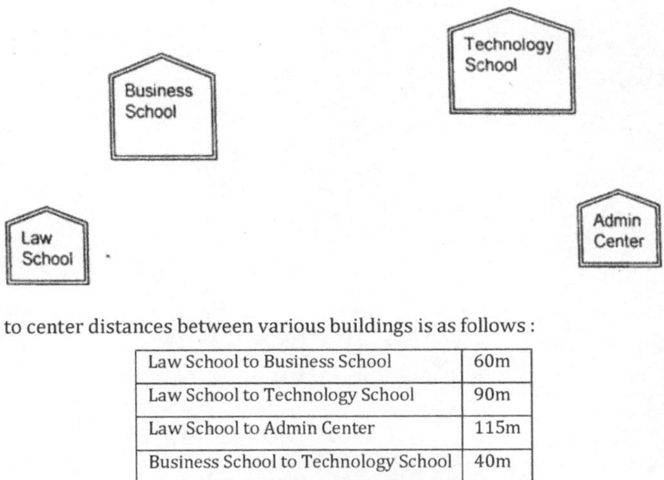

Center to center distances between various buildings is as follows :

Law School to Business School	60m
Law School to Technology School	90m
Law School to Admin Center	115m
Business School to Technology School	40m
Business School to. Admin Center	45m
Technology School to Admin Center	25m

Number of Computers in each of the Schools/Center is follows:

Law School	25
Technology School	50
Admin Center	125
Business School	35

(i) Suggest the most suitable place (i.e. School/Center) to install the server of this university with a suitable reason.

(ii) Suggest an ideal layout for connecting these schools/ center for a wired connectivity.

(iii) Which device will you suggest to be placed/installed in each of these schools/ center to efficiently connect all the computers within these schools center?

(iv) The university is planning to connect its admission office in the closest big city, which is more than 350 km from the university. Which type of network out of LAN, MAN or WAN will be formed? Justify your answer.

(f) Compare Open Source Software and Proprietary Software. 1

(g) What are cookies? 1

Question Paper Code 91/1

Expected Answers

1.

a) What is the difference between Local Variable and Global Variable? Also, give a suitable C++ code to illustrate both. **2**

Ans.

Local Variables: Local variables are those variables which are declared within a function or a compound statement and these variables can only be used within that function/scope.

Global Variables: Global variables are those variables which are not declared within any function or scope. So, these variables can be accessed by any function of the program.

Example

```
#include<iostream.h>
#include<conio.h.>
int G;                              // Global variable declared
void Fun ( )
{
int L = 25; // Local variable of function Fun ( ) assigned value 25
G=5;                                // Global Variable is accessed and assigned value 5
Cout<<G<<endl;                      // Value of global variable is displayed as 5
Cout<<L<<endl;                      // Value of local variable is displayed as 25
}
void main ( )
{
Fun ( ) ;                           // Function call
G = G + 5;                          // Global variable is incremented by 5
cout<<G<<endl;                      // Global variable is displayed as 10
}
```

(½ Mark for each correct explanation of Local Variable and Global Variable)

(½ Mark for each correct example of Local variable and Global Variable)

OR

(Full 2 Maries for correct example(s) demonstrating the meaning of / difference between Local Variable and Global Variable)

OR

(Only 1 Mark to be awarded if Explanation without supporting examples)

b) Write the names of the header files, which is/are essentially required to run/ execute the following C++ code:

```
void main ( )
{
        char C, String [ ] = "Excellence Overload";
        for (int I=0; String [ I ] ! = '\ 0'; I ++ )
        if (String [I] ==' ')
                cout<<end1;
        else
        {
                C=toupper(String[I]);
                cout<<C ;
        }
}
```

Ans iostream.h

ctype.h

(½ Mark for writing each correct header file)

c) Rewrite the following program after removing the syntactical errors (if any). Underline each correction. 2

```
#include[iostream.h]
typedef char Text(80) ;
void main ( )
{
        Text T= "Indian";
        int Count=strlen(T) ;
        cout<<T<<'has'<<Count<< 'characters' <<end1;
}
```

Ans

```
#include<iostream.h>
#include<string.h>
typedef char Text [80];
void main ( )
{
        Text T= "Indian";
        int Count=str1en(T);
```

```
        cout<<T<< "has" <<Count<< "cbaracters"<<end1;
    }
```

(½ Mark for writing # include<iostream.h>

(½ Mark for writing # include<string.h>

(½ Mark for writing typedef char Text(80];

(½ Mark for writing "has" and "characters")

d) Find the output of the following program. **3**

```
#inc1ude<iostream.h>
void ChangeArray(int Number, int ARR[ ], int Size)
    {
        for (int L =0; L<Size; L++)
        if (L<Number)
            ARR [L] +=L;
        e1se
            ARR [L] *=L;
    }
    void Show (int ARR [ ], int Size)
    {
        for (int L=0; L<Size; L++)
            (L%2!=0) ?cout<<ARR[L] <<"#": cout<<ARR[L]<<end1 ;
    }
    void main ( )
    {
        int Array [ ] = {30, 20, 40, 10, 60, 50};
        ChangeArray (3, Array, 6) ;
        Show (Array, 6) ;
    }
```

Ans 30

21#42

30#240

250#

(½ Mark for each correct value)

Note:

Deduct ½ Mark for not writing # at proper places

Deduct ½ Mark for not considering endl at proaer places

(e) Find the output of the following program: 2

```
#include<iostream.h>
void main ( )
{
int Track [ ] = {10, 20, 30, 40}, *Striker ;
Stxiker=Track :
Track [1] += 30 ;
cout<<"Striker>"<<*Striker<<end1 ;
Striker - =10 ;
Striker++ ;
cout<<"Next@"<<*Striker<<end1 ;
Striker+=2 ;
cout<<"Last@"<<*Striker<<end1 ;
cout<< "Reset To" <<Track[0] <<end1 ;
}
```

Ans Striker>10

Next@50

Last@40

Reset to 0

(½ for writing each line of output correctly).

Note:

Deduct ½ Mark if any/all special characters are missing

Deduct ½ Mark if endl is not considered at the right positions.

e) Go through the C++ code shown below, and find out the possible output or outputs from the suggested Output Options (i) to (iv). Also, write the least value and highest value, which can be assigned to the variable Guess. **2**

```
#include <iostream.h>
#include <stdlib.h>
void main ( )
{
        randomize ( ) ;
        int Guess, High=4;
        Guess=random{High)+ 50 ;
```

```
        for{int C=Guess ; C<=55 ; C++)
        cout<<C<<"#" ;
    }
```

(i) 50 # 51 # 52 # 53 # 54 # 55 #

(ii) 52 # 53 # 54 # 55

(iii) 53 # 54 #

(iv) 51 # 52 # 53 # 54 # 55

Ans

(i) 50 # 51 # 52 # 53 # 54 # 55 #

Least value 50

Highest value 53

(1 Mark for mentioning correct option (i))

(½ Mark for mentioning correct Least value of Guess)

(½ Mark for mentioning correct Highest value of Guess)

2.

a) **Differentiate between members, which are present within the private visibility mode with those which are present within the public visibility modes.** **2**

Ans.

Private members of a class are accessible only to the member functions of the same class.

Public members of a class are accessible to the member functions of the same class as well as member functions of its derived class(es) and also to an object of the class.

```
Example:
class Base
{
        int N;
public:
        void Assign ()
        {
                N=10;
        }
};
class Derived: public Base
{
        int X;
```

```
public:
      void DisplayBase()
      {
            cout<<N;     //Not Accessible
            Assign ( ) ; //Accessible
      }
};
void main ( )
{
      Base B;
      B.Assign( ) ;          //Accessible
}
```

(1 Mark for correct explanation OR example illustrating non accessibility of Private Members inside Derived class).

(1 Marie for correct explanation OR example illustrating accessibility of Public Members inside Derived Class and to object of the class).

b) Write the output of the following C++ code. Also. Write the name of feature of Object Oriented Programming used in the following program jointly illustrated by the function [I] to [IV]. **2**

```
#include<iostream.h>
void Print ( ) // Function [I]
{
      for (int K=1 ; K<=60 ; K++) cout<< "-" ;
            cout<<end1 ;
}
void Print (int N) // Function [II]
{
      for (int K=1 ; K<=N ; L++) cout<<"*" ;
            cout<<end1 ;
}
void Print (int A, int.B)
{
      for (int K=1. ;K<=B ;K++) cout <<A*K ;
```

```
            cout<<end1 ;
    }
    void Print (char T, int N)      // Function [IV]
    {
        for (int K=1 ; K<=N ; K++) cout<<T ;
            cout<<end1;
    }
    void main ( )
    {
            int U=9, V=4, W=3;
            char C='@' ;
            Print (C,V) ;
            Print (U,W) ;
    }
```

Ans. @@@@

91827

OR

No Output as L is not declared in void Print (int N)

Polymorphism

OR

Function Overloading

(½ Mark for writing each correct line of output)

(1 Mark for writing the feature name correctly)

c) Define a class Candidate in C++ with following description. **4**

Private Members

A data member RNo (Registration Number) of type long A data member Name of type string.

A data member Score of type float.

A data member Remarks of type string.

A member function AssignRem( ) to assign Remarks as per the Score obtained by a candidate. Score range and the respective Remarks are shown as follows:

Score	**Remarks**
>=50	Selected
less than 50	Not selected

Public Members

A function ENTER ( ) to allow user to enter values for RNo, Name, Score & call function AssignRem( ) to assign the remarks.

A function DISPLAY ( ) to allow user to view the content of all the data members.

Ans

```
class Candidate
{
        long RNo;
        char Name[20];
        float Score;
        char Remarks[20];
        void AssignRem( ) ;
public:
        void Enter( );
        void Display( );
} ;
void Candidate: :AssignRem( )
        {
                if (Score>=50)
                        strcpy (Remarks,"Selected") ;
                else
                        strcpy(Remarks,"Not Selected") ;
        }
void Candidate: : Enter ( )
{
        cin>>RNo ;
        gets (Name) ; cin>>Score;
        AssignRem( ) ;
}
void Candidate: :Display()
{
        cout<<RNo<<Name<<Score<<Remarks<<end1;
}
```

(½ Mark for correct syntax for class header)

(½ Mark for correct declaration of data members)

(1 Mark for correct definition of AssignRem())

(1 Mark for correct definition of Enter() with proper invocation of AssignRem() function)

(1 Mark for correct definition of Display())

NOTE:

Deduct ½ Mark to be deducted if Assignrem() is not invoked properly inside Enter( ) function

No marks to be deducted if member function definitions are written inside the class

d) Answer the questions (i) to (iv) based on the following: class Strident

```
(
    int Rno;
    char Name [20];
    float Marks;
protected:
    void Result( ) ;
public:
    Student( ) ;
    void Register( ); void Display( ) ;
} ;
class Faculty
{
    long FCode;
    char FName[20];
protected:
    float Pay;
public :
    Faculty ( ) ;
    void Enter ( ) ;
    void Show ( ) ;
} ;
class Course : public Student, private Faculty
{
    long CCode [10]; char CourseName [50] ;
    char StartDate[8], EndDate[8] ;
```

```
public:
        Course ( ) ;
        void Commence ( ) ;
        void CDetail ( ) ;
};
```

(i) Which type of inheritance is illustrated in the above C++ code?

Ans Multiple Inheritance

(1 Mark for correct answer)

(ii) Write the names of the all data members, which is/are accessible from member function Commence of class Course.

Ans CCode, CourseName, StartDate, EndDate, Pay

(1 Mark for correct answer)

Note: No marks to be awarded for any other alternative answer

(iii) Write the names of member functions, which are accessible from objects of class Course.

Ans Commence( ), CDetail( ), Register( ), Display( )

(1 Mark for correct answer)

Note:

No marks to be awarded for any other alternative answer Constructor functions to be ignored

(iv) Write the name of all the members, which are accessible from objects of class Faculty.

Ans Enter( ), Show( )

(1 Mark for correct answer)

Note:

No marks to be awarded for any other alternative answer Constructor functions to be iqnored

3.

a) Write a Get1From2 ( ) function in C++ to transfer the content from two arrays FIRST[ ] and SECOND[ ] to array ALL[ ]. The even places (0, 2, 4,...) of array ALL[ ] should get the content from the array FIRST[ ] and odd places (1, 3, 5,) of the array ALL[] should get the content from the array SECOND[ ].

Example:

If the FIRST[ ] array contains

30, 60, 90

And the SECOND[ ] array contains

10, 50, 80

The ALL[ ] array should contain

30, 10, 60, 50, 90, 80

Ans

```
void Get1From2 (int ALL[],int FIRST[],int SECOND[],
                int N,int M)
    {
        for(int I=0,J=0,K=0;i<N+M; I++)
            if (I%2==0)
                ALL[I]=FIRST[J++];
            else
                ALL[I]=SECOND[K++];
    }
    OR
    void Get1From2(int ALL[],int FIRST[],int SECOND[],
                int N, int M)
    {
        int J=0,K=0;
        for(int I=0;i<N+M; I++)
        {
            if (I%2==0)
            {
                ALL [I] =FIRST [J] ;
                J++;
            }
            else
            {
                ALL[I]=SECOND[K];
                K++;
            }
        }
    }
```

(1 Mark for correct loop)

(½ Mark for checking even locations)

(½ Mark for checking even locations or writing else for odd locations)

(1 Mark for incrementing FIRST and SECOND Array Locations)

b) An array P[20] [50] is stored in the memory along the column with each of its element occupying 4 bytes, find out the 1ocation of P[15][10], if P[0][0] is stored at 5200. **3**

Ans

Assuminq LBR=LBC=0

B=5200

W=4 bytes

Number of Rows(N)=20

Number of Columns(M)=50

LOC(Arr[I] [J]) = B +(I + J*N)*W

LOC(Arr[15][10]) = 5200+(15+10*20)*4

= 5200 + (215*4)

= 5200 + 860

= 6060

(1 Mark for writing correct formula (for row major) OR substituting formula with correct values for calculating Address)

(2 marks for calculating correct address)

Note:

1 Mark to be awarded for writing only the correct answer (i.e. 6060)

c) Write a function in C++ to perform Insert: operation on a dynamically allocated Queue containing Passenger details as given in the following definition of NODE. **4**

```
struct NODE
{
        long Pno;              //passenger Number
        char Pname[20] ; //passenger Name
        NODE *Link.;
};
```

Ans

```
class Queue
{
        NODE *Front, *Rear;
public:
        Queue ( ) {Front = NULL; Rear = NULL; }
        void QueInsert ( ) ;
        void QueDel ( ) ;
        void QueDis ( ) ;
```

```
        ~Queue ( ) ;
    } ;
    void Queue: : QueInsert ( )
    {
        NODE*Temp=new NODE;
        cin>>Temp->Pno; gets (Temp->Pname) ;
        Temp->Link = NULL;
        Rear->Li.nk = Temp;
        Rear = Temp ;
    }
```

(1 Mark for creating a new NODE dynamically)

(1 Mark for assigning NULL to Link of new NODE)

(1 Mark for linking the Rearmost NODE to the new NODE)

(1 Mark for making the new NODE as the Rearmost NODE)

d) Write a COLSUM( ) function in C++ to find sum of each column of a NxM Matrix. **2**

Ans

```
void COLSUM(int A[] [100], int N, int M)
{
        int SUMC;
        for (int j=0; j<M; j++)
        {
            SUMC = 0;
            for (int i=0; i<N; i++)
                SUMC = SUMC + A[i] [j] ;
            Cout<< "Sum of Column "<<j<<" = "<<SUMC ;
    }
}
```

(½ Mark for writing correct outer loop)

(½ Mark for initializing SUMC with 0 for each column)

(½ Mark tor writing correct inner loop)

(½ Mark for finding sum of each column)

(e) Evaluate the following postfix notation of expression: 2

50, 60, + , 20, 10, -, *

Ans

Element Scanned	STACK
50	50

60	50, 60
+	110
20	110, 20
10	110, 20, 10
-	110, 10
*	1100

(2 Mark for evaluating 1100 as the final answer)

Note:

(½ Mark for writing only the final answer as 1100 without showing the operations or Stack)

4.

a) Observe the program segment given below carefully and fill the blanks marked as Statement 1 and Statement 2 using seekg( ), seekp( ), tellp( ) and tellg( ) functions for performing the required task. **1**

```
#include<fstream.h>
class PRODUCT
{
        int Pno; char Pname[20]; int Qty;
public :
        :
        void ModifyQty( ) ;
        // The function is to modify quantity of a PRODUCT
} ;
void PRODUCT: :ModifyQty ( )
{
        fstream File ;
        Fil.open ("PRODUCT.DAT", ios::binary |ios : : in| ios: :out) ;
        int MPno;
        cout<<"Product No to modify quantity : "; cin>>MPNo;
        While (Fil.read ((char*) this, sizeof (PRODUCT))
        {
                if (MPno == Pno)
                {
                Cout<<"Present Quantity:"<<Qty<<end1 ;
                cout<<"Changed Quantity:";cin>>Qty ;
                int Position = ___________; //Statement 1
```

```
                    ____________; // Statement 2
                    Fil.write ((char*) this, sizeof (PRODUCT));
                                    //Re-writing the record
                    }
            }
            Fil.close () ;
    }
```

Ans

Option 1

Statement 1:	File. tellp () ;
OR	File.tellg () ;
Statement 2:	File.seekp (FilePos - sizeof (PRODUCT)) ;
OR	File.seekp (-sizeof (PRODUCT), ios: :cur));
OR	File.seekg (FilePos - sizeof (PRODUCT));
OR	File.seekg (-sizeof (PRODUCT), ios: :cur));

Option 2

Statement 1:	File.tellp () - sizeof (PRODUCT) ;
OR	File.tellg () - sizeof (PRODUCT) ;
Statement 2:	File. seekp (FilePos) ;
OR	File.seekg (FilePos) ;

(½ Mark for writing Statement 1 correctly)

(½ Mark for writing Statement 2 correctly)

Note:

File / Fil both are acceptable as the name of the File object

b) Write a function in C++ to count the no. of "Me" or "My" words present in a text file "DIARY. TXT". **2**

If the file "DIARY.TXT" content is as follows:

My first book was Me and My

family. It gave me chance to be known to the world.

The output of the function should be Count of Me/My in file : 4

Ans
```
void COUNT ()
{
        ifstream Fil ("DIARY. TXT") ;
        char STR [10] ;
```

```
        int count = 0 ;
        while (!Fil.eof ( ))
        {
            Fil>>STR;
            if (strcmp (STR, "Me")==0 | | strcmp (STR, "My") ==0)
                count++;
        }
        Cout<<"Count of Me/My in file : "<<count<<end1;
        Fil.close( ) ; //Ignore
    }
```

OR

Any other correct function definition performing the desired operation

(½ Mark for opening DIARY. TXT correctly)

(½ Mark for reading each word (Whichever method adopted) from, the file)

(½ Mark for comparing the word with 'Me' and 'My' and incrementing counter)

(½ Mark for displaying the number of 'Me/My' with/without the Text Message)

NOTE:

Ignore case sensitivity check for Me/My

c) Write a function in C++ to search for a laptop from a binary file "LAPTOP.DAT" containing the objects of class LAPTOP (as defined below). The user should enter the Model No and the function should search and display the details of the laptop. **3**

```
class LAPTOP
{
        long ModelNo ;
        float RAM, HDD ;
        char Details [120] ;
public:
        void StockEnter ( )
        {cin>>ModelNo>>RAM>>HDD; gets (Details);}
        void StockDisplay ( )
        {cout<<ModelNo<<RAM<<HDD<<Details<<endl;}
        long ReturnModelNo ( ) {return ModelNo ;}
};
```

Ans

```
void Search( )
{
    LAPTOP L;
    long modelnum;
    cin>>modelnum;
    ifstream fin;
    fin.open ("LAPTOP.DAT", ios: :binary | ios: :in);
     while(fin.read ((char*) &L,sizeof (L)))
     {
        if (L.ReturnModelNo ( ) == modelnum)
            L.StockDisplay ( );
  }
  Fin.close() ; //Ignore
}
```

OR

```
void Search (long modelnum)
{
  LAPTOP L;
  ifstream fin;
  fin.open ("LAPTOP.DAT", ios: :binary | ios: :in) ;
  while (fin.read ((char*) &L,sizeof (L)))
  {
      if (L.ReturnModelNo ( ) == modelnum)
          L.StockDisplay ( ) ;
  }
  fin.close ( ) ; //Ignore
}
```

(½ Mark for declaring and entering a model number for a LAPTOP to search OR passing it as a parameter to the function)

(½ Mark for opening LAPTOP.DA T correctly)

(½ Mark for reading each record from LAPTOP.DA T)

(½ Mark for correct loop / checking end of file)

(½ Mark for comparing value returned by ReturnModelNo() with model

number entered)

(½ Mark for displaying the matching record)

5 (a) What do you understand by Union & Cartesian Product operations in relational algebra? 2

Ans Cartesian Product (binary operator): It operates on two relations and is denoted by X. For example Cartesian product of two relations R1 and R2 is represented by R = R1 X R2. The degree of R is equal to sum of degrees of R1 and R2. The cardinality of R is product of cardinality of R1 and cardinality of R2.

Example:

Relation: R1

Roll No	Student Name	Class
1	Akash	XII
4	Debakar	X
10	Rishi	XI

Relation: R2

Teacher Code	Teacher Name
102	Ms Rinee
309	Mr Tanmoy

Resultant: R = R1 × R2

Col1	Col2	Col3	Col4	Col5
1	Akash	XII	102	Ms Rinee
1	Akash	XII	309	Mr Tanmoy
4	Debakar	X	102	Ms Rinee
4	Debakar	X	309	Mr Tanmoy
10	Rishi	XI	102	Ms Rinee
10	Rishi	XI	309	Mr Tanmoy

Union (binary operator): It operates on two relations and is indicated by U. For example, R=R1 U R2 represents union operation between two relations R1 and R2. The degree of R is equal to degree of R1. The cardinality of R is sum of cardinality of R1 and cardinality of R2. Following have to be considered for the operation R1 U R2.

Degree of R1 = Degree of R2

jth attribute of R1 and jth attribute of R2 must have a common domain.

Example:

Relation: R1

Student_I D	Name
R490	Fatima
R876	Faraz
R342	Gauri

Relation: R2

Student_Code	Student_Name
S123	Rekha
S456	Tushi

Resultant Relation: R = R1 U R2

Column 1	Column2
R490	Fatima
R876	Faraz
R342	Gauri
S123	Rekha
S456	Tushi

(1 Marie for explaining Union correctly)

(1 Marie for explaining Cartesian Product correctly)

Consider the following tables WORKER and PAYYLEVEL and answer

(b) and (c) parts of this question: 4

Table: WORKER

ECODE	NAME	DESIG	PLEVEL	DOJ	DOB
11	Radhe Shyam	Supervisor	P001	13-Sep- 2004	23-Aug-1981
12	Chander Nath	Operator	P003	22-Feb-2010	12-Jul-1987
13	Fizza	Operator	P003	14-Jun-2009	14-0ct-1983
15	Ameen Ahmed	Mechanic	P002	21-Aug-2006	13-Mar-1984
18	Sanya	Clerk	P002	19-Dec-2005	09-Jun-1983

Table: Paylevel

PLEVEL	PAY	ALLOWANCE
P001	26000	12000
P002	22000	10000
P003	12000	6000

(b) Write SQL commands for the following statements:

(i) To display the details of all WORKERs in descending order of DOB.

SELECT FROM WORKER ORDER BY DOB DESC;

(1 Mark for correct query)

(½ Mark for partially correct answer)

(ii) To display NAME and DE; SIG of those WORKERs, whose PLEVEL is either P001 or P002.

SELECT NAME, DESIG FROM WORKER

WHERE PLEVEL IN ('P001', 'P002');

OR

SELECT NAME, DESIG FROM WORKER

WHERE PLEVEL = 'P001' OR PLEVEL= 'P002';

(1 Marie for correct query)

(½ Marie for partially correct answer)

(iii) To display the content of all the WORKERs table, whose DOB is in between '19-JAN-1984' and '18-JAN-1987'.

SELECT * FROM WORKER

WHERE DOB BETWEEN '19-JAN-1984' AND '18-JAN-1987';

OR

SELECT * FROM WORKER

WHERE DOB >= '19-JAN-1984' AND DOB<='18-JAN-1987';

OR

SELECT * FROM WORKER

WHERE DOB > '19-JAN-1984' AND DOB<'18-JAN-1987';

(1 Mark for correct query)

(½ Mark for partially correct answer)

(iv) To add a new row with the following:

19, 'Daya Kishore', 'Operator', 'P003', '19-Jun-2008', '11-Jun-1984'

INSERT INTO WORKER

VALUES (19, 'Daya Kishore', 'Operator' , 'P003' , '11-Jun-1984');

(1 Mark for correct query)

(½ Mark for partially correct answer)

(c) Give the output of the following SQL queries: 2

(i) SELECT COUNT (PLEVEL), PLEVEL FROM WORKER GROUP BY PLEVEL;

Ans.

COUNT (PLEVEL)	PLEVEL
1	P001
2	P002
2	P003

(½ Mark for correct output)

(ii) SELECT MAX (DOB), MIN (DOJ) FROM WORKER;

MAX (DOB)	MIN (DOJ)
12-Jul-1987	13-Sep-2004

(Mark for correct output)

(iii) SELECT Name, Pay FROM WORKER W, PAYLEVEL P

WHERE W. PLEVEL = S. PLEVEL AND P.ECODE<13;

Name	Pay
Radhe Shyam	26000
Chander Nath	12000

OR

P.ECode does not exist

(½ Mark for correct output)

OR

(Mark for writing No Output)

(iv) SELECT PLEVEL, PAY+ALLOWANCE FROM PAYLEVEL

WHERE PLEVEL= 'P003';

PLEVEL	PAY+ALLOWANCE
P003	118000

(½ Mark for correct output)

6 (a) Verify the following using Truth Table. 2

U. (U' +V) = (U + V)

Ans

U	V	U'	U'+V	U.(U'+)	U+V
0	0	1	1	0	0
0	1	1	1	0	1
1	0	0	0	0	1
1	1	0	1	1	1

VERIFIED FALSE

(2 Marks to be awarded if Truth Table is made OR any equivalent term conveying the same meaning).

(b). Write the equivalent Boolean Expression for the following logic Circuit. **2**

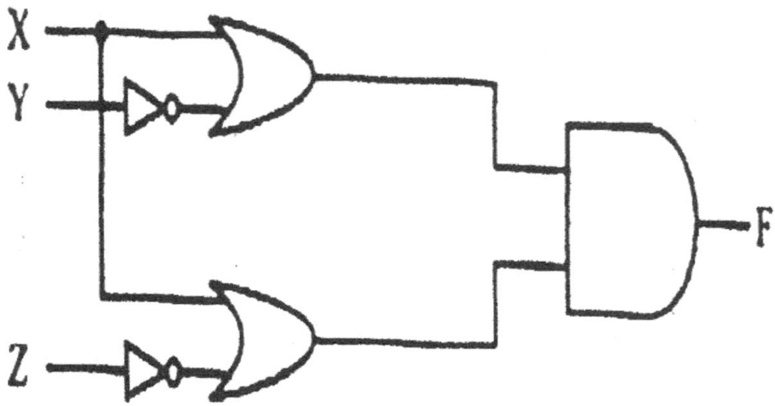

Ans

F=(X+Y').(X+Z')

(2 Marks for the final expression (X+Y').(X+Z')

OR

(1 Mark for anyone of the correct terms out of (X+Y') or (X+ Z')

(C). Write the POS form of a Boolean function F, which is represented in a truth table as follows. **1**

A	B	C	F
0	0	0	0
0	0	1	1
0	1	0	1
0	1	1	0
1	0	0	1
1	0	1	0
1	1	0	0
1	1	1	1

Ans F(A,B,C) = (A+B+C).(A+B'+C').(A'+B+C').(A'+B'+C)

(1 Mark for the correct POS form)

Note: Deduct ½ mark if wrong variable names are used

(d) Reduce the following Boolean Expression using K-Map:

F(P, Q, R, S) = E (0,1,2,4,5,6,8, 12)

	P'Q'	P'Q	PQ	PQ'
R'S'	1	1	1	1
R'S	1	1		
RS				
RS'	1	1		

OR

	R'S'	R'S	RS	RS'
P'Q'	1	1		1
P'Q	1	1		1
PQ	1			
PQ'	1			

Ans

F(P,Q,R,S) = P'R' + R'S' + P'S'

(½ Mark for placing all 1s at correct positions in K-Map)

(½ Mark for each grouping)

(1 Mark for writing final expression in reduced/minimal form)

Note: Deduct ½ mark if wrong variable names are used

7.

a) Differentiate between packet switching and message switching technique in network communication. **1**

Ans

Packet switching: In packet switching, a fixed size of data packet that can be transmitted across the network is specified and then the data packets are sent through switching stations to the final destination. All the packets are stored in the main memory instead of disk. As a result accessing time of packets is reduced.

Message switching: The source computer sends data (message) to the switching station, which stores data in a buffer. It then looks for a free link to another switching station and sends data to that station. This process continues until data is delivered to the destination computer. This type of switching technique is also known as "store and forward" switching.

(½ Marks for written OR diagrammatic explanation of correct Packet Switching).

(½ Marks for written OR diagrammatic explanation of correct Message Switching).

b) Differentiate between BUS and STAR topology of networks. **1**

Ans

Bus Topology	**Star Topology**
Slower as compared to star Slower as compared to star.	Expensive as compared to Bus Expensive as compared to Bus.
Breakage of wire at any point disturbs the entire network	Long wire length

(½ Marks for written or diagrammatic explanation of correct Bus Topology).

(½ Marks for written or diagrammatic explanation of correct Star Topology).

c) What is VoIP? **1**

Ans

Voice over Internet Protocol (Voice over IP, VoIP) is communication protocols and transmission technologies for delivery of voice communications and multimedia sessions over Internet Protocol (IP) networks, such as the Internet. Also, we can say, VoIP are IP telephony, Internet telephony and broadband telephony.

(1 Mark for explaining VoIP).

Note: 1 Mark for writing full form of VoIP.

d) Out of the following, identify client side script (s) and server side script(s). **1**

a) ASP.

b) Javascript.

c) VBScript.

d) JSP.

Ans

Java script & VB script are client side scripts.

JSP & ASP are server side scripts.

(½ Mark for writing correct Client Side Scripts)

(½ Mark for writing correct Server Side Scripts)

(e) Quick learn University is setting up its Academic blocks at Prayag Nagar and planning to set up a network. The university has 3 academic blocks and one Human Resource Center as shown in the diagram below. **4**

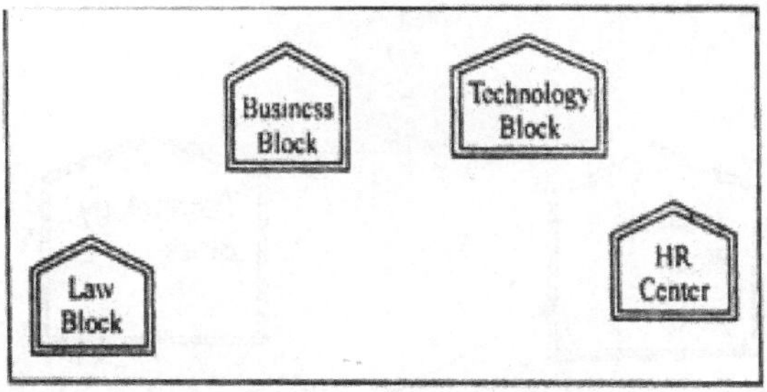

Center to center distance between various block/center is as follows"

Law Block to Business Block	40m
Law Block to Technology Block	80m
Law Block to HR Center	105m
Business Block to Technology Block	30m
Business Block to HR Center	35m
Technology Block to HR Center	15m

Number of Computers in each of the Blocks/Centre is follows:

Law Block	15
Technology Block	40
HR Center	115
Business Block	25

(e1) Suggest the most suitable place (i.e. Block/Center) to install the server of this university with a suitable reason.

Ans HR center:

Reason as it has the maximum number of computers

OR

Business Block

Reason as it is closest to all other Centers (minimum cable length required)

(½ Mark for mentioning any correct place)

(½ Mark for correct reason)

OR

(1 Mark for any other location with a valid reason)

(e2) Suggest an ideal layout for connecting these blocks/centers for a wired connectivity.

Ans. Option 1:

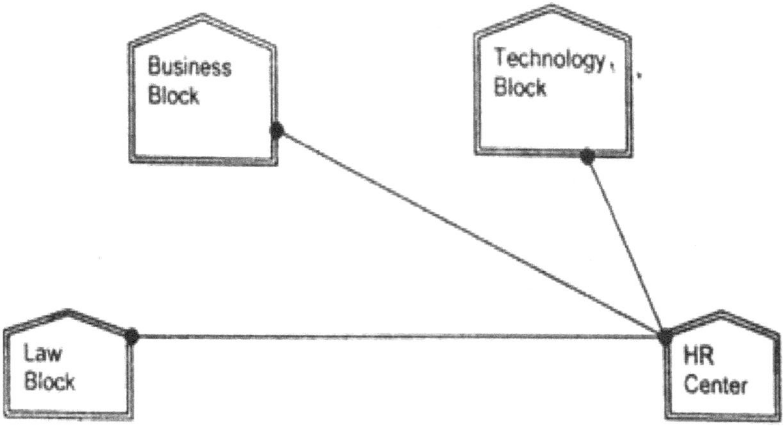

Option 2:

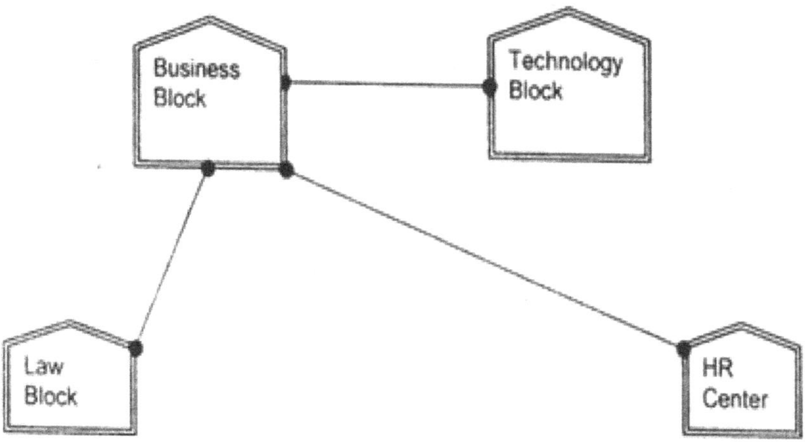

(1 Mark for mentioning any valid connectivity or topology or diagram connecting various compounds inside the campus)

(e3). Which device you will suggest to be placed/installed in each of these blocks/ center to efficiently connect all the computers with in these blocks/center.

Ans

Switch

(1 Mark for mentioning correct device)

Note:

(1 mark to be awarded if Switch / Hub is mentioned)

(e4) The university is planning to connect its admission office in the closest big city, which is more than 250 km from university, which type of network out of LAN, MAN or WAN will be formed? Justify your answer.

Ans

WAN as the given distance is more than the range of LAN and MAN.

(1 Mark for correct network type)

(f) Which of the following will come under Cyber Crime? **1**

(i) Theft of a brand new sealed pack Laptop

(ii) Access to a bank account for getting unauthorized Money Transaction

(iii) Modification in a company data with unauthorized access

(iv) Photocopying a printed report

Ans. (ii) and (iii)

Note:

No marks to be awarded for any other alternative answer

(½ Mark for each correct option)

(g) Compare open source software and proprietary software. **1**

Ans.

Open source software refers to a program or software in which the source code (the form of the program when a programmer writes a program in a particular programming language) is available to the general public for use and/or modification from its original design free of charge.

Proprietary software is software that is owned by an individual or a company (usually the one that developed it). There are almost always major restrictions on its use, and its source code is almost always kept secret.

(½ Mark for each correct explanation/comparison)

Marking Scheme Computer Science Question Paper Code 91 Expected Answers

1.

a) What is the difference between Type Casting and Automatic Type conversion? Also, give a suitable C++ code to illustrate both.

Ans

Automatic Type Conversion: It is an implicit process of conversion of a data from one type to another. For example:

```
int N = 65;
char C = N; // Automatic type conversion ; conversion
cout<<C;
```

Type Casting: It is an explicit process of conversion of a data from one type to another. For example

```
int A=1, B=2;
float C = (float) A/B; //Type Casting
cout<<C;
```

(½ Mark for each correct explanation of Automatic Type Conversion and Type Casting)

(½ Mark for each correct example of Automatic Type Conversion and Type Casting)

OR

(Full 2 Marks for correct example(s) demonstrating the meaning of / difference between Automatic Type Conversion and Type Casting)

OR

(Only 1 Mark to be awarded if Explanation is given without supporting example)

b) Write the names of the header files, which is/are essentially required to run/ execute the following c++ code:

```
void main ( )
{
        char CH,Text[ ] ="+ve Attitude";
        for (int I=0 ; Text[I] ! ='\0' ;I++)
                if (Text[I]== ' ')
                        cout<<end1;
                else
                {
```

```
                CH=toupper (Text [I]) ;
                cout<<CH;
            }
    }
```

Ans

```
iostream.h
ctype.h
```

(½ Mark for writing each correct header file)

c) Rewrite the following program after removing the syntactical errors (if any). Underline each correction. **2**

```
include<iostream.h>
typedef char [80] String;
void main ( )
{
    String S= "Peace";
    int L=strlen(S) ;
    cout<<S<< 'has'<<L<< 'characters'<<end1;
}
```

Ans

```
#include<string.h>
#include<iostream.h>
typedef char String [80];
void main ( )
{
    String S = "Peace";
    int L= strlen(S) ;
    cout<<S<< "has" << L << "characters"<<end1;
}
```

(½ Mark for writing # include<string.h>

(½ Mark for adding # before include<iostream.h> (½ Mark for writing typedef char string[80];) (½ Mark for writing "has" and "characters")

d) Find the output of the following program. **3**

```
#include<iostream.h>
    void SwitchOver(int A [ ], int N, int Split)
    {
```

```
for (int K=0 ; K<N; K++)
        if (K<Split)
                A(K]+ =K;
        else
                A [K]*=K;
}
void Display (int A [ ], int N)
{
        for (int K=0 ; K<N ; K++)
                (K%2==0)? cout<<A[K]<<"%":cout<<A(K]<<end1;
}
void main ( )
{
        int H[ ]= {30,40,50,20,10,5};
        SwitchOver (H, 6, 3);
        Display (H, 6);
}
```

Ans 30%41

52%60

40%25

(1 Mark for each line with correct values)

Note:

Deduct ½ Mark if any/all '% t missing

Deduct ½ Mark if endl is not considered at the right positions

(e) Find the output of the following program: **2**

```
#include<iostream.h>
void main ( )
{
        int *Queen, Moves [ ] = {11, 22, 33, 44};
        Queen = Moves;
        Moves [2] + = 22;
        Cout<< "Queen @"<<*Queen<<end1;
        *Queen - = 11;
        Queen + = 2;
```

```
cout<< "Now @"<<*Queen<<end1;
Queen++;
cout<< "Finally@"<<*Queen«end1;
cout<< "New Origin @"<<Moves[0]<<end1;
}
```

Ans Queen @11

Now @55

Finally @44

New origin @0

(½ Mark for writing each line of output correctly)

Note:

Deduct ½ Mark if any/all '@' missing or/and endl is not considered at the right positions.

(f) Go through the C++ code shown below, and find out the possible output or outputs from the suggested Output Options (i) to (iv). Also, write the minimum and maximum values, which can be assigned to the variable MyNum. **2**

```
#include<iostream.h>
#include <stdlib.h>
void main ( )
{
randomize ( ) ;
int MyNum, Max=5;
MyNum = 20 + random (Max) ;
for (int N=MyNum; N<=25;N++)
cout<N<"*";
}
```

(i) 20*21*22*23*24*25

(ii) 22*23*24*25*

(iii) 23*24*

(iv) 21*22*23*24*25

Ans

ii) 22*23*24*25*

Minimum value 20

Maximum value 24

(1 Marie for mentioning correct option)

(½ Mark for mentioning correct minimum value of MyNum)

(½ Marie for mentioning correct maximum value of MyNum)

2.

a) Differentiate between Constructor and Destructor function with respect to Object Oriented Programming.

Ans

Constructor

It is a special member function of class with the following unique features:

It has same name as the name of the class they belong to.

It has no return type.

It is defined in public visibility mode.

It is automatically called and executed at the time of creation/declaration of the object Constructor can be overloaded.

```
class Trial
}
int a,b;
public:
Trial () {a=0;b=0;}//Constructor
void Disp ()
{
cout<<a<<b<<endl;
}
};
void main ()
{
Trial T; //Constructor invoked
T . Disp ();
  }
```

Destructor

It is a special member function of class with the following unique features:

It has same name as the name of the class preceded by a symbol ~ (tilde).

It has no return type.

It is defined in public visibility mode.

It is automatically called and executed when scope of an object gets over.

Moreover, destructor functions can NOT be overloaded.

```
class Item
{
public:
Item ()
{cout<<"Item Manufactured.."<<endl}
void Working ()
{cout<<"Item is Working"<<endl;}
~Item()//Destructor
{cout<<"Item destroyed..."«end1}
};
void main ()
{
Item I;
I . Working ();
for (int C=0; C<2; C++)
{
Item J;
J.Working ();
}// Call of Destructor for J
}// Call of Destructor for I
```

(1 Marie for correct explanation OR example illustrating a Constructor)

(1 Marie for correct explanation OR example illustrating a Destructor)

b) Write the output of the following C++ code. Also, write the .name of feature of Object Oriented Programming used in the following program jointly illustrated by the function [I] to [IV]. **2**

```
#include<iostream.h>
void Line ( )                                                    //Function [I]
{
        for (int L=1;L<=80;L++)          cout<<"-";
        cout<<end1;
}
void Line (int N)                                                //Function[II]
{
        for (int L=l;L<=N;L++)           Cout<<"*";
        cout<<endl;
}
void Line (char C, int N)                                        //Function [III]
{
        for (int L=l;L<=N;L++)           cout<<C;
        cout<<end1;
}
void Line (int M, int, N)                                        //Function [IV]
{
        for (int L=1;L<=N;L++)           cout<<M*L;
        cout<<end1;
}
void main ( )
{
        int A=9, B=4, C=3;
        char K= '#' ;
        Line (K,B);
        Line (A,C);
}
```

Ans

####

91827

Polymorphism OR Function Overloading

(½ Mark for writing each correct line of output)

(1 Mark for writing the feature. name correctly)

c) Define a class Applicant in C++ with following description. **4**

Private Members

A data member ANo (Admission Number) of type long

A data member Name of type string

A data member Agg (Aggregate Marks) of type float

A data member Grade of type char

A member function GradeMe() to find the Grade as per the Aggregate Marks obtained by a student. Equivalent Aggregate Marks range and the respective Grades are shown as follows:

Aggregate Marks	**Grade**
>=80	A
less than 80 and >=65	B
less than 65 and >=50	C
less than 50	D

Public Members

A function ENTER () to allow user to enter values for ANo, Name, Agg & call function GradeMe() to find the Grade.

A function_RESULT( ) to allow user to view the content of all the data members.

Ans

```
class Applicant
{
        long ANo;
        char Name [20] ;
        float Agg;
        char Grade;
void Grademe ( ) ;
public:
        void Enter ( ) ;
        void Result ( ) ;
} ;
```

```
void Applicant: :GradeMe( )
{
	if (Agg>=80)
		Grade=' A';
	else if(Agg>=65)
		Grade=' B';
	else if(Agg>=50)
		Grade=' C' ;
	else
		Grade=' D';
}
void Applicant: :Enter ( )
{
	cin>>ANo;
	gets (Name) ;
	cin>>Agg;
	GradeMe() ;
}
void Applicant: :Result ( )
{
	cout<<ANo<<Name<<Agg<<Grade<<end1;
}
```

(½ Mark for correct syntax for class header)

(½ Mark for correct declaration of data members)

(1 Mark for correct definition of GradeMe( ))

(1 Mark for correct definition of Enter() with proper invocation of GradeMe( ) function)

(1 Mark for correct definition of Result())

NOTE:

½ mark to be deducted if Grademe() is not invoked within Enter()

No marks to be deducted if member function definitions are inside the Class.

d) *Answer the questions (i) to (iv) based on the* following. **4**

```
class Student
{
	int Rollno:
```

```
        char SName[20];
        float Marksl;
    protected:
        void Result ( ) ;
    public:
        Student ( ) ;
        void Enroll ( ) ;void Display ( ) ;
    } ;
    class Teacher
    {
        long TCode;
        char TName [20];
    protected:
        float Salary;
    public:
        Teacher ( );
        void Enter ( ) ;
        void Show ( ) ;
    } ;
    class Course: public Student, private Teacher
    }
        long CCode [10]; char CourseName [50];
        char StartDate [8] , EndDate [8];
    public:
        Course ( );
        void Commence ( );
        void CDetail ( ) ;
    } ;
```

(i) Write the names of member functions, which are accessible from objects of class Course.

Ans Commence( )

CDetail( )

Enroll( )

Display( )

(1 Mark for correct answer)

Note:

No marks to be awarded for a partially correct answer Constructor functions to be ignored.

(ii) Write the names of all the data members, which is/are accessible from member function Commence of class Course.

Ans CCode

CourseName

StartDate

EndDate

Salary

(1 Mark for correct answer)

Note: No marks to be awarded for a partially correct answer

(iii) Write the names of all the-members, which are accessible from objects of class Teacher.

Ans

Enter( ), Show( )

(1 Mark for correct answer)

Note:

No marks to be awarded for a partially correct answer Constructor functions to be ignored

(iv) Which type of Inheritance is illustrated in the above C++ code? Ans Multiple Inheritance.

(1 Mark for correct answer)

Note: No marks to be awarded for a partially correct answer

3.

a) Write a Get2From1 () function in C++ to transfer the content from one array ALL[] to two different arrays Odd[] and Even[]. The Odd[] array should contain the values from odd positions (1,3,5,...) of ALL[] and Even [] array should contain the values from even positions (0, 2, 4,.....) of ALL [].3

Example

If the ALL[] array contains

12, 34, 56, 67, 89, 90

The Odd[] array should contain

34, 67, 90

And the Even [] array should contain

12,56,89

Ans

```
voil Get2From1 (int All [],int Even [], int Odd [], int Size)
{
        int J=0,K=0;
        for (int I=0 ;I<Size; 1++)
        {
                if (I%2==0)
                {
                        Even [J]=All[I] ;
                        J++;
                }
                else
                {
                        Odd[K]=All[I);
                        K++;
                }
        }
}
```

(1 Mark for correct loop).

(½ Mark for checking even locations).

(½ Mark for checking odd locations or writing else for even locations).

(½ Mark for assigning elements to the corresponding Even and Odd Array).

(½ Mark for incrementing Even and Odd Array Locations).

b) An array G[50][20] is stored in the memory along the row with each of its elements occupying 8 bytes. Find out the location of G[10][15], if G[0][0] is stored at 4200. **3**

Ans Assuming LBR=LBC=0

B=4200

W=8 bytes

Number of Rows(N)=50

Number of Columns (M)=20

LOC(Arr[I] [J]) = B +(I*M + J) *W

LOC (Arr [10] [15]) = 4200+ (10*20+15)*8

= 4200 + (215*8)

= 4200+1720

= 5920

(1 Mark for writing correct formula (for row major).

OR substituting formula with correct values for calculating Address).

(2 marks for calculating correct address).

Note:

1 mark to be awarded for writing only the correct answer i.e. 5920, without showing any formula/calculation.

c) Write a function in C++ to perform Delete operation on a dynamically allocated Queue containing Members details as given in the following definition of NODE. **4**

```
struct NODE
{
    long Mno                        //Member Number
    char Mname[20];                 //Member Name
            NODE *Link;
        };
```

Ans
```
        class Queue
        {
            NODE *Front, *Rear;
        public:
            Queue ( ) {Front = NULL; Rear = NULL; }
            void QueAdd ( );
            void QueDel ( );
            void QueDis ( );
            ~Queue();
        } ;
        void Queue: :QueDel ( )
        {
            if (Front!=NULL)
            {
                NODE *Temp=Front;
                cout<<Front->Mno<< " " ;
                cout<<Front->Mname<< "Deleted";
                Front=Front->Link;
                delete Temp;
                if (Front==NULL) Rear=NULL;
```

```
        }
        else
            cout<<"Underflow ! Queue is empty..";
    }
```

(1 Mark for checking Empty Queue)

(½ Mark for assigning Front to Temp)

(1 Mark for reassigning Front with Front->Link)

(1 Mark for deleting Temp)

(½ Mark for assigning Rear with NULL if Queue becomes Empty)

d) Write a DSUMO function in C++ to find sum of Diagonal Elements from a NxN Matrix. **2**
(Assuming that the N is a odd number)

Ans

```
void DSUM (int A [ ] [100] ,int N)
{
    int SUMR =0, SUML=0;
    for (int i=0; i<N;i++}
    {
        SUMR=SUMR + A[i] [i] ;
        SUML = SUML + A[i] [N-1-i] ;
    }
    cout<< " Sum of Diagonal Elements = "<<SUMR + SUML –
A[N/2] [N/2] ;
}
OR
void DSUM (int A[] [100], int N)
{
    int SUMR =0, SUML=0;
    for (int i=0; i<N; i++)
    {
        SUMR = SUMR + A[i] [i] ;
        SUML = SUML + A[i] [N-1-i] ;
    }
```

```
        cout<< "Sum of Right Diagonal Elements =
        "<<SUMR<<end1; cout<< "Sum of Left Diagonal
        Elements = "<<SUML<<end1;
    }
    OR
    void DSUM (int A[] [100] , int N)
    {
        int SUMR =0, SUML=0;
        for (int i = 0; i<N; i++)
        {
            for (int j = 0; j<N; j++)
            {
                if (i==j)
                    SUMR=SUMR + A[i] [j] ;
                else if (i+j == N-1)
                    SUML = SUML + A[i] [j];
            }
        }
        cout<< "Sum of Diagonal Elements ="<< SUMR + SUML - A[N/2] [N/2];
    }
```

(½ Mark for writing correct Function Header)

(½ Mark for writing correct loop)

(1 Mark for finding sum of Right Diagonal Elements and/or Left Diagonal Elements)

e) Evaluate the following postfix notation of expression. **2**

True, False, NOT, AND, True, True, AND,OR

Ans Element Scanned	STACK Status
True	TRUE
False	TRUE, FALSE
NOT	TRUE, TRUE
AND	TRUE
True	TRUE, TRUE
True	TRUE, TRUE, TRUE
AND	TRUE, TRUE
OR	TRUE
	Final Result: TRUE

(½ Mark for evaluating each operator correctly)

OR

(½ Mark only for writing TRUE as the final answer without showing any calculation/Stack)

4.

a) Observe the program segment given below carefully and fill the blanks marked as Statement 1 and Statement 2 using seekg( ), seekp( ) tellp( ) and tellg( ) functions for performing the required task. **1**

```
#include <fstream.h>
class ITEM
{
        int Ino;char Iname[20]; float Price;
        public:
        void ModifyPrice() ;//The function is to modify
                price of a particular ITEM
};
void item: :ModiyPrice()
{
        fstream File;
        File.open ("ITEM.DAT", ios::binary | ios::in |
        ios: :out) || ; int CIno;
        cout<<"Item No to modify price:";cin>>CIno;
        while (file.read ((char*) this, sizeof (ITEM)))
        {
                if (CIno==Ino)
                {
                        cout<<"Present Price:"<<Price<<end1;
                        cout<<"Changed price:"; cin>>Price;
                        int FilePos = ________ ; //Statement 1,
                        ______________; //Statement 2
                        File.write((char*)this, size of(ITEM)) ;
                                        //Re-writing the record
                }
        }
        File.close( ) ;
```

}

Ans

Option 1

Statement 1: File.tellp ( ) ; OR File. tellg ( ) ;

Statement 2: File.seekp (FilePos - sizeof (ITEM)) ;

OR File.seekp (-sizeof (ITEM), ios: :cur));

OR File.seekg(FilePos - sizeof (ITEM));

OR. File.seekg(-sizeof (ITEM), ios: :cur));

Ogtion 2

Statement 1: File. tellp ( ) – sizeof (ITEM) ;

OR File.tellg()- sizeof (ITEM) ;

Statement 2: File.seekp (FilePos) ;

OR File.seekg (FilePos) ;

(½ Mark for writing Statement 1 correctly)

(½ Mark for writing Statement 2 correctly)

b) Write a function in C++ to count the no. of "He" or "She" words present in a text file "STORY. TXT".2

If the file "STORY. TXT" content is as follows:

He is playing in the ground. She is

Playing with her dolls.

The output of the function should be

Count of He/She in file: 2

Ans

```
void COUNT ( )
{
    ifstream Fil ("STORY.TXT");
    char STR [10];
    int count = 0;
    while (!Fil.eof ( ))
    {
        Fil>>STR ;
        if (strcmp (STR, "He") ==0 | | strcmp (STR, "She") = =0)
        count++;
    }
```

```
        Cout<<"Count of He/She in file : "<<count<<end1;
        Fil.close( ); //Ignore
    }
    OR
```

Any other correct function definition performing the desired operation

(½ Mark for opening STORY. TXT correctly)

(½ Mark for reading each word (Whichever method adopted) from the file)

(½ Mark for comparing the word with 'He' and 'She' and incrementing counter)

(½ Mark for displaying the count of 'He/She' with/without the Text Message)

Note: Ignore case sensitivity for He/She

c) Write a function in C++ to search for a camera from a binary file "CAMERA.DAT" containing the objects of class" CAMERA (as defined below). The user should enter the Model No and the function should search display the details of the camera. **3**

```
class CAMERA
    {
        long ModelNo;
        float MegaPixel;
        int Zoom;
        char Details[120];
public:
    void Enter ( ) {cin>>ModelNo>>MegaPixel>>Zoom;gets(Details);}
    void Display ( )
    {cout<<ModelNo<<MegaPixel<<Zoom<<Details<<endl;}
    long GetModelNo ( ) {return ModelNo;}
};
```

Ans

```
void Search ( )
{
    CAMERA C;
    long modelnum;
    cin>>modelnum;
    ifstream fin;
    fin.open ("CAMERA.DAT", ios: :binary | ios: :in) ;
    while (fin.read((char*) &C,sizeof (C)))
```

```
{
        if (C. GetModelNo ( ) modelnum)
                C.Display() ;
}
Fin.close( ) ; //Ignore
}
OR
void Search (long modelnum)
{
        CAMERA C;
        ifstream fin;
        fin.open ("CAMERA.DAT", ios: :binary | ios: :in);
        while(fin.read((char*)&C,sizeof(C)))
        {
                if (C.GetModelNo() = = modelnum)
                        C. Display ();
        }
        Fin.close( );//Ignore
}
```

(½ Mark for declaring and entering a model number for a camera to search OR passing it as a parameter to the function)

(½ Marie for opening CAMERA.DAT in correct mode)

(½ Marie for reading each record from CAMERA.DAT)

(½ Marie for correct loop / checking end of file)

(½ Marie for comparing value returned by GetModelNo() with model number entered)

(½ Marie for displaying the matching record)

5.

a) What do you understand by Selection & Projection operations in relational algebra? **2**

Ans. Projection for selecting the columns of table.

Selection for selecting the rows of table

(1 Marie for correct explanation of Projection).

(1 Marie for correct explanation of Selection correctly*).*

OR

(Full 2 Marks for correct example(s) demonstrating the meaning of Projection & Selection).

Consider the following tables EMPLOYEE and SALGRADE and answer and (c) parts of this question:

Table: Employee

ECODE	NAME	DESIG	SGRADE	DOJ	DOB
101	Abdul Ahmad	EXECUTIVE	S03	23-Mar-2003	13-Jan-1980
102	Rav:i. Chander	HEAD-IT	S02	12-Feb-2010	22-Jul-1987
103	John Ken	RECEPTIONIST	S03	24-June-2009	24-Feb-1983
105	Nazar Ameen	GM	S02	11-Aug-2006	03-Mar-1984
108	Priyam Sen	CEO	S01	29-Dec-2004	19-Jan-1982

Table: Salgrade

SGRADE	SALARY	HRA
S0l	56000	18000
S02	32000	12000
S03	24000	8000

b) Write SQL commands for the following statements:

(i) To display the details of all EMPLOYEEs, in descending order of DOJ.

Ans

SELECT * FROM EMPLOYEE ORDER BY DOJ DESC; *(1 Mark for correct query)*

OR

(½ Mark for partially correct answer)

(ii) To display NAME and DE51G of those EMPLOYEEs, whose 5ALGRADE is either 502 or 503

Ans

SELECT NAME, DESIG FROM EMPLOYEE WHERE SGRADE = 'S02' OR SGRADE= 'S03';

OR

SELECT NAME, DESIG FROM EMPLOYEE WHERE SALGRADE ='S02' OR SALGRADE='S03'; *(1 Mark for correct query)*

OR

(½ Mark for partially correct answer)

(iii) To display the content of all the EMPLOYEEs table, whose DOJ is in between'09-Feb-2006' and '08-Aug-2009'.

Ans SELECT * FROM EMPLOYEE

WHERE DOJ BETWEEN '09-Feb-2006'and '08-Aug-2009';

OR

SELECT * FROM EMPLOYEE

WHERE DOJ > = '09-Fab-2006' and DOJ <='08-Aug-2009';

OR

SELECT * FROM EMPLOYEE

WHERE DOJ > '09-Feb-2006' and DOJ <' 08-Aug-2009" ;

(1 Mark for correct query)

OR

(½ Mark for partially correct answer)

(iv) To add a new row with the following:

109, 'Harish Roy', 'HEAD-IT', 'S02', '09-Sep-2007, '21-Apr-1983'

Ans INSERT INTO EMPLOYEE

VALUES(109,'Harish Roy' ,'HEAD-IT' ,'S02' ,'09-Sep-2007' ,'21-Apr-1983') ;

(1 Mark for correct query)

OR

(½ Mark for partially correct answer)

(c) Give :the output of the following SQL queries: **2**

(i) SELECT COUNT (SGRADE), SGRADE FROM EMPLOYEE GROUP BY SGRADE;

Ans

COUNT (SGRADE)	SGRADE
1	S01
2	S02
2	S03

(½ Mark. for correct output)

(ii) SELECT MIN(DOB), MAX (DOJ) FROM EMPLOYEE;

Ans

MIN (DOB)	MAX (DOJ)
13-Jan-1980	12-Feb-2010

(½ Mark for correct output)

(iii) SELECT NAME, SALARYFROM EMPLOYEE E, SALGRADE S WHERE E.SGRADE= S.SGRADE AND E.ECODE<103;

Ans

Name	Salary
Abdul Ahmad	24000
Ravi Chander	32000

(½ Mark for correct output)

(iv) SELECT SGRADE, SALARY+HRA ET:)M SALGRADE WHERE SGRADE= 'S02';

Ans

SGRADE	SALARY+HRA
S02	44000

(½ Mark for correct output)

6(a) Yerify the following using Truth Table: 2

X+Y. Z=(X+Y).(X+Z)

Ans

X	Y	Z	Y.Z	X+Y.Z	X+Y	X+Z	(X+Y).(X+Z)
0	0	0	0	0	0	0	0
0	0	1	0	0	0	1	0
0	1	0	0	0	1	0	0
0	1	1	1	1	1	1	1
1	0	0	0	1	1	1	1
1	0	1	0	1	1	1	1
1	1	0	0	1	1	1	1
1	1	1	1	1	1	1	1

VERIFIED

(2 Mark for correct verification using Truth Table)

NOTE: No marks are to be awarded if only algebraic proof is given.

(b). Write the equivalent Boolean Expression for the following Logic Circuit. 2

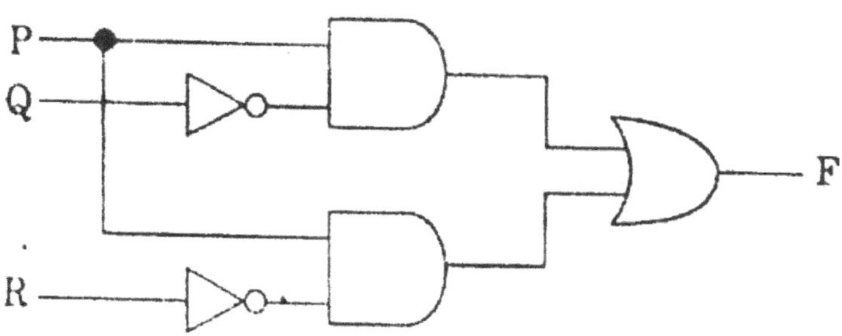

Ans F = P.Q' + P.R'

(2 Marks for the final expression P.Q'+P.R')

OR

(1 Mark for anyone of the correct terms out of P .Q' or P .R'

(c) Write the SOP form of a Boolean function F, which is represented in a truth table as follows. **1**

U	V	W	F
0	0	0	1
0	0	1	0
0	1	1	1
1	0	0	0
1	0	1	0
1	1	0	1
1	1	1	1

Ans F(U, V, W) = U'.V'.W'+ U'.V.W + U.V.W'+ U.V.W

(1 Mark for the correct SOP form)

Note: Deduct ½ mark if wrong variable names are used

(d) Reduce the following Boolean Expression using K-Map: **3**

F(A, B,C, D) = Σ (0,1, 2, 4, 5, 6, 7, 8, 10)

	A'B'	A' B	AB	AB'
C'D'	1	1		1
C'D	1	1		
C D				
C D'	1	1		1

OR

	C'D'	C'D	CD	CD'
A' B'	1	1		1
A' B	1	1		1
A B				
A B'	1			1

Ans F (A,B,C,D) = A 'C'+ A'D' + B'D'

(½ Mark for placing all 1s at correct positions in K-Map)

(½ Mark for each grouping)

(1 Mark for writing final expression in reduced/minimal form)

Note : Deduct ½ mark if wrong variable names are used

7. (a) In networking, what-is WAN? How is it different from LAN? 1

Ans. A WAN (wide area network), is not restricted to a geographical location, although it might be confined within the bounds of a state or country. A WAN connects several LANs, and may be limited to an enterprise (a corporation or an organization) or accessible to the public. The technology is high speed and relatively expensive. The Internet is an example of a worldwide public WAN.

A LAN (local area network) is a group of computers and network devices connected together, usually within the same building or campus.

(½ Marks for writing WAN correctly)

(½ Marks for writing LAN correctly)

(b) Differentiate between XML and HTML. **1**

Ans The Extensible Markup Language (XML) was initially visualized as a language for defining new document formats for the World Wide Web. XML is text- based formats that provide mechanisms for describing document structures with the help of user defined Tags.

HTML - short for Hypertext Markup Language is the predominant markup language for the creation of web pages. It provides a means to describe the structure of text-based information in a document by denoting certain text as headings, paragraphs, lists, and to supplement that text with interactive forms, embedded images, and other objects using predefined Tags.

(½ Marks for explaining XML correctly)

(½ Marks for explaining HTML correctly)

OR

(½ Mark Only if correct expansion of both the terms XML and HTML are given)

(c) What is WEB2.0? **1**

Ans The term Web 2.0 is associated with **web applications that facilitate participatory information sharing,** interoperability, **user-centered design, and collaboration on the World Wide Web.** Web 2.0 is also used for social networking. Example: **Social Networking Sites, Blogs, Facebook,** Video Sharing Sites, Video Conferencing Applications etc.

(1 Mark for correctly explaining Web 2.0 - anyone of the highlighted text to be consider appropriate)

Note: Only ½ Mark for mentioning an example or an improved Web Application of WWW

(d) Out of the following, identify client side script (s) and server side script (s). **1**

(i) Javascript

(ii) ASP

(iii) vbscript

(iv) JSP

Ans.

Javascript & vbscript are client side scripts

JSP & ASP are server side scripts

(½ Mark for writing correct 'Client Side Scripts)

(½ Mark for writing correct Server Side Scripts)

(e) Great Studies University is setting up its Academic schools at Sunder Nagar and planning to set up a network. The university has 3 academic schools and one administration center as shown in the diagram below. **4**

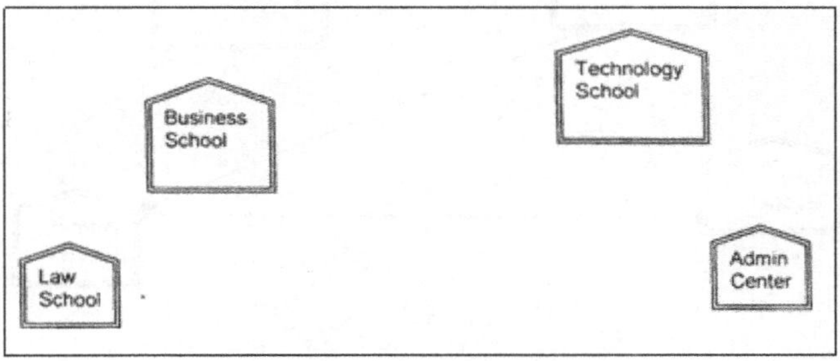

Center to center distances between various buildings is as follows :

Law School to Business School	60m
Law School to Technology School	90m
Law School to Admin Center	115m
Business School to Technology School	40m
Business School to. Admin Center	45m
Technology School to Admin Center	25m

Number of Computers in each of the Schools/Center is follows:

Law School	25
Technology School	50
Admin Center	125
Business School	35

(i) Suggest the most suitable place (i.e. School/Center) to install the server of this university with a suitable reason. **1**

Ans

Option 1:

Admin center as it has the most number of computers Option 2.

Business School as it will require minimum cable length to connect other blocks *(½ Mark for mentioning the correct place) (½ Mark for mentioning a valid reason)*

OR

(1 Mark for any other location with a valid reason)

(ii) Suggest an ideal layout for connecting these schools/ center for a wired connectivity. **1**

Ans Option 1:

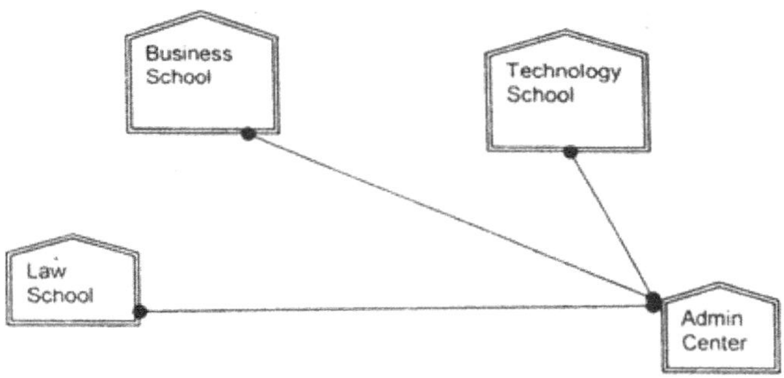

Option 2:

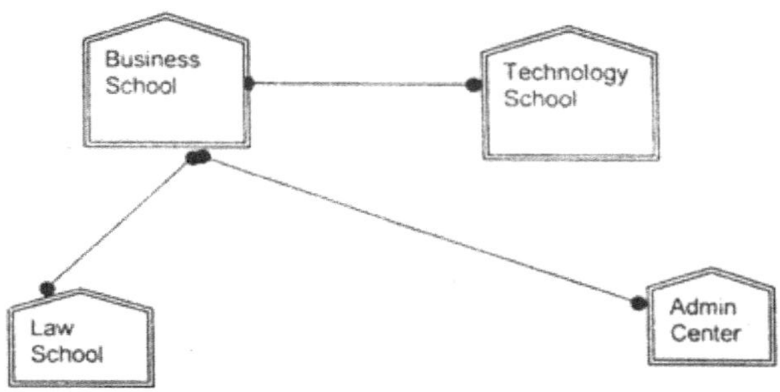

(1 Mark for mentioning any valid connectivity or topology or diagram connecting various compounds inside the campus)

(iii) Which device will you suggest to be placed/installed in each of these schools / center to efficiently connect all the computers within these schools / center? **1**

Ans Switch

(1 Mark for mentioning correct device)

NOTE: Award 1 full mark if Hub/Switch is mentioned.

(iv) The university is planning to connect its admission office in the closest big city, which is more than 350 km from the university. Which type of network out of LAN, MAN or WAN will be formed? Justify your answer. **1**

Ans WAN as the distance is more than the range of LAN or MAN. **1**

(1 Mark for correct network type)

(f) Compare Open Source Software and Proprietary Software. **1**

Ans Open source software refers to a program or software in which the source code (the form of the program when a programmer writes a program in a particular programming language) is available to the general public for use and/or modification from its original design free of charge.

Proprietary software is software that is owned by an individual or a company (usually the one that developed it). There are almost always major restrictions on its use, and its source code is almost always kept secret.

(1 Mark for correct/valid comparison)

OR

(Mark for defining each term correctly)

(g) What are cookies? **1**

Ans A small piece of information that a server sends to a client. When a person visits a Web site with cookie capabilities, its server sends certain information about him/her to the browser, which is stored on his/her hard drive as a text file. At some later time (such as returning to the site the next day), the server retrieves the cookie.

(1 Mark for correct definition)

COMPUTER SCIENCE

Time allowed: 3 hours **Maximum Marks: 70**

Instructions

(i) All questions are compulsory.

(ii) Programming Language: C+ +.

Question Paper Code 91/1

1.

a) What is the difference between automatic type conversion and type casting? Also, give a suitable C++ code to illustrate both. **2**

b) Which C++ header file(s) will be essentially required to be included to run/ execute the following C++ code? **1**

```
void main( )
{
    int Eno=123, char Ename[ ]="Rehan Swamp";
    cout<<setw(5)<<Eno<<setw(25)<<EName<<endl;
}
```

c) Rewrite the following c++ program code after removing the syntax error(s) (if any). Underline each correction. **2**

```
include <iostream.h>
class TRAIN
{
    long TrainNo;
    char Description[25];
public
    void Entry ( )
    {
        cin >>TrainNo; gets(Description);
    }
    Void Display ( )
    {
        cout<<TrainNo<<":"<<Description<<endl;
    }
```

```
};
void main( )
{
        TRAIN  T;
        Entry. T( ); Display. T( );
}
```

d) Find the output of the following program. **3**

```
#inc1ude  <iostream.h>
struct  POINT
{int X, Y, Z;};
void StepIn(POINT & P, int Step=1)
{
        P.X+=Step;
        P.Y  -=Step;
        P.Z+=Step;
}
void StepOut(POINT & P, int Step=1)
{
P.X-=Step;
P.Y+=Step;
P.Z-=Step;
}
void main ( )
{
        POINT P1={15, 25, 5}, P2={10, 30, 20};
        StepIn(P1);
        StepOut(P2,4);
        cout<<P1.X<<","<<P1.Y<<","<<P1.Z<<endl;
        cout<<P2.X<<","<<P2.Y<<","<<P2.Z<<endl;
        StepIn(P2,12);
        cout<<P2.X<<","<<P2.Y<<","<<P2.Z<<endl;
}
```

e) Find the output of the following program. **2**

```
#include <iostream.h>
#include <ctype.h>
void ChangeIt(char Text[ ], char C)
{
        for (int K=0;Text[K]!='\0';K++)
        {
                 if (Text[K]>='F' && Text[K]<='L')
                    Text[K]=tolower(Text[K]);
                else
                if (Text[K]='E' || Text[K]=='e')
                        Text[K]= =C;
                else
                if (K%2==O)
                        Text[K]=toupper(Text[K]);
                else
                        Text[K]=Text[K-l];
        }
}
void main ( )
{
        char OldText[ ]="pOwERALone";
        ChangeIt(OldText,'%');
        cout<<"New        TEXT:"<<OldText<<endl;
}
```

f) The following code is from a game, which generates a set of 4 random numbers. Yallav is playing this game, help him to identify the correct option(s) out of the four choices given below as the possible set of such numbers generated from the program code so that he wins the game. Justify your answer. 2

```
#include <iostream.h>
#include <stdlib.h>
const int LOW=15;
void main ( )
{
```

```
        randomize( ) ;
        int POINT=5, Number;
        for (int 1=1;I<=4;I++)
        {
            Number=LOW+random(POINT) ;
            cout<<Number<<":" ;
            POINT--;
        }
    }
```

(i) 19:16:15:18:

(ii) 14:18:15:16:

(iii) 19:16:14:18:

(iv) 19:16:15:16:

2.

a) What do you understand by Polymorphism.? Also, give an example in C++ to illustrate the same. **2**

b) Answer the questions (i) and (ii) after going through the following class. **2**

```
class TEST
{
    int Regno, Max, Min, Score;
public:
    TEST()                                          //Function 1
    {
        Regno= 101;Max=100;Min=40;Score=75;
    }
    TEST(int Pregno,int Pscore)                     //Function 2
    {
        Regno=Pregno;Max=100;Min=40;Score=Pscore;
    }
    ~TEST()                                         //Function 3
    {
        cout<<"TEST Over"<<endl;
    }
            void Display() //Function 4
```

```
{
cout<<Regno<<":"<<Max<<":"<<Min<<endl;
cout<<"[Score]"<<Score<<endl;
}
};
```

(i) As per Object Oriented Programming, which. concept is illustrated by **Function 1 and Function 2** together?

(ii) What is **Function 3** specifically referred as? When do you think, **Function 3** will be invoked/called?

c) Define a class ITEM in C++ with following description. **4**

Private Members

Code of type integer (Item Code)

Iname of type string (Item Name).

Price of type float (Price of each item).

Qty of type integer (Quantity of item in stock).

Offer of type float (Offer percentage on the item).

A member function GetOffer() to calculate Offer percentage as per the following rule:

If Qty<=50	Offer is 0
If 50<Qty<=100	Offer is 5
If Qty>100	Offer is 10

Public Members

A function GetStock() to allow user to enter values for Code, Iname, Price, Qty and call function GetOffer() to calculate the offer

A function ShowItem() to allow user to view the content of all the data members.

d) Answer the questions (i) to (iv) based on the following. **4**

```
class Chairperson
{
 long CID;                //Chairperson Identification Number
      char CName[20];
protected:
      char Description [40];
      void Allocate();
public:
      Chairperson();
      void Assign();
```

```
        void Show();
    };
    class Director
    {
        int DID;                        //Director ID
        char Dname[20];
    protected:
        char Profile[30];
    public:
        Director();
        void Input();
        void output();
    };
    class Company: private Chairperson, public Director
    {
        int CID;                    //Company ID
        char City[20], Country[20];
    public:
        Company();
        void Enter();
        void Display();
};
```

(i) Which type of inheritance out of the following is specifically is illustrated in the above C++ code?

 (a) Single Level Inheritance.

 (b) Multi Level Inheritance.

 (c) Multiple Inheritance.

(ii) Write the names of data members, which are accessible by objects of class type Company.

(iii) Write the names of all member functions, which are accessible by objects of class type Company.

(iv) Write the names of all members, which are accessible from member functions of class Director.

3.

a) Write a function CHANGEO in C++, which accepts an array of integer and its size as parameters and divide all those array elements by 7 which are divisible by 7 and multiply other-array elements by 3. **3**

Sample Input Data of the array

A[0]	A[1]	A[2]	A[3]	A[4]
21	12	35	42	18

Content of the array after Calling CHANGE() function

A[0]	A[1]	A[2]	A[3]	A[4]
3	36	5	6	54

b) An array P[50][60] is stored in the memory along the column with each of the element occupying 2 bytes, find out the memory location for the element P[10] [20], if the Base Address of the array is 6800. **3**

c) Write a complete program in c++ to implement a dynamically allocated Stack containing names of Countries. **4**

d) Write a function int SKIPSUM(int A[ ] [3], int N,int M) in C++ to find and return the sum of elements from all alternate elements of a two-dimensional array starting from A[0][0]. **2**

Hint:

If the following is the content of the array

A[0][0]	A[0][1]	A[0][2]
4	5	1
A[1][0]	A[1][1]	A[1][2]
2	8	7
A[2][0]	A[2][1]	A[2][2]
9	6	3

The function SKIPSUM() should add elements A[0][0], A[0][2], A[1][l], A[2][0] and A[2][2].

e) Evaluate the following postfix notation of expression. **2**

(Show status of Stack after each operation)

False, True, NOT, OR, True, False, AND, OR

4.

a) Observe the program segment given below carefully and fill the blanks marked as Statement 1 and Statement 2 using tellg() and seekp() functions for performing the required task. **1**

```
#include <fstream.h>
class Client
{
        long Cno; char Name[20], Email[30] ;
public:
        //Function to allow user to enter the Cno, Name, Email
        void Enter() ;
        //Function to allow user to enter (modify) Email void
        Modify() ;
        long ReturnCno() {return Cno;}
};
void ChangeEmail()
{Client C;
    fstream F;
    F.open ("INFO.DAT",ios::binary|ios::in|ios::out);
    long Cnoc;//Client's no. whose Email needs to be changed
    cin>>Cnoc;
    while (F.read((char*)&C, sizeof(C)))
    {
            if (Cnoc= =C.ReturnCno())
            {
                    C.Modify();
                                                    //Statement 1
                    int Pos =        ________//To find the current
                                     position of file pointer
                                                    // Statement 2
```

```
              ____________//To move the file
                           pointer to write the
                                  //modified record
                                  back onto the file
                                  //for the desired Cnoc
F.write((char*)&C, sizeof(C));
              }
          }
          F.close();
      }
```

b) Write a function in C++ to count the words "this" and "these" present in a text file "ARTICLE.TXT". **2**

[Note that the words "this" and "these" are complete words]

c) Write a function in C++ to search and display details of all flights, whose destination is "Mumbai" from a binary file "FLIGHT.DAT". Assuming the binary file is containing the objects of the following class. **3**

```
class FLIGHT
{
      int Fno;                    //Flight Number
      char From[20];              //Flight Starting Point
      char To[20];                //Flight Destination
public:
      char* GetFrom() {return From;}
      char* GetTo() {return To;}
   void Enter() {cin>>Fno;gets(From);gets(To);}
   void Display(){cout<<Fno<<":"<<From<<":"<<To<<endl;}
};
```

5.

a) What do you understand by Candidate Keys in a table? Give a suitable example of Candidate Keys from a table containing some meaningful data. **2**

b) Consider the following tables STORE and SUPPLIERS and answer (bl) and (b2) parts of this question:

Table: Store

ItemNo	Item	Scode	Qty	Rate	LastBuy
2005	Sharpener Classic	23	60	8	31-Jun-09
2003	Ball Pen 0.25	22	50	25	01-Feb-10
2002	Gel Pen Premium	21	150	12	24-Feb-10
2006	Gel Pen Classic	21	250	20	11-Mar-09
2001	Eraser Small	22	220	6	19-Jan-09
2004	Eraser Big	22	110	8	02-Dec-09
2009	Ball Pen 0.5	21	180	18	03-Nov-09

Table: Suppliers

Scode	Sname
21	Premium Stationers
23	Soft Plastics
22	Tetra Supply

(b1). Write SQL commands for the following statements. **4**

(i) To display details of all the items in the Store table in ascending order of LastBuy.

(ii) To display ItemNo and Item name of those items from Store table whose Rate is more than 15 Rupees.

(iii) To display the details of those items whose Supplier code (Scode) is 22 or Quantity in Store (Qty) is more than 110 from the table Store.

(iv) To display Minimum Rate of items for each Supplier individually as per Scode from the table Store.

(b2) Give the output of the following SQL queries. **2**

(i) SELECT COUNT(DISTINCT Scode) FROM Store;

(ii) SELECT Rate*Qty FROM Store WHERE ItemNo=2004;

(iii) SELECT Item,Sname FROM Store S, Suppliers P WHERE S.Scode=P.Scode AND ItemNo=2006;

(iv) SELECT MAX(LastBuy) FROM Store;

6.

a) Verify the following algebraically. **2**

(A'+B').(A +B)=A'.B+A.B'

b) Write the equivalent Boolean Expression for the following Logic circuit. **2**

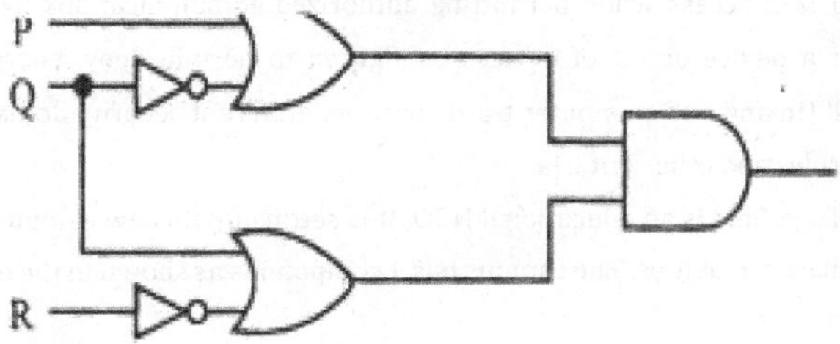

c) Write the POS form of a Boolean function H, which is represented in a truth table as follows. **1**

X	Y	Z	H
0	0	0	1
0	0	1	0
0	1	0	1
0	1	1	1
1	0	0	1
1	0	1	0
1	1	0	0
1	1	1	1

d) Reduce the following Boolean Expression using K-Map. **3**

F (U, V, W, Z) = Σ (3, 5, 7, 10, 11, 13, 15)

7.

a) What was the role of ARPANET in the Computer Network? **1**

b) Which of the following is not an unit for data transfer rate? **1**

(i) bps.

(ii) abps.

(iii) gbps.

(iv) kbps.

c) What is the difference between Trojan Horse and Virus in terms of computers? **1**

d) What term we use for a software/hardware device, which is used to block, unauthorized access while permitting authorized communications. This term is also used for a device or set of devices configured to permit, deny, encrypt, decrypt, or proxy all (in and out) computer traffic between different security domains based upon a set of rules and other criteria. **1**

e) "Learn Together" is an educational NGO. It is setting up its new campus at Jabalpur for its web based activities. The campus has 4 compounds as shown in the diagram below: **4**

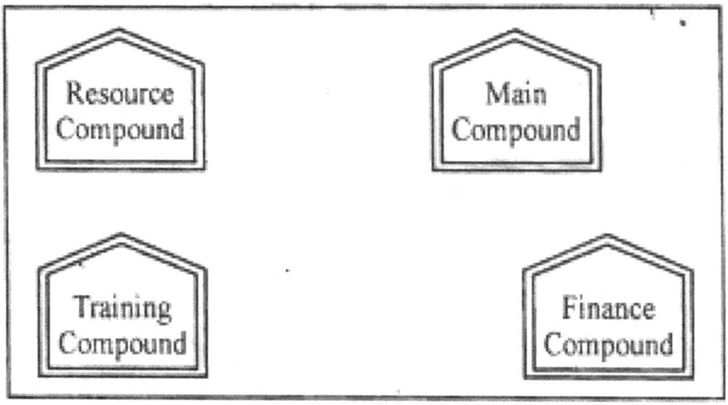

Center to center distances between various Compounds as per architectural drawings (in Metre) is as follows.

Main Compound to Resource Compound	110 m
Main Compound to Training Compound	115 m
Main Compound to Finance Compound	35 m
Resource Compound to Training Compound	25 m
Resource Compound to Finance Compound	135 m
Training Compound to Finance Compound	100 m

Expected Number of Computers in each Compound is as follows.

Main Compound	5
Resource Compound	15
Training Compound	150
Accounts Compound	20

(e1). Suggest a cable layout of connections between the compounds.

(e2). Suggest the most suitable place (i.e. compound) to house the server for this NGO. Also, provide a suitable reason for your suggestion.

(e3).Suggest the placement of the following devices with justification.

(i) Repeater.

(ii) Hub/Switch.

(e4). The NGO is planning to connect its International office situated in Mumbai, which out of the following wired communication link, you will suggest for a very high speed connectivity?

(i) Telephone Analog Line.

(ii) Optical Fiber.

(iii) Ethernet Cable.

f) Write the full forms of the following. **1**

(i) (f1) GNU.

(ii) (f2) XML.

g) Write one advantage of each for Open Source Software and Proprietary Software. **1**

Question Paper Code 91

1.

a) What is the difference between call by value and call by reference? Also, give a suitable C++ code to illustrate both. **2**

b) Which C++ header file(s) will be essentially required to be included to run/ execute the following C++ code. **1**

```
void main()
{
        int Rno=24; char Name[] ="Amen Singhania";
        cout<<setw(lO)<<Rno<<setw(20)<<Name<<endl;
}
```

c) Rewrite the following C++ program code after removing the syntax error(s) (if any). Underline each correction. **2**

```
include <iostream.h>
class FLIGHT
{
      long FlightCode;
      char Description[25];
  public
      void AddInfo()
      {
            cin>>FlightCode; gets (Description) ;
      {
      void ShowInfo()
      (
            cout<<FlightCode<<":"<<Description<<endl;
            }
};
      void main()
      {
        FLIGHT F;
        AddInfo.F(); ShowInfo.F();
      }
```

d) Find the output of the following program. **3**

```
#include <iostream.h>
struct THREE_D
{int X,Y,Z;};
void Moveln(THREE_D &T, int Step=l)
}
        T.X+=Step;
        T.Y-=Step;
        T.Z+=Step;
}
void MoveOut(THREE_D &T, int Step=l)
{
        T.X-=Step;
        T.Y+=Step;
        T.Z-=Step;
}
void main ()
{
        THREE_D    Tl={lO,20,5},T2={30,lO,40};
        Moveln(T1);
        MoveOut(T2,5);
        cout<<Tl.X<<","<<Tl.Y<<","<<T1.Z<<endl;
        cout<<T2.X<<","<<T2.Y<<","<<T2.Z<<endl;
        Moveln(T2,l0);
        cout<<T2.X<<","<<T2.y<<","<<T2.Z<<endl;
}
```

e) Find the output of the following program. **2**

```
#include <iostream.h>
#include <ctype.h>
void MyCode (char Msg [], char CH)
{
        for (int (Cnt=O;Msg[Cnt]!='\0';Cnt++)
        {
        if (Msg[Cnt]>='B' && Msg[Cnt]<='G')
```

```
            Msg[Cnt]=tolower(Msg[Cnt]);
            else
                if (Msg[Cnt]=='A'|| Msg[Cnt]=='a')
                Msg[Cnt]=CH;
            else
            if (Cnt%2==0)
                Msg[Cnt]=toupper(Msg[Cnt]);
            else
                Msg[Cnt]=Msg[Cnt-l];
        }
}
void main ()
{
        char MyText [] =" ApEACeDriVE";
        MyCode(MyText,'@');
        cout<<"NEW     TEXT:"<<MyText<<endl;
}
```

f) The following code is from a game, which generates a set of 4 random numbers. Praful is playing this game, help him to identify the correct option(s) out of the four choices given below as the possible set of such numbers generated from the program code so that he wins the game. Justify your answer. **2**

```
#include <iostream.h>
#include <stdlib.h>
const int LOW=25;
void main ()
{
        randomize();
        int P01NT=5,Number;
        for (int I=1;I<=4;I++)
          {
                Number=LOW+random(POINT);
                Cout<<Number<<":";
                P0INT --;
          }
```

```
}
```

(i) 29:26:25:28:

(ii) 24:28:25:26:

(iii) 29:26:24:28:

(iv) 29:26:25:26:

2.

a) What do you understand by Data Encapsulation and Data Hiding ?' Also, give an example in C++ to illustrate both. **2**

b) Answer the questions (i) and (ii) after going through the following class. **2**

```
class Exam
{
        int Rno,MaxMarks,MinMarks,Marks;
public:
        Exam()                                          //Module 1
        {
                Rno=101;MaxMarks=l00;MinMarks=40;Marks=75;
        }
        Exam(int Prno, int Pmarks)                      //Module 2
        {
        Rno=Prno;MaxMarks=l00;MinMarks=40;Marks=Pmarks;
        }
        ~Exam()                                         //Module 3
      {
              cout<<"Exam Over"<<endl;
      }
      void Show ()                                      //Module 4
      {
              cout<<Rno<<":"<<MaxMarks<<":"<<MinMarks<<endl;
              cout<<"[Marks Got]"<<Marks<<endl;
      }
};
```

(i) As per Object Oriented Programming, which concept is illustrated by **Module 1** and **Module 2** together?

(ii) What is **Module 3** referred as ? When do you think, **Module 3** will be invoked/called?

c) Define a class STOCK in C++ with following description. **4**

Private Members

ICode of type integer (Item Code).

Item of type string (Item Name).

Price of type float (Price of each item).

Qty of type integer (Quantity in stock).

Discount of type float (Discount percentage on the item).

A member function FindDisc() to calculate discount as per the following rule:

If Qty<=50	Discount is 0
If 50<Qty<=100	Discount is 5
If Qty>100	Discount is 10

Public Members

A function Buy() to allow user to enter values for ICode, Item, Price, Qty and call function FindDisc() to calculate the Discount.

A function ShowAll( ) to allow user to view the content of all the data members.

d) Answer the questions (i) to (iv) based on the following. **4**

```
        class Director
        {
        long DID;       //Director Identification Number
        char Name[20];
 protected:
        char Description[40];
        void Allocate();
 public:
        Director();
        void Assign();
        void Show();
};
        class Ractory:public Director
}
            int FID; //Factory ID
            char Address[20];
protected:
        int NOE;        //No. of Employees
```

```
public:
        Factory();
        void Input();
        void Output();
};
class ShowRoom:private Factory
{
        int SID;                        //Showroom ID
        char City[20];
public:
        ShowRoom();
        void Enter();
        void Display();
};
```

(i) Which type of inheritance out of the following is illustrated in the above C++ code?

(a) Single Level Inheritance.

(b) Multi Level Inheritance.

(c) Multiple Inheritance.

(ii) Write the names of data members, which are accessible by objects of class type Show Room.

(iii) Write the names of all member functions which are accessible by objects of class type Show Room.

(iv) Write the names of all members, which are accessible from member functions of class Factory.

3.

a) Write a function REASSIGNO in C++, which accepts an array of integers and its size as parameters and divide all those array elements by 5 which are divisible by 5 and multiply other array elements by 2. **3**

Sample Input Data of the array.

A[0]	A[1]	A[2]	A[3]	A[4]
20	12	15	60	32

Content of the array after calling REASSIGNO function.

A[0]	A[1]	A[2]	A[3]	A[4]
4	24	3	12	64

b) An array T[90][100] is stored in the memory along the column with each of the elements occupying 4 bytes. Find out the memory location for the element T[10][40], if the Base Address of the array is 7200. **3**

c) Write a complete program in C++ to implement a dynamically allocated Queue containing names of Cities. **4**

d) Write a function `int ALTERSUM (int B[ ] [5], int N, int M` in C++ to find and return the sum of elements from all alternate elements of a two-dimensional array starting from B[0][0]. **2**

Hint:

If the following is the content of the array.

B[0][0]	B[0][1]	B[0][2]
4	5	1
B[1][0]	B[1][1]	B[1][2]
2	8	7
B[2][0]	B[2][1]	B[2][2]
9	6	3

The function should add elements B[0][0], B[0][2], B[l][l], B[2][0] and B[2][2].

e) Evaluate the following postfix notation of expression. **2**

(Show status of Stack after each operation).

True, False, NOT, OR, False, True, OR, AND.

4.

a) Observe the program segment given below carefully and fill the blanks mar-ked as Statement 1 and Statement 2 using tellg() and seekp() functions for performing the required task. **1**

```
#include <fstream.h>
class Customer
{
        long Cno;char Name[20],Mobile[12];
public:
      //Function to allow user to enter the Cno, Name, Mobile
   void Enter();
      //Function to allow user to enter (modify) mobile number
   void Modify();
      //Function to return value of Cno
```

```
        long GetCno () {return Cno;}
};
void ChangeMobile()
{
        Customer C;
        fstream F;
        F.open("CONTACT.DAT",ios::binary|ios::in|ios::out);
        long Cnoc; //Customer no.whose mobile number needs to be changed
        cin>>Cnoc;
        while (F.read((char*)& C,sizeof(C)))
        {
                if (Choc==C.GetCno())
                {
                        C.Modify ();
                                                                  //Statement 1
          int Pos=___________//To find the current position of file pointer
                                                                  //Statement 2
                ____//To move the file pointer to write the
                    //modified record back onto the file
                    //for the desired Cnoc
                F.write((char*)&C,          sizeof(C));
                }
        }
        F. close () ;
}
```

b) Write a function in C++ to count the words "to" and "the" present in a text file "POEM.TXT". **2**

[Note that the words "to" and "the" are complete words]

c) Write a function in C++ to search and display details. of all trains, whose **destination** is "Delhi" . from a binary file "TRAIN.DAT". Assuming the binary file is containing the objects of the following class. **3**

```
    class TRAIN
    {
        int Tno;                                    // Train Number
```

```
        charFrom[20];                    // Train Starting Point
        charTo [20];                          // Train Destination
    public:
        char*       GetFrom(){return From;}
        char*       GetTo(){return To;}
        void Input(){cin>>Tno;gets(From);gets(To);}
        void Show(){cout<<Tno<<":"<<From<<":"<<To<<endl;}
    };
```

5.

a) What do you understand by Primary Key? Give a suitable example of Primary Key from a table containing some meaningful data. **2**

Consider the following tables STOCK and DEALERS and answer.

(b1) and (b2) parts of this question:

Table: STOCK

ItemNo	Item	Dcode	Qty	UnitPrice	StockDate
5005	Ball Pen 0.5	102	100	16	31-Mar-10
5003	Ball Pen 0.25	102	150	20	01-Jan-10
5002	Gel Pen Premium	101	125	14	14-Feb-10
5006	Gel Pen Classic	101	200	22	01-Jan-09
5001	Eraser Small	102	210	5	19-Mar-09
5004	Eraser Big	102	60	10	12-Dec-09
5009	Sharpener Classic	103	160	8	23-Jan-09

Table: DEALERS

Dcode	Dname
101	Reliable Stationers
103	Classic Plastics
102	Clear Deals

(b1). Write SQL commands for the following statements. **4**

(i) To display details of all Items in the Stock table in ascending order of StockDate.

(ii) To display ItemNo and Item name of those items from Stock table whose UnitPrice is more than Rupees 10.

(iii) To display the details of those items whose dealer code (Dcode) is 102 or Quantity in Stock (Qty) is more than 100 from the table Stock.

(iv) To display Maximum UnitPrice of items for each dealer individually as per Dcode from the table Stock.

(b2). Give the output of the following SQL queries. **2**

(i) SELECT COUNT(DISTINCT Dcode) FROM Stock;

(ii) SELECT Qty*UnitPrice FROM Stock WHERE ItemNo=5006;

(iii) SELECT Item,Dname FROM Stock S, Dealers D WHERE S.Dcode=D.Dcode AND ItemNo=5004.

(iv) SELECT MIN(StockDate) FROM Stock.

6.

a) Verify the following algebraically. **2**

X'.Y + X.Y' = (X'+Y').(X+Y)

b) Write the equivalent Boolean Expression for the following Logic Circuit. **2**

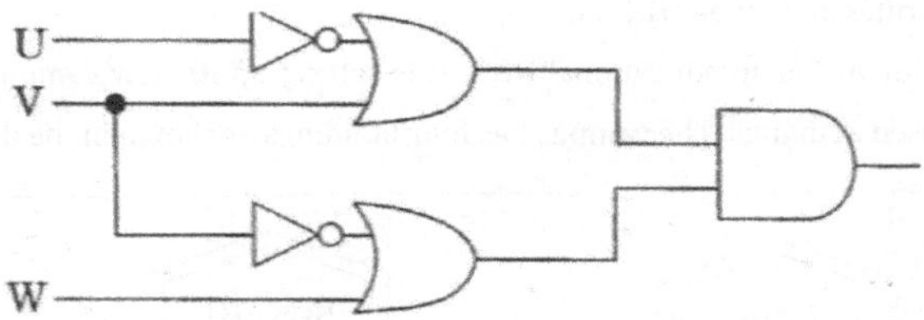

(c) Write the SOP form of a Boolean function G, which is represented in a truth table as follows. **1**

P	Q	R	G
0	0	0	0
0	0	1	0
0	1	0	1
0	1	1	1
1	0	0	1
1	0	1	0
1	1	0	1
1	1	1	1

(d) Reduce the following Boolean Expression using K-Map.

F(A,B,C,D)= Σ (3,4,5,6,7,13,15) **3**

7.

a) What was the role of ARPANET in the Computer Network?. **1**

b) Which of the following is not a unit for data transfer rate?. **1**

(i) mbps.

(ii) kbps.

(iii) sbps.

(iv) gbps.

c) What is the difference between Virus and Worms in the computers?. **1**

d) What term do we use for a software/hardware device, which is used to block unauthorized access while permitting authorized communications? This term is also used for a device or set of devices configured to permit, deny, encrypt, decrypt, or proxy all (in and out) computer traffic between different security domains based upon a set of rules and other criteria. **1**

e) "Vidya for All" is an educational NGO. It is setting up its new campus at Jaipur for its web-based activities. The campus has four buildings as shown in the diagram below. **4**

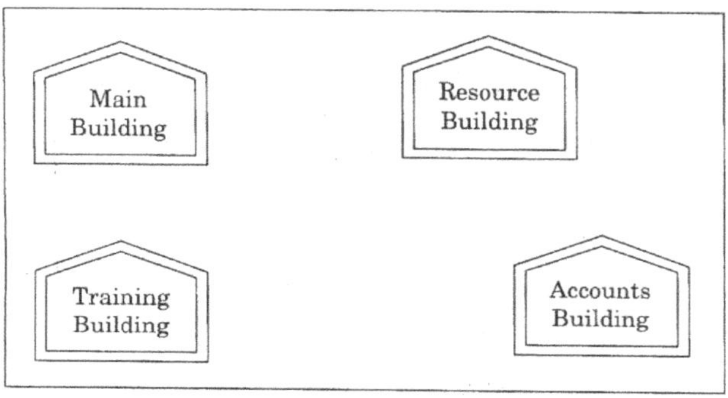

Center to center distances between various buildings as per architectural drawings (in meters) is as follows:

Main Building to Resource Building	120 m
Main Building to Training Building	40 m
Main Building to Accounts Building	135 m
Resource Building to Training Building	125 m
Resource Building to Accounts Building	45 m
Training Building to Accounts Building	110 m

Expected Number of Computers in each Building is as follows:

Main Building	15
Resource Building	25
Training Building	250
Accounts Building	10

(el). Suggest a cable layout of connections between the buildings.

(e2). Suggest the most suitable place (i.e. building) to house the server for this NGO. Also, provide a suitable reason for your suggestion.

(e3). Suggest the placement of the following devices with justification.

(i) Repeater.

(ii) Hub/Switch.

(e4). The NGO is planning to connect its International office situated in Delhi. Which out of the following wired communication links, will you suggest for a very high speed connectivity ?

(i) Telephone Analog Line.

(ii) Optical Fiber.

(iii) Ethernet Cable.

f) Write the full forms of the following. **1**

(i) FTP.

(ii) FSF.

g) Name any two common Web browsers. **1**

Question Paper Code 91/1

Expected Answers

1.

a) What is the difference between automatic type conversion and type casting?

Also, give a suitable C++ code to illustrate both. **2**

Ans. Automatic Type Conversion: it is an implicit process of conversion of a data from one type to another. For example

```
int N = 65;
char C = N; // Automatic type conversion
cout<<C;
```

<u>OUTPUT:</u>

A

Type Casting: It is an explicit process of conversion of a data from one type to another.

For example.

```
int A=1, B=2;
float C = (float)A/B; //Type Casting
cout<<C;
```

OUTPUT:

0.5

(½ Mark for each correct explanation of Automatic Type Conversion and Type Casting).

(½ Mark for each correct example of Automatic Type Conversion and Type Casting).

OR

(Full 2 Marks for correct example(s) demonstrating the meaning of / difference between Automatic Type Conversion and Type Casting).

OR

(Only 1 Mack to be awarded if Explanation without supporting examples).

Note: Output is optional.

b) Which C++ header file(s) will be essentially required to be included to run/ execute the following C++ code?. **1**

```
void main( )
{
    int  Eno=123,  char  Ename[  ]="Rehan  Swamp";
    cout<<setw(5)<<Eno<<setw(25)<<EName<<endl;
```

```
}
```

Ans.

(i) iostream.h

(ii) iomanip.h

OR

iomanip.h - (As iostream.h is included in iomanip.h)

(½ Mark for writing each correct header file)

OR

(Full 1 Mark for mentioning only iomanip.h)

Note: Ignore any other header files, if mentioned.

c) Rewrite the following c++ program code after removing the syntax error(s) (if any). Underline each correction. **2**

```
include <iostream.h>
class TRAIN
{
        long TrainNo;
        char Description[25];
public
        void Entry ( )
        {
                cin >>TrainNo; gets(Description);
        }
        Void Display ( )
        {
                cout<<TrainNo<<":"<<Description<<endl;
        }
};
void main( )
{
        TRAIN T;
        Entry. T( ); Display. T( );
}
```

Ans. #include<iostream.h>

<u>#include<stdio.h></u>

```
class TRAIN
{
        long TrainNo;
        char Description [25];
public:
        void Entry          ()
        {
                cin>>TrainNo; gets (Description);
        }
        void Display ()
        {
                cout<<TrainNo<<":"<<Description<<end1;
        }
};
void main ()
{
        TRAIN T;
        T.Entry();          T.Display();
}
```

(½ Mark for writing # before include<iostream.h>

(½ Mark for writing # include <stdio.h>

(½ Mark for writing: after public)

(½ Mark for writing T.Entry(); and T.Display(); correctly)

d) Find the output of the following program. **3**

```
#inc1ude      <iostream.h>
struct POINT
{int  X,Y, Z;};
void StepIn(POINT & P, int Step=1)
{
        P.X+=Step;
        P.Y-=Step;
        P.Z+=Step;
}
void StepOut(POINT & P, int Step=1)
```

```
{
        P.X-=Step;
        P.Y+=Step;
        P.Z-=Step;
}
void main ( )
{
        POINT P1={15, 25, 5}, P2={10, 30, 20};
        StepIn(P1);
        StepOut(P2,4);
        cout<<P1.X<<","<<P1.Y<<","<<P1.Z<<endl;
        cout<<P2.X<<","<<P2.Y<<","<<P2.Z<<endl;
        StepIn(P2,12);
        cout<<P2.X<<","<<P2.Y<<","<<P2.Z<<endl;
}
```

Ans. 16, 24, 6

6, 34, 16

18, 22, 28

(1 Mark for each line with -correct values)

OR

(½ Mark for any two correct values in each line)

Note:

Deduct (½ Mark if any/all ',' missing

Deduct (½ Mark if endl is not considered at the right positions

e) Find the output of the following program. **2**

```
#include <iostream.h>
#include <ctype.h>
void ChangeIt(char Text[ ], char C)
{
        for (int K=0;Text[K]!='\0';K++)
        {
                if (Text[K]>='F' && Text[K]<='L')
                        Text[K]=tolower (Text[K]);
                else
```

```
            if (Text[K]='E' || Text[K]=='e')
                Text[K]==C;
            else
            if (K%2==O)
                Text[K]=toupper(Text[K]);
            else
                Text[K]=Text[K-l];
        }
}
void main ( )
{
        char OldText[ ]="pOwERALone";
        ChangeIt(OldText,'%');
        cout<<"New      TEXT:"<<OldText<<endl;
}
```

Ans. New TEXT : PPW % RR11N%

(½ Mark for writing PPW as the first three characters)

(½ Mark for writing %RR as the next three characters)

(½ Mark for writing 11 as the next two characters)

(½ Mark for writing N% as the next two characters)

Note: Deduct X Mark for not mentioning New TEXT.

f) The following code is from a game, which generates a set of 4 random numbers. Yallav is playing this game, help him to identify the correct option(s) out of the four choices given below as the possible set of such numbers generated from the program code so that he wins the game. Justify your answer. **2**

```
#include <iostream.h>
#include <stdlib.h>
const int LOW=15;
void main ( )
{
        randomize( ) ;
        int POINT=5, Number;
        for (int 1=1;I<=4;I++)
        {
```

```
            Number=LOW+random(POINT) ;
            cout<<Number<<":" ;
            POINT--;
        }
    }
```

(i) 19:16:15:18:

(ii) 14:18:15:16:

(iii) 19:16:14:18:

(iv) 19:16:15:16:

Ans. (iv) 19:16:15:16:

Justification is as follows:

I	POINT	Number	
		Minimum	Maximum
1	5	15	19
2	4	15	18
3	3	15	17
4	2	15	16

The only option that satisfies these values is option (iv).

(1 Mark for mentioning correct option)

(1 Mark for any valid justification)

Note: Only ½ Mark to be given if only options (i) & (iv) are mentioned as correct options; no other combination of options is acceptable.

2.

a) What do you understand by Polymorphism? Also, give an example in C++ to illustrate the same. **2**

Ans. The process of using an -operator or a function in different ways for different set of inputs given is known- as polymorphism. Function overloading is- an example of polymorphism, where the functions having same name with different set of parameters perform different operations.

Example:

```
void Disp ( )                         //Function 1
{
        cout<<"Hello"<<endl;
}
```

```
void Disp(int N)                    //Function 2
{
    for(int I=1;I<=N;I++)
        cout<<I<<endl;
}
void Disp (int N,int M)             //Function 3
{
    for(int I=N;I<=M; I++)
    cout<<N<<"x"<<I<<"="<<N*I<<endl;
}
void main ( )
{
    int x=5, y=10;
    Disp(x);       //Function 2 called-Prints numbers from 1 to 5
    Disp(x,y) ;    //Function 3 called- Prints from multiples of 5
                   //ranging from 5 to 10
    Disp () ;      //Function 1 called- Prints Hello
    }
```

(1 Mark for correct explanation of Polymorphism)

(1 Mark for a valid example of Polymorphism)

b) Answer the questions (i) and (ii) after going through the following class. **2**

```
    class TEST
    {
    int Regno, Max, Min, Score;
public:
    TEST()                                          //Function 1
    {
        Regno=    101;Max=100;Min=40;Score=75;
    }
    TEST(int Pregno,int Pscore)                     //Function 2
    {
        Regno=Pregno;Max=100;Min=40;Score=Pscore;
    }
   ~TEST()                                          //Function 3
```

```
{
        cout<<"TEST    Over"<<endl;
}
void Display()                          //Function 4
{
  cout<<Regno<<":"<<Max<<":"<<Min<<endl;
  cout<<"[Score]"<<Score<<endl;
  }
};
```

(i) As per Object Oriented Programming, which. concept is illustrated by **Function 1 and Function 2** together?

Ans. Polymorphism

OR

Function Overloading

OR

Constructor Overloading

(1 Mark for naming the concept correctly)

(ii) What is **Function 3** specifically referred as ? When do you think, **Function 3** will be invoked/called?

Ans. Destructor, invoked or called when scope of an Object gets over.

(½ Mark for naming Destructor correctly).

(½ Mark for mentioning correctly when it is invoked).

c) Define a class ITEM in C++ with following description. **4**

Private Members

Code of type integer (Item Code) Iname of type string (Item Name).

Price of type float (Price of each item).

Qty of type integer (Quantity of item in stock).

Offer of type float (Offer percentage on the item).

A member function GetOffer() to calculate Offer percentage as per the following rule:

If Qty<=50	Offer is 0
If 50<Qty<=100	Offer is 5
If Qty>100	Offer is 10

Public Members

A function GetStock() to allow user to enter values for Code, Iname, Price, Qty and call function GetOffer() to calculate the offer

A function ShowItem() to allow user to view the content of all the data members

Ans. class ITEM

```
{
        int Code;
        char Iname [20] ;
        float Price;
        int Qty;
        float Offer;
        void GetOffer() ;
public:
        void GetStock ()
        {
                cin>>Code;
                gets (Iname) ; // OR cin.getline (Iname, 80); OR cin>>Iname;
                cin>>Price>>Qty;
                GetOffer() ;
}
void ShowItern ( )
{
        cout<<Code<<Iname<<Price<<Qty<<Offer;
};
void ITEM: : GetOffer ()
{
        if (Qty<=50)
                Offer = 0;
        else if (Qty <=100)
                Offer = 5;      / /OR Offer = 0.05;
        else
                Offer = 10;     / /OR Offer = 0.1;
}
```

(½ Mark for correct syntax for class header)

(½ Mark for correct declaration of data members)

(1 Mark for correct definition of GetOffer())

(1 Mark for correct definition of GetStock () with proper invocation of GetOffer() function)

(1 Mark for correct definition of ShowItem())

NOTE:

Deduct ½ Mark if GetOffer() is not invoked properly inside GetStock()function

d) Answer the questions (i) to (iv) based on the following. **4**

```
class Chairperson
{
        long CID;                       //Chairperson Identification Number
        char CName[20];
protected:
        char Description [40];
        void Allocate();
public:
        Chairperson();
        void Assign();
        void Show();
};
class Director
{
        int DID;                                //Director ID
        char Dname[20];
protected:
        char Profile[30];
public:
        Director();
        void Input();
        void output();
};
class Company: private Chairperson, public Director
{
        int CID;                                //Company ID
        char City[20], Country[20];
public:
        Company();
        void Enter();
```

```
        void Display();
    };
```

i. Which type of inheritance out of the following is specifically is illustrated in the above C++ code?

(a) Single Level Inheritance.

(b) Multi Level Inheritance.

(c) Multiple Inheritance.

Ans. (c) Multiple Inheritance.

(1 Mark for writing correct inheritance type).

ii. Write the names of data members, which are accessible by objects of class type Company.

Ans. None

(1 Mark for writing None or No data members)

iii. Write the names of all member functions, which are accessible by objects of class type Company.

Ans. Enter(), Display(), Input(), output()

(1 Mark for writing correct member functions)

Note:

Both output() or Output() are acceptable as correct answer since differentiation between small and capital O is very difficult.

No marks to be awarded for any other *alternative answer Ignore mention of Constructor(s)*

(iv) Write the names of all members, which are accessible from member functions of class Director.

Ans. Enter(), Display(), Input(), output()

(1 Mark for writing correct members)

Note:

Both output() or Output() are acceptable as correct answer since differentiation between small and capital O is very difficult.

No marks to be awarded for any other alternative answer Ignore mention of Constructor(s)

3.

a) Write a function CHANGEO in C++, which accepts an array of integer and its size as parameters and divide all those array elements by 7 which are divisible by 7 and multiply other-array elements by 3. **3**

Sample Input Data of the array.

A[0]	A[1]	A[2]	A[3]	A[4]
21	12	35	42	18

Content of the array after Calling CHANGE() function

A[0]	A[1]	A[2]	A[3]	A[4]
3	36	5	6	54

Ans.
```
void CHANGE (int A[ ], int N)
    {
        for(int I = 0; I<N; I++)
        {
            if (A[I]%7 = = 0)
                A [I] = A [I] /7;
            else
                A[I] = A[I] * 3;
        }
    }
```

OR

Any other correct equivalent function definition

(½ Mark for correct Function Header)

(½ Mark for correct loop)

(½ Mark for correct checking of divisibility of array elements by 7)

(½ Mark for correct else OR correct checking of non divisibility of array elements by 7)

(½ Mark for each correct assignment)

b) **An array P[50] [60] is stored in the memory along the column with each of the element occupying 2 bytes, find out the memory location for the element P[10] [20], if the Base Address of the array is 6800.** **3**

Ans. Loc(P[I] [J]) = Base(P)+W(I+J*M)

i Loc(P[10][20]) = Base(P)+ 2(10+20*50)

Loc(P[10] [20]) = 6800 + 2(10+20*50)

= 6800 + 2 (10+1000)

= 6800 + 2*1010

= 6800 + 2020

= 8820

OR

Address of P[i] [j] = BaseAddress + W((i–L1)+(j–L2)*M)

Address of P[10] [20]= 6800 + 2((10-0)+(20-0)x50)

= 6800 + 2 x 1010

= 6800 + 2020

= 8820

OR

Address of P[I] [J] along the column

= BaseAddress + W((I–LBR)+(J–LBC)*M)

(where N is the number of rows, LBR = LBC = 1)

Address of P[10][20]=6800+2((10-1)+(20-l)x50)

= 6800 + 2 (9 + 19 x 50)

= 6800 + 2 x 959

= 6800 + 1918

= 8718

(1 Mark for writing correct formula (for column major) OR substituting formula with correct values for calculating Address)

(2 marks for calculating correct address)

c) Write a complete program in c++ to implement a dynamically allocated Stack containing names of Countries. **4**

Ans.
```
#include<iostream.h>
#include<stdio.h>
struct Node
{
        char Country [20] ;
        Node *Link;
};
class Stack
{
        Node *Top;
public:
        Stack(){ Top = NULL; }
        void Push() ;
        void Pop() ;
```

```
		void Display() ;
		~Stack ();
	};
	void Stack::Push()
	{
		Node *Temp = new Node;
		gets(Temp  ->  Country);
		Temp -> Link = Top;
		Top = Temp;
	}
	void Stack::Pop()
	{
		if (Top  !=NULL)
		{
			Node *Temp = Top;
			Top = Top -> Link;
			delete Temp;
		}
		else
			cout<<"stack  Empty";
	}
	void Stack::Display()
	{
		Node *Temp = Top;
		while (Temp! = NULL)
		{
			cout<<Temp  ->  Country <<endl;
			Temp = Temp -> Link;
		}
	}
	Stack::~Stack  ()
	{
		while (Top!=NULL)
		{
```

```
                NODE *Temp=Top;
                Top=Top->Link;
                delete Temp;
            }
}
    void main ( )
    {
        Stack ST; char Ch;
        do
        {
            cout<<"p/O/D/Q" ;
            cin>>Ch;
            switch (Ch)
            {
                case 'P' : ST.Push(); break;
                case 'O' :ST.Pop();  break;
                case 'D' :ST.Disp();
            }
        } while (Ch!='Q');
    }
```

d) Write a function int SKIPSUM (int A[ ] [3], int N,int M) in C++ to find and return the sum of elements from all alternate elements of a two-dimensional array starting from A[0][0]. **2**

Hint:

If the following is the content of the array

A[0][0]	A[0][1]	A[0][2]
4	5	1
A[1][0]	A[1][1]	A[1][2]
2	8	7
A[2][0]	A[2][1]	A[2][2]
9	6	3

The function SKIPSUM() should add elements A[0][0], A[0][2], A[1][l], A[2][0] and A[2][2].

Ans.

```
int SKIPSUM(int A[ ][ 3 ], int N, int M)
    {
        int S=0:
        for(int I = 0; 1< N; 1++)
            for (int J = (I%2)?1:0; J<M; J = J+2)
                S = S + A [I][J];
        return S;
    }
```

OR

```
int SKIPSlJM(int A[ ][3], int N, int M)
{
    int S=0;
    for (int I = 0; 1< N; I++)
        for (int J = (I%2==0)? 0:1 ; J<M; J = J+2)
            S = S + A [I][J];
    return S;
}
```

OR

```
int SKIPSUM(int A[][3], int N, int M)
{
    int I,J, S=O;
    for (I = 0; 1 < N; 1++)
    {
  if (I%2) //OR (1%2 !=0 ) OR (I%2 == 1)
            J = l;
  else
            J = 0;
 for ( ; J<M; J = J+2)
            S = S + A[I][J];
    }
    return S;
}
```

OR

```
int SKIPSUM(int A[][3], int N, int M)
{
        int S=0, C=0;
        for(int I = 0; 1< N; 1++)
                for (int J = 0; J<M; J++ )
                {
                        if (C%2 == 0)
                                S = S + A[I][J];
                        C++;
                }
        return S;
}
```

OR

```
int SKIPSUM(int A[][3], int N, int M)
{
        int S=0, C=l;
        for(int I = 0; I<N; I++)
                for (int J = 0; J<M; J++)
                {
                        if (C%2 != 0)
                                S = S + A[I][J];
                        C++;
                }
        return S;
}
```

OR

```
int SKIPSUM (int A[][3], int N, int M)
{
        int S=0;
        for(int I = 0; l< N; l++)
                for (int J = 0; J<M; J++ )
                {
                        if ((I+J)%2 == 0)
```

```
                    S = S + A[I][J];
            }
        return S;
    }
```

OR

Any other correct equivalent function definition

(½ Mark for correct function header)

(½ Mark for each correct loop)

(½ Mark for checking alternate cells)

(½ Mark for finding Sum of elements)

(½ Mark for returning

e) Evaluate the following postfix notation of expression: *the Sum)* **2**

(Show status of Stack after each operation)

False, True, NOT, OR, True, False, AND, OR

Ans.

Element Scanned	Stack
False	False
True	False, True
NOT	False, False
OR	False
True	False, True
False	False, True, False
and	False, False
OR	False

RESULT = False

OR

Step 1: Push

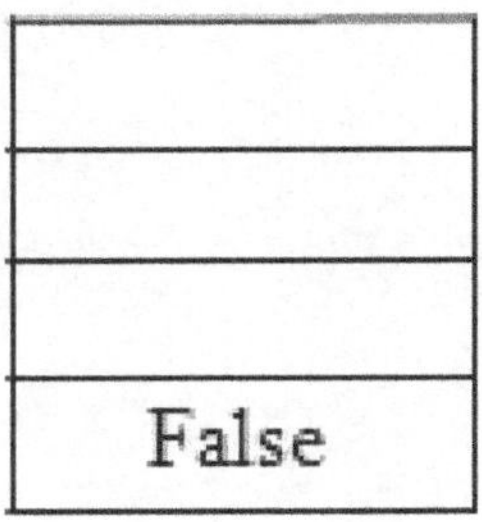

Step 2: Push

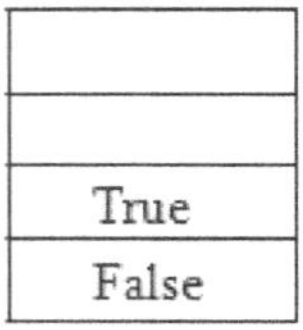

Step 3: NOT

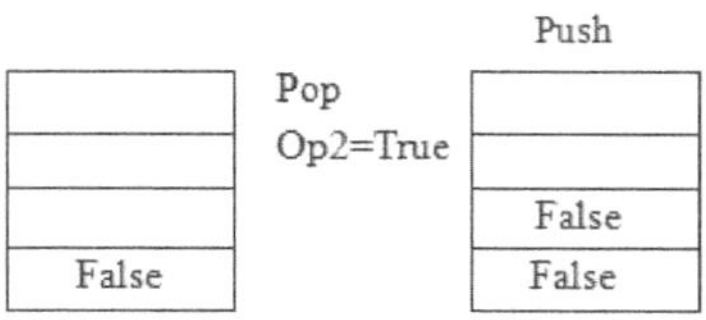

Step 4 OR

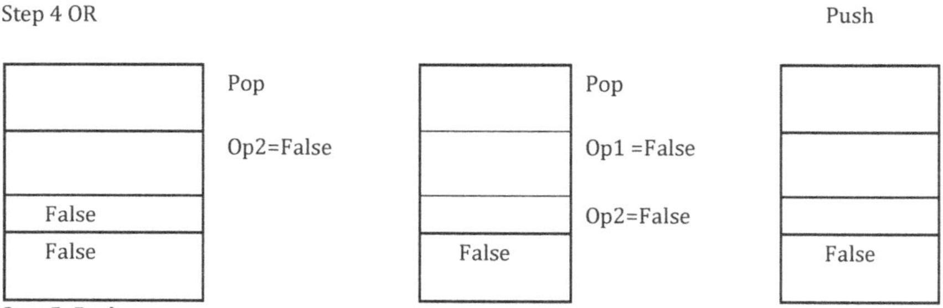

Step 5: Push

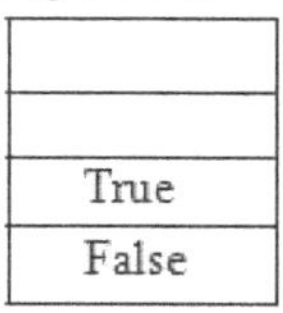

Step 6: Push

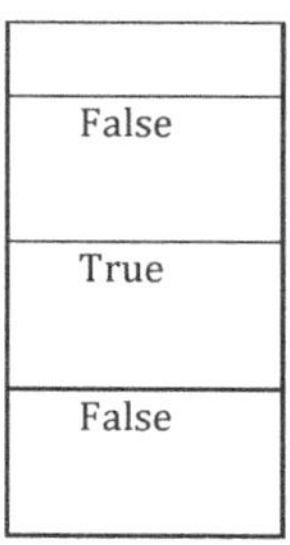

Step 7: AND

Push

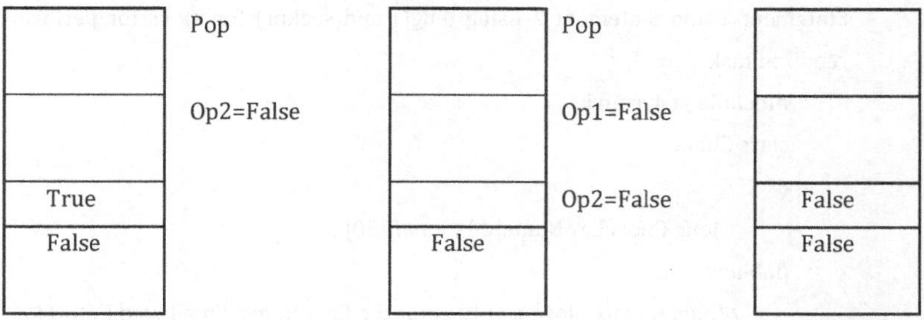

Step 8: OR

Push

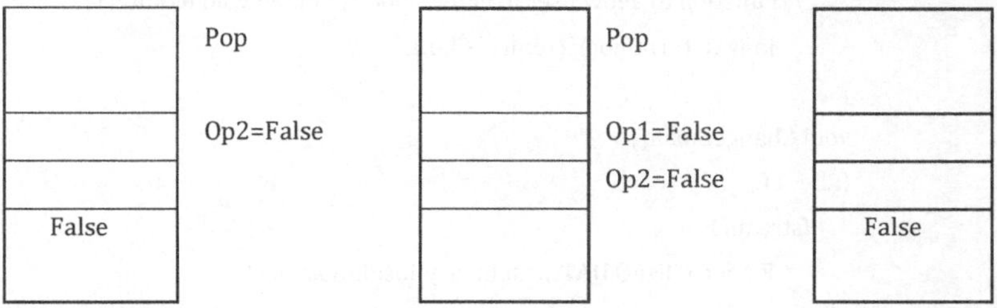

Step 9: Pop

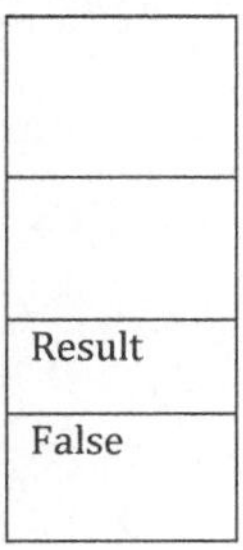

OR

Any other method for evaluating the given postfix expression showing the Stack Status.

(½ Mark for correctly evaluating expression up to each operator

(1 Mark only to be given for writing correct answer without showing the Stack Status)

4.

a) Observe the program segment given below carefully and fill the blanks mar-ked as Statement 1 and Statement 2 using tellg() and seekp() functions for performing the required task. **1**

```
#include <fstream.h>
class Client
{
        long Cno; char Name[20], Email[30] ;
public:
     //Function to allow user to enter the Cno, Name, Email void Enter() ;
     //Function to allow user to enter (modify) Email void Modify() ;
        long ReturnCno() {return  Cno;}
};
void ChangeEmail()
{Client C;
    fstream F;
        F.open ("INFO.DAT",ios::binary|ios::in|ios::out);
        long Cnoc;//Client's no. whose Email needs to be changed
        cin>>Cnoc;
        while (F.read((char*)&C, sizeof(C)))
        {
               if (Cnoc==C.ReturnCno())
               {
                       C.Modify();
                                                     //Statement 1
                       int Pos =        ________//To find the current
                                          position of file pointer
                                                     // Statement 2
                       ______________//To move the file
                                          pointer to write the
                                               //modified record
                                               back onto the file
                                               //for the desired Cnoc
                       F.write((char*)&C,        sizeof(C));
```

```
            }
        }
        F.close();
    }
```

Ans. Statement 1:

F. tellg ();

Statement 2:

F. seekp(Pos-sizeof(C)) ;

OR

F.seekp(-sizeof(C), ios::cur);

OR

Any equivalent correct method

(½ Mark for each correct statement)

b) Write a function in C++ to count the words "this" and "these" present in a text file "ARTICLE.TXT". **2**

[Note that the words "this" and "these" are complete words]

Ans.

```
void COUNT ( )
{
ifstreamFil;                          OR ifstream Fil("ARTICLE.TXT");

Fil.open("ARTICLE.TXT");
char Word [80]
        int C1 = 0, C2 = 0
        while (!Fil.eop())
        {
            Fil>>Word;
            if (strcmp(Word,"this") ==0)
                Cl++;
            else if (strcmp(Word,"these") ==0)
                C2++;
        }
        cout<<"Count of -this- in file:"<<Cl;
```

```
cout<<"Count of -these- in file:"<<C2;

OR cout<<"Count of -this- and -these- -in file:"<<C1+C2;

Fil.close(); //gnore
}
OR
void COUNT( )
{                                               OR
if stream Fil("ARTICLE.TXT");                   ifstream Fil;
char Word[80] ;                                 Fil.open("ARTICLE. TXT");
    int C = 0;
    while(!Fil.eof())
        { Fil>>Word;
        if (strcmp(Word,"this")==0||strcmp(Word,"these") ==0) C++;
    }
    cout<<"Count of -this- and -these- in file:"<<C;
    Fil.close(); //Ignore
    }
    OR
    void COUNT( )
    {
        Ifstream Fil("ARTICLE.TXT");
        //OR fstream Fil;
        //   Fil. open("ARTICLE. TXT", ios: : in);
        char STR[l0];
        int Cl=0, C2=0;
        while (Fil.getline (STR,l0, ''))
        {
            if    (strcmp(STR,"this")==0)
                Cl++;
            else if (strcmp(STR,"these")==0) C2++;
```

```
        }
    }
    cout<<"Count    of    -this-    in    file:"<<Cl;
    cout<<"Count of -these- in file:"<<C2; Fil.close()
    ;//Ignore
      OR cout<<"Count of -this- and -these- in file:"<<Cl+C2;
    }
    OR
    void COUNT ( )
    {
        ifstream Fil;
                                          OR
        ifstreamFil("ARTICLE.TXT");   Fil. open("ARTICLE.TXT");
        char Word[80],Ch;
        int Cl =0, C2 = 0, I=O;
        while(Fil.get(Ch))
        {
            if (Ch! = ' ')
                Word[I++]  =  Ch;
            else
            {
                Word[I]  =  '\0';
                if (strcmp  (Word,"this")==0)
                    Cl++;
                else if  (strcmp(Word,"these")==0)
                    C2++;
                I=0,
            }
        }
        cout<<"Count  of  -this-  in  file:" <<Cl;
        cout<<"Count  of  -these-  in  file:" <<C2;
        OR
        cout<<"Count  of  -this-  and  -these-  in  file:  "<<Cl+C2;
```

```
        cout<<"Count of -this- and -these- in file: "<<Cl+C2;
        Fil.close(); //Ignore
    }
```

OR

Any other correct function definition

(½ Mark for opening ARTICLE. TXT correctly)

(½ Mark for reading each word (Whichever method adopted) from the file)

(½ Mark for comparing the word with 'this' and 'these' and incrementing counter(s)

(½ Mark for displaying the individual count of 'this' and 'these' or the total count of 'this' and 'these' with/without the Text Message)

c) Write a function in C++ to search and display details of all flights, whose destination is "Mumbai" from a binary file "FLIGHT.DAT". Assuming the binary file is containing the objects of the following class.

```
class FLIGHT
{
int Fno;                          //Flight    Number
char       From[20];              //Flight    Starting    Point
char       To[20];                //Flight    Destination
public:
char*      GetFrom() {return From;}
char*      GetTo()      {return      To;}
void       Enter()      {cin>>Fno;gets(From);gets(To);}
void       Display(){cout<<Fno<<":"<<From<<":"<<To<<endl;}
};
```

Ans.
```
void Read     ()
{
FLIGHT F;
ifstream fin;

fin.open("FLIGHT.DAT",                ios::binary) ;
    OR ifstream fin ("FLIGHT. DAT", iC;s: :binary) ;

while(fin.read((char*)&F, sizeof(F))) {
if (strcmp(F. GetTo(),"Mumbai"))
F.Display() ;
        }
        fin.close(); //Ignore
    }
```

OR

```
void Read ()
{
        FLIGHT F;
        ifstream fin;
        fin" open ("FLIGHT. DAT", ios:: binary) ;
        OR ifstream fin ("FLIGHT. DAT" , ios:: binary;

        if (fin)
        {
        fin.read((char*)&F, sizeof (F));
        while(!fin.eof())
        {
                if (strcmp(F. GetTo(),"Mumbai"))
                                F.Display();
                fin.read((char*)&F,sizeof(F))
        }
        fin.close(); //Ignore
}
```

OR

Any other correct function definition

(½ Mark for opening FLIGHT DAT correctly)

(½ Mark for reading each record from FLIGHT.DAT)

(½ Mark for correct loop / checking end of file)

(1 Mark for comparing value returned by GetTo() with "Mumbai"} (½ Mark for displaying the matching record)

5.

a) What do you understand by Candidate Keys in a table? Give a suitable example of Candidate Keys from a table containing some meaningful data. **2**

Ans. A table may have more than one such attribute/group of attribute that identi-fies a tuple uniquely, all such attribute(s) are known as Candidate Keys.

Table: Item

Ino	Item	Qty
I01	Pen	560
I02	Pencil	780
I04	CD	450
I09	Floppy	700
I05	Eraser	300
I03	Duster	200

(1 Mark for writing correct definition of Candidate Key)

(1 Mark for giving suitable example)

(b) Consider the following tables STORE and SUPPLIERS and answer (bl) and (b2) parts of this question:

Table: STORE

ItemNo	Item	Scode	Qty	Rate	LastBuy
2005	Sharpener Classic	23	60	8	31-Jun-09
2003	Ball Pen 0.25	22	50	25	01-Feb-10
2002	Gel Pen Premium	21	150	12	24-Feb-10
2006	Gel Pen Classic	21	250	20	11-Mar-09
2001	Eraser Small	22	220	6	19-Jan-09
2004	Eraser Big	22	110	8	02-Dec-09
2009	Ball Pen 0.5	21	180	18	03-Nov-09

Table: SUPPLIERS

Scode	Sname
21	Premium Stationers
23	Soft Plastics
22	Tetra Supply

(b1). Write SQL commands for the following statements. **4**

(i) To display details of all the items in the Store table in ascending order of LastBuy.

Ans. SELECT * FROM STORE ORDER BY LastBuy;

(1 Mark for correct query).

(½ Mark for partially correct answer).

(ii) To display ItemNo and Item name of those items from Store table whose Rate is more than 15 Rupees.

Ans. SELECT ItemNo, Item..In FROM STORE WHERE Rate >15;

(1 Mark for correct query)

(½ Mark for partially correct answer).

(iii) To display the details of those items whose Supplier code (Scode) is 22 or Quantity in Store (Qty) is more than 110 from the table Store.

Ans. SELECT * FROM STORE WHERE Scode = 22 OR Qty >110;

(1 Mark for correct query).

(½ Mark for partially correct answer).

(iv) To display Minimum Rate of items for each Supplier individually as per Scode from the table Store.

Ans. SELECT Scode, MIN (Rate) FROM STORE GROUP BY Scode;

(1 Mark for correct query).

(½ Mark for partially correct answer).

(b2). Give the output of the following SQL queries. **2**

Note: In all output Questions ignore Column Headings

(i) SELECT COUNT(DISTINCT Scode) FROM Store.

Ans. <u>COUNT(DISTINCT Scode)</u>

(½ Mark for correct Output)

(ii) SELECT Rate*Qty FROM Store WHERE ItemNo=2004;

Ans. <u>RATE*QTY</u>

880

(½ Mark for correct Output)

(iii) SELECT Item,Sname FROM Store S, Suppliers P WHERE S.Scode=P.Scode AND ItemNo=2006;

Ans. ITEM	SNAME
Gel Pen Classic	Premium Stationers

(½ Mark for correct Output)

(iv) SELECT MAX(LastBuy) FROM Store;

Ans. MAX (LASTBUY)

24-Feb-10

(½ Mark for correct Output)

6.

a) Verify the following algebraically. **2**

(A'+B').(A +B)=A'.B+A.B'

Ans. LHS

(A' +B').(A+B)

= A'.A + A'.B + A.B' + B'.B

= 0 + A'.B + A.B'+ 0

= A'.B + A.B'

= RHS (Verified)

OR

Any other valid algebraic verification

(2 Marks for verifying LHS = RHS OR RHS = LHS)

b) Write the equivalent Boolean Expression for the following Logic circuit. **2**

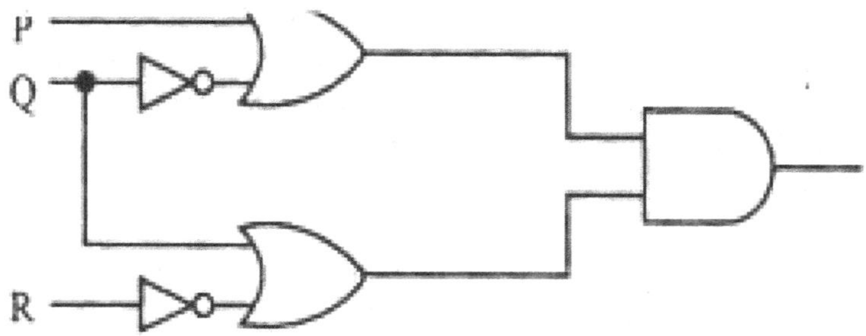

Ans. (P + Q').(Q + R')

(2 Marks for the final expression (P + Q').(Q + R'))

OR

(1 Mark for any of the correct terms out of (P + Q') or (Q + R'))

c) Write the POS form of a Boolean function H, which is represented in a truth table as follows: **1**

X	Y	Z	H
0	0	0	1
0	0	1	0
0	1	0	1
0	1	1	1
1	0	0	1
1	0	1	0
1	1	0	0
1	1	1	1

Ans. (X + Y + Z').(X'+ Y + Z') . (X'+ Y'+ Z)

OR

H(X,Y,Z) = Π (1, 5, 6)

(1 Mark for the correct POS form)

Note:

Deduct % mark if wrong variable names are used

(d) Reduce the following Boolean Expression using K-Map :

Ans. F(U, V, W, Z) = Σ (3, 5, 7, 10, 11, 13, 15)

	U' V'	U' V	UV	UV'
W' Z'	0	4	12	8
W' Z	1	1 5	1 13	9
W' Z	1 3	1 7	1 15	1 11
W Z'	2	6	14	1 10

OR

	W' Z'	W' Z	WZ	WZ'
U' V'	0	1	1 3	2
U' V	4	1 5	1 7	6
U V	12	1 13	1 15	14
U V'	8	9	1 11	1 10

F(U,V,W,Z) = WZ + VZ + UV'W

(½ Mark for drawing K-Map with correct variable names)

(½ Mark for placing all 1s at correct positions in K-Map)

(½ Mark for each grouping)

(½ Mark for writing final expression in reduced/minimal form)

7.

a) What was the role of ARPANET in the Computer Network? **1**

Ans. The first computer network was jointly designed by The Advanced-Research Projects Agency (ARPA) and Department of Defence (DoD) of United States in 1969 and was called ARPANET. It was an experimental project, which connected a few computers from some of the reputed universities of USA and DoD. ARPANET allowed access to computer resource sharing projects. This ARPANET was handed over to Defence Communication Agency (DCA) for further development.

(1 Mark for mentioning that ARPANET was the first computer network)

OR

(½ Mark if only the expansion of ARPANET is mentioned)

b) Which of the following is not an unit for data transfer rate? **1**

(i) bps.

(ii) abps.

(iii) gbps.

(iv) kbps.

Ans.(ii) abps

(1 Mark for writing correct option)

c) What is the difference between Trojan Horse and Virus in terms of computers? **1**

Ans. TROJAN HORSE: "Malware" computer programs presented as useful or harmless in order to induce the user to install and run them.

VIRUS: Virus is a malicious program that damages data and files and causes harm to computer system.

(1 Mark for mentioning anyone valid difference)

OR

(½ Mark for correct definition of each term)

d) What term we use for a software/hardware device, which is used to block, Unauthorized access while permitting authorized communications. This term is also used for a device or set of devices configured to permit, deny, encrypt, decrypt, or proxy all (in and out) computer traffic between different security domains based upon a set of rules and other criteria. **1**

Ans. Firewall

(1 Mark for writing £orrect term)

e) "Learn Together" is an educational NGO. It is setting up its new campus at Jabalpur for its web based activities. The campus has 4 compounds as shown in the diagram below. **4**

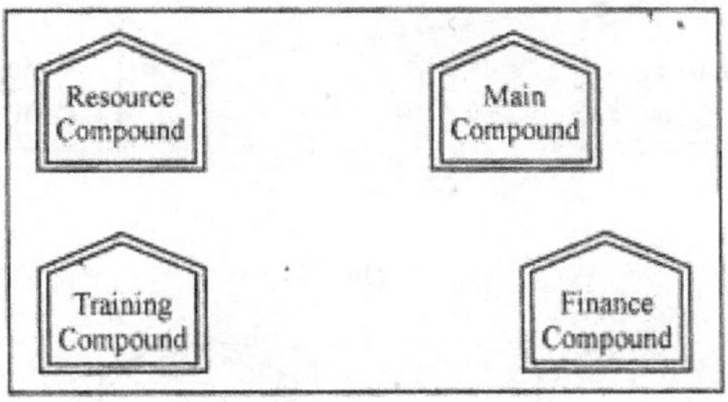

Center to center distances between various Compounds as per architectural drawings (in Metre) is as follows:

Main Compound to Resource Compound	110 m
Main Compound to Training Compound	115 m
Main Compound to Finance Compound	35 m
Resource Compound to Training Compound	25 m
Resource Compound to Finance Compound	135 m
Training Compound to Finance Compound	100 m

Expected Number of Computers in each Compound is as follows:

Main Compound	5
Resource Compound	15
Training Compound	150
Accounts Compound	20

(e1). Suggest a cable layout of connections between the compounds. **1**

Ans.

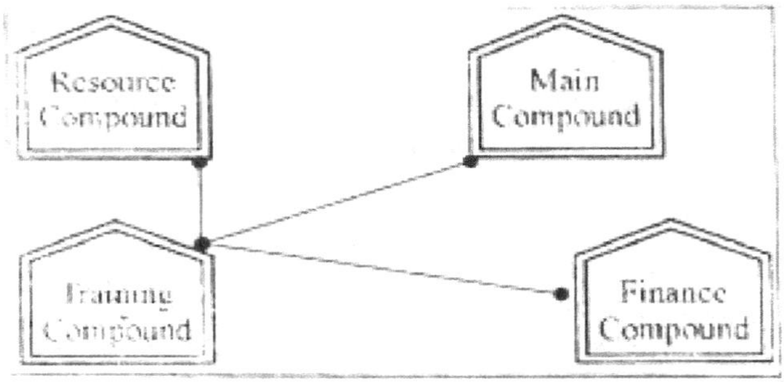

OR

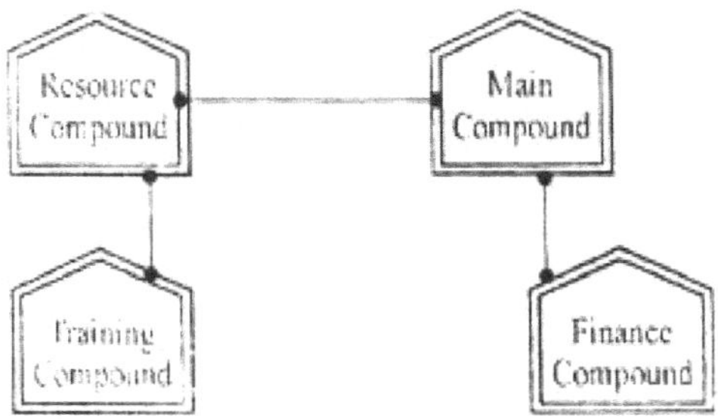

(1 Mark for mentioning any valid connectivity or topology or diagram connecting various compounds inside the campus)

(e2). Suggest the most suitable place (i.e. compound) to house the server for this NGO. Also, provide a suitable reason for your suggestion. **1**

Ans. Training Compound as it contains maximum number of computers.

(½ Mark for mentioning the correct compound)

(½ Mark for correct justification)

OR

(1 Mark for any other location with a valid justification)

(e3). Suggest the placement of the following devices with justification. **1**

i. Repeater.

ii. Hub/Switch.

Ans.

(i) A Repeater should be placed when the distance between any two connecting compounds exceeds 70 m. Every compound will need one Hub I Switch, to send signals to all of the workstations connected to it.

OR

Any diagrammatic representation with valid justification

(½ Mark for each correct placement of Devices with valid justifications)

(e4). The NGO is planning to connect its International office situated in Mumbai, which out of the following wired communication link, you will suggest for a very high speed connectivity? **1**

(i) Telephone Analog Line.

(ii) Optical Fiber.

(iii) Ethernet Cable.

Ans. (ii). Optical Fiber

(1 Mark for correct option /answer)

f) Write the full forms of the following **1**

(i) (f1) GNU

(ii) (f2) XML

Ans

(f1) GNU's not Unix

(f2) eXtensible Markup Language

(½ Mark for each full form)

g) Write one advantage of each for Open Source Software and Proprietary Software. **1**

Ans. An Open Source Software is freely and liberally licensed because of which users have right to study, change and improve its design and source code.

A Proprietary Software has a copyright owner, who can restrict the user's control over the software, its modification, or restrictions in publishing of modified or unmodified versions.

(½ Mark for writing correct advantage / definition for Open Source Software).

(½ Mark for writing correct advantage / definition for Proprietary Software).

Question Paper Code 91

Expected Answers

1.

a) What is the difference between call by value and call by reference? Also, give a suitable C++ code to illustrate both. **2**

Ans. Call by value: The formal parameter makes a copy of actual parameter. It does not make the changes In actual parameter If the changes are done In formal parameters.

Call by reference: The formal parameter Is an alias of actual parameter. The changes made In the formal parameter are reflected In actual parameter. It is preceded by &.

```
vcid Caloulato(int A,int & B )          // A is call by value
{                                        // B is call by reference
        A++;
        a+=A;
}
```

(½ Mark for each correct explanation of Call by value and Call by reference)

(½ Mark for each correct example, of Call by value and Call by reference) OR

(Full 2 Marks for correct examples demonstrating the *difference between Call by value and Call by reference)*

OR

(Only 1 Mark to be awarded for Explanation given without supporting examples)

b) Which C++ header file(s) will be essentially required to be included to run/ execute the following C++ code. **1**

```
void main()
{
        int Rno=24; char Name [] =" Amen Singhania";
        cout<<setw(lO)<<Rno<<setw(20)<<Name<<endl;
}
```

Ans. iostream.h

iomanip.h

OR

iomanip.h -(As iostream.h is included in iomanip.h)

(½ Mark for writing each correct header file)

OR

(Full Mark for mentioning only iomanip.h)

Note: Ignore any other header files, if mentioned.

c) Rewrite the following C++ program code after removing the syntax error(s) (if any). Underline each correction. **2**

```
include <iostream.h>
class FLIGHT
{
        long FlightCode;
        char Description[25];
public
        void AddInfo ( )
        {
                cin>>FlightCode; gets (Description) ;
        {
        void ShowInfo ()
        (
                cout<<FlightCode<<":"<<Description<<endl;
        }
};
void main()
{
        FLIGHT F;
        AddInfo.F(); ShowInfo.F();
}
```

Ans.

```
#include <iostream.h>        //    Error  1
#include <stdio.h>           //    Error  2
class FLIGHT
{
        char Description[25];
public:                      // / Error 3
        void AddInfo ( )
        {
                cin>>FlightCode; gets (Description) ;
        }
        void ShowInfo ( )
```

not required if gets( ) is replaced with cin.getline() or cin

```
        {
                cout<<FlightCode<<":"<<Description<<endl;
        }
};
void main ( )
{
        FLIGHT F;
        F.AddInfo( ) ; F. ShowInfo ( ) ; / / Error 4
}
```

(½ Mark for each correction)

OR

(1 mark for identifying at least three errors, without suggesting correction)

d) Find the output of the following program. **3**

```
#include <iostream.h>
struct THREE_D
{int X,Y,Z;};
void Moveln(THREE_D &T, int Step=l)
}
        T.X+=Step;
        T.Y-=Step;
        T.Z+=Step;
}
void MoveOut(THREE_D &T, int Step=l)
{
        T.X-=Step;
        T.Y+=Step;
        T.Z-=Step;
}
void main ()
{
        THREE_D     Tl={lO,20,5},T2={30,lO,40};
        Moveln(T1);
        MoveOut(T2,5) ;
        cout<<Tl.X<<","<<Tl.Y<<","<<T1.Z<<endl;
```

```
        cout<<T2.X<<","<<T2.Y<<","<<T2.Z<<endl;
        MoveIn(T2,l0);
        cout<<T2.X<<","<<T2.y<<","<<T2.Z<<endl;
    }
```

Ans. 11, 19, 6

25, 15, 35

35, 5, 45

(1 Mark for each line with correct values)

OR

(½ Mark for any two correct values in each line)

Note:

Deduct ½ Mark if any/all ',' missing

Deduct ½ Mark if endl is not considered at the right positions

e) Find the output of the following program. **2**

```
#include <iostream.h>
#include <ctype.h>
void MyCode (char Msg [], char CH)
{
    for (int (Cnt=O;Msg[Cnt]!='\0';Cnt++)
    {
    if  (Msg[Cnt]>='B'   &&   Msg[Cnt]<='G')
        Msg[Cnt]=tolower(Msg[Cnt]); else
            if (Msg[Cnt]=='A'|| Msg[Cnt]=='a')
            Msg[Cnt]=CH;
        else
        if (Cnt%2==0)
            Msg[Cnt]=toupper(Msg[Cnt]);
        else
            Msg[Cnt]=Msg[Cnt-l];
    }
}
void main ()
{
    char MyText [] =" ApEACeDriVE";
```

```
        MyCode(MyText,'@');
        cout<<"NEW      TEXT:"<<MyText<<endl;
    }
```

Ans. NEW TEXT:@@e@ccddIIe

(½ Mark for writing @,@,e as the first three characters)

(½ Mark for writing @,c,c as the next three characters)

(½ Mark for writing d,d, I as the next three characters)

(½ Mark for writing I,e as the next two characters)

Note: Deduct ½ Mark for not mentioning ***NEW TEXT:***

f) The following code is from a game, which generates a set of 4 random numbers. Praful is playing this game, help him to identify the correct option(s) out of the four choices given below as the possible set of such numbers generated from the program code so that he wins the game. Justify your answer. **2**

```
#include <iostream.h>
#include <stdlib.h>
const int LOW=25;
void main ()
{
        randomize() ;
        int P01NT=5,Number;
        for (int I=1;I<=4;I++)
        {
                Number=LOW+random(POINT);
                Cout<<Number<<":";
                P0INT--;
        }
}
```

(i) 29:26:25:28:

(ii) 24:28:25:26:

(iii) 29:26:24:28:

(iv) 29:26:25:26:

Ans. (iv). 29:26:25:26:

Justification is as follows:

I	POINTNumber	Minimum	Maximum
1	5	25	29
2	4	25	28
3	3	25	27
4	2	25	26

The only option that satisfies these values is option (iv).

(1 Mark for mentioning correct option)

(1 Mark for any valid justification)

Note: Only ½ Mark to be given if only options (i) & (iv) are mentioned as correct options; no other combination of options is acceptable;

2.

a) What do you understand by Data Encapsulation and Data Hiding ?' Also, give an example in C++ to illustrate both. **2**

Ans. Data Encapsulation: Wrapping up of data and functions together in a single unit is known as Data Encapsulation. In a class, we wrap up the data and functions together in a single unit.

Data Hiding: Keeping the data in private/protected visibility mode of the class to prevent it from accidental change is known as Data Hiding.

```
class Computer
{
        char CPU[lO] ;int RNM;                //Data Hiding
public:                                        //Data Encapsulation
        void STOCK();
        void SHOW();
};
```

(½ Mark for each correct explanation of Data Encapsulation and Data Hiding)

(½ Marie for each correct example of Data Encapsulation and Data Hiding)

OR

(2 Marks for explaining the concept of the terms through suitable examples)

OR

(Only 1 Mark to be awarded for Explanation given without any example)

b) Answer the questions (i) and (ii) after going through the following class. **2**

```
class Exam
```

```
{
        int    Rno,MaxMarks,MinMarks,Marks;
public:
        Exam ( )                                                        //Module 1
        {
                Rno=101;MaxMarks=l00;MinMarks=40;Marks=75;
        }
        Exam (int Prno, int Pmarks)                                     //Module 2
        {
        Rno=Prno;MaxMarks=l00;MinMarks=40;Marks=Pmarks;
        }
        ~Exam ()                                                        //Module 3
        {
                cout<<"Exam  Over"<<endl;
        }
        void Show ()                                                    //Module  4
        {
                cout<<Rno<<":"<<MaxMarks<<":"<<MinMarks<<endl;
                cout<<"[Marks Got]"<<Marks<<endl;
        }
};
```

(i) As per Object Oriented Programming, which concept is illustrated by **Module 1** and **Module 2** together?

Ans. Polymorphism

OR

Constructor Overloading

OR

Function Overloading

(1 Mark for mentioning the correct concept)

(ii) What is **Module 3** referred as ? When do you think, **Module 3** will be invoked/called?

Ans. Destructor. It is invoked as soon as the scope of the object gets over.

(½ Mark for identifying it as Destructor)

(½ Mark for mentioning correctly when it be called/invoked)

c) Define a class STOCK in C++ with following description. **4**

Private Members

ICode of type integer (Item Code) Item of type string (Item Name)

Price of type float (Price of each item) Qty of type integer (Quantity in stock)

Discount of type float (Discount percentage on the item)

A member function FindDisc() to calculate discount as per the following rule:

If Qty<=50	Discount is 0
If 50<Qty<=100	Discount is 5
If Qty>100	Discount is 10

Public Members

A function Buy() to allow user to enter values for ICode, Item, Price, Qty and call function FindDisc() to calculate the Discount.

A function ShowAll() to allow user to view the content of all the data members.

Ans. class STOCK

```
{
        int ICode,Qty;
        char Item[20];
        float Price,Discount;
        void FindDisc();
public:
        void Buy();
        void ShowAll();
};
void STOCK::Buy()
{
        cin>>ICode;
        gets(Item);
        cin>>Price;
        cin»Qty;
        FindDisc();
}
void STOCK::FindDisc()
{
        if (Qty<=50)
                Discount=0;
```

```
        else if (Qty<=100)
                Discount=5;                     // =0.05;
        else
                Discount=10;                    // =0.1;
}
void STOCK::ShowAll()
{
        cout<<ICode<<'\t'<<Item<<'\t'<<Price<<'\t'<<Qty
        <<'\t'<<Discount<<endl;
}
```

(½ Mark for correct syntax for class header)

(½ Mark for correct declaration of data members)

(1 Mark for correct definition of FindDisc())

(1 Mark for correct definition of Buy() with proper invocation of FindDisc() function)

(1 Mark for correct definition of ShowAll())

NOTE:

Deduct ½ Mark if FindDisc() is not invoked properly inside Buy() function

d) Answer the questions (i) to (iv) based on the following. **4**

```
class Director
{
        long        DID;            //Director Identification Number
        char        Name[20];
protected:
        char        Description[40];
        void        Allocate        ();
public:
        Director()              ;
        void        Assign      ();
        void        Show ()         ;
};
        class Ractory:public  Director
        }
                int FID;                //Factory  ID
                char Address[20];
```

```
protected:
        int NOE;                //No. of Employees
public:
        Factory();
        void Input ();
        void Output  ();
};
class ShowRoom:private  Factory
{
        int SID;                //Showroom ID
        char City[20];
public:
        ShowRoom();
        void Enter ();
        void Display  ();
};
```

i. Which type of inheritance out of the following is illustrated in the above C++ code?

(a) Single Level Inheritance.

(b) Multi Level Inheritance.

(c) Multiple Inheritance.

Ans. (b) Multilevel Inheritance

(1 Mark for mentioning correct option)

ii. Write the names of data members, which are accessible by objects of class type ShowRoom.

Ans. None

(1 Mark for correct answer)

Note: No marks to be awarded for any partial/*alternative answer*

iii. Write the names of all member functions which are accessible by objects of class type ShowRoom.

Ans. Enter(), Display()

(1 Mark for correct answer)

Note:

No marks to be awarded for any partial/alternative answer Ignore mention of Constructor(s)

iv. Write the names of all members, which are accessible from member functions of class Factory.

Ans. FID, Address, NOE, Description,

Input(), Output(), Assign(), Show(), Allocate()

(1 Mark for correct answer)

Note:

No marks to be awarded for any partial/alternative answer Ignore mention of Constructor(s)

3.

a) Write a function REASSIGNO in C++, which accepts an array of integers and its size as parameters and divide all those array elements by 5 which are divisible by 5 and multiply other array elements by 2. **3**

Sample Input Data of the array.

A[0]	A[1]	A[2]	A[3]	A[4]
20	12	15	60	32

Content of the array after calling REASSIGNO function.

A[0]	A[1]	A[2]	A[3]	A[4]
4	24	3	12	64

Ans.
```
void REASSIGN (int Arr[ ], int Size)
{
    for (int i=0;i<Size;i++)
    if (Arr[i]%5==0)
            Arr[i]/=5;
        else
            Arr[i]*=2;
}
```

OR

```
void REASSIGN(int Arr[ ],int Size)
{
    for (int i=0;i<Size;i++)
        Arr[i]%5 ? Arr[i]/=5: Arr[i]*=2;
}
```

OR

Any other correct equivalent function definition

(½ Mark for correct Function Header)

(½ Mark for correct loop)

(½ Mark for correct checking of divisibility of array elements by 5)

(½ Mark for correct placing of else OR correct checking of non divisibility of array elements by 5)

(½ Mark for each correct assignment)

b) An array T[90][100] is stored in the memory along the column with each of the elements occupying 4 bytes. Find out the memory location for the element T[10][40], if the Base Address of the array is 7200. **3**

Ans. Loc(T[I][J]) = Base(T)+W(I+J*N)

(where N is the number of rows, LBR = LBC = 0)

= 7200 + 4[10 + 40 x 90]

= 7200 + 4[10+3600]

= 7200 + 4 x 3610

= 7200 + 14440

= 21640

OR

Address of T[I][J] along the column

= BaseAddress + W [(I-LBR)+(J-LBC)* N] (where N is the number of rows, LBR=LBC = 1)

Address of T[10][40]=BaseAddress + 4[(10 - 1) +(40 - l)x 90]

= 7200+4[9 + 39 x 90]

= 7200+4[9 + 3510]

= 7200+4 x 3519

= 7200+14076

= 21276

(1 Mark for writing correct formula (for column major) OR. substituting formula with correct values for calculating Address)

(2 marks for calculating correct address)

c) Write a complete program in C++ to implement a dynamically allocated Queue containing names of Cities. **4**

Ans.
```
#include <iostream.h>
#include <conio.h>
struct NODE
{
        char City[20];
        NODE *Next;
};
class Queue
{
        NODE *Rear,*Front;
puplic:
        Queue() {Rear=NULL;Front=NULL;}
        void Qinsert();
        void Qdelete();
        void Qdisplay ();
        ~Queue();
} ;
void Queue::Qinsert()
{
        NODE *Temp;
        Temp=new NODE;
        cout<<"Data:";
        gets (Temp->City);
        Temp->Next=NULL;
        if (Rear==NULL)
        {
                Rear=Temp;
                Front=Temp;
        }
        else
        {
                Rear->Next=Temp;
```

```
            Rear=Temp;
        }
}
void Queue::Qdelete()
{
        if (Front!=NULL)
        {
                NODE *Temp=Front;
                cout<<Front->City<<"Deleted\n";
                Front=Front->Next;
                delete Temp;
                if (Front==NULL)  Rear=NULL;
        }
        else
                cout<<"Queue Empty..";
}
Queue:: Qdisplay  ()
{
        NODE *Temp=Front;
        while (Temp!=NULL)
        {
                cout<<Temp->City<<endl;
                Temp=Temp->Next;
        }
}
Queue:: ~Queue()//Destructor  Function
{
        while (Front!=NULL)
        {
                NODE    *Temp=Front;
                Front=Front->Next; delete Temp;
        }
}
void main ()
```

```
{
        Queue QU; char Ch;
        do
        {
                :
                :
        } while (Ch!='Q');
}
```

(4 Marks for correct program)

OR

(Full 4 Marks for correct logic of either Insertion OR Deletion functions for Dynamically Allocated Queue.)

OR

(2 Marks for defining class with Constructor, function prototypes for Insertion & deletion and Destructor or equivalent using Structures.)

d) Write a function int ALTERSUM (int B[ ] [5], int N, int M in C++ to find and return the sum of elements from all alternate elements of a two-dimensional array starting from B[0][0]. **2**

Hint: If the following is the content of the array:

B[0][0]	B[0][1]	**B[0][2]**
4	5	**1**
B[1][0]	**B[1][1]**	B[1][2]
2	**8**	7
B[2][0]	B[2][1]	**B[2][2]**
9	6	**3**

The function should add elements B[0][0], B[0][2], B[l][l], B[2][0] and B[2][2].

Ans. //Sample Code 1

```
int ALTERSUM(int B[][5] ,int N,int M)
{
        int Sum=0;
        for (int I=0;I<N;I++)
```

```
		for (int J=(I%2==0)?0:1;J<M;J+=2)
			Sum+=B[I][J] ;
	return Sum;
}
```

OR

```
//Sample Code 2
int ALTERSUM(int B[][5],int N,int M)
{
	int Sum=0,J=0;
	for (int I=0;I<N;I++)
	{
		for (;J<M;J+=2)
			Sum+=B[I][J] ;
		J-=M;
	}
	return Sum;
}
```

OR

```
//Sample Code 3
int ALTERSUM(int B[][5],int N,int M)
{
	int *P=&B[0][0],Sum=0;
	for (int I=0;I<M*N;I+=2)
	{
		Sum+=(*P);
		P+=2;
	}
	return Sum;
}
```

OR

```
//Sample Code 4
int ALTERSUM (int B[][5], int N, int M)
{
	int S=0, C=0;
```

```
        for(int I = 0; 1< N; 1++)
            for (int J = 0; J<M; J++ )
            {
                if (C%2 == 0)
                    S = S + B[I][J];
                C++;
            }
        return S;
    }
```

OR

```
//Sample Code 5
    int ALTERSUM(int B[][5],int N,int M)
    {
      int     Sum=0;
      for     (int I=0;1<N;1++)
              for    (int J=0;J<M;J++)
                      if ((1+J)%2==0)
                           Sum+=B [I][J] ;
      Return Sum;
  }
```

OR

```
  //Sample Code 6
  int ALTERSUM(int B[][5],int N,int M)
  {
      int     Sum=0;
      for     (int I=0;1<N;1++)
              for      (int J=0;J<M;J++)
              {
                 if ((1%2==0 && J%2=0)||(1%2!=0 && J%2!=0))
                        Sum+=B [I][J] ;
              }
      return Sum;

  }
```

Note: Kindly note Sample Code 5 and 6 will not work in case of Even Dimensional Arrays, but keeping in view of the Sample given for 3x3 array the solution is acceptable.

(½ Mark for correct loops)

(1 Mark for finding Sum of alternate cells)

(½ Mark for returning the Sum)

(e) Evaluate the following postfix notation of expression: 2

(Show status of Stack after each operation)

True, False, NOT, OR, False, True, OR, AND

Ans.

Element Scanned	Stack Content
True	True
False	True, False
NOT	True, True
OR	True
False	True, False
True	True, False, True
OR	True, True
AND	True

OR

Step 1: Push

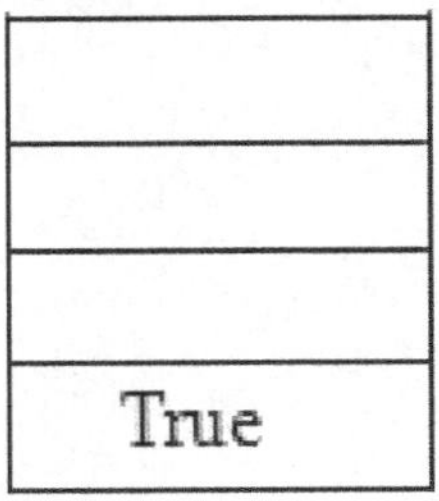

Step 2: Push

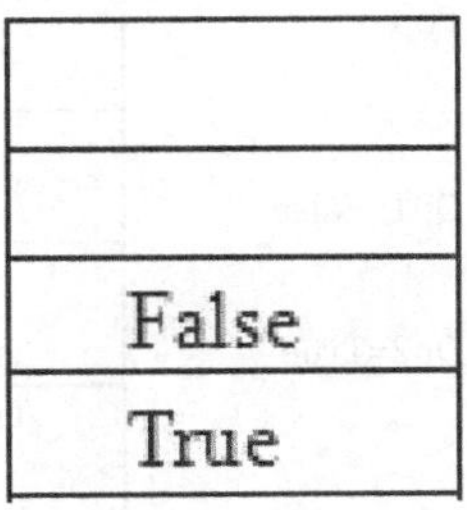

Step 3: NOT

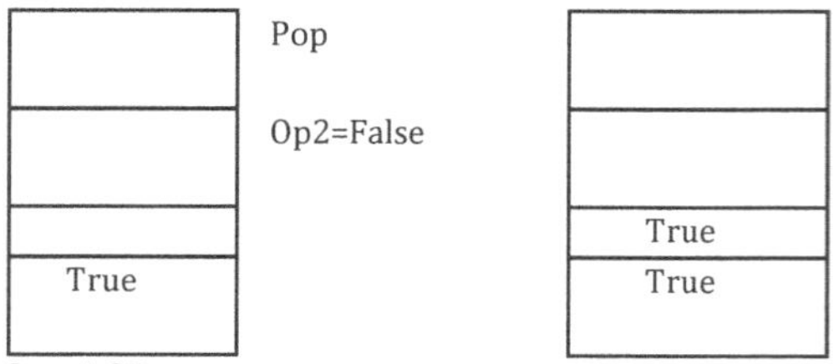

Step 4 OR

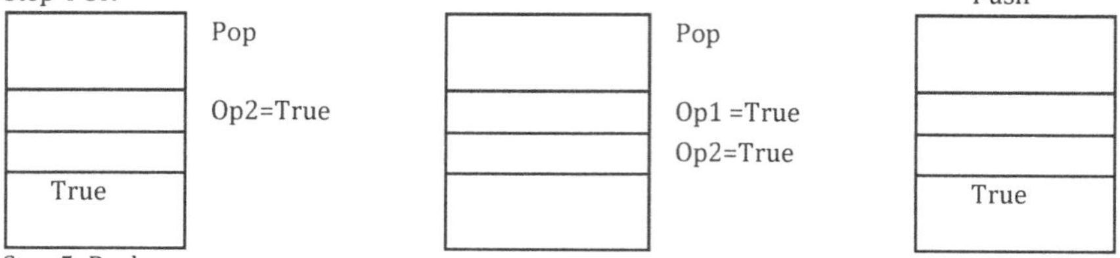

Step 5: Push

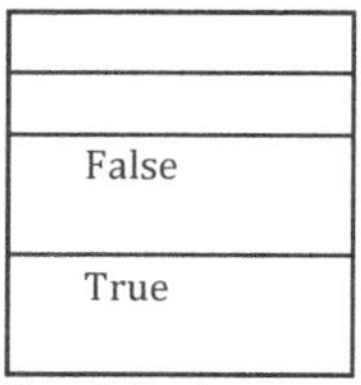

Step 6: Push

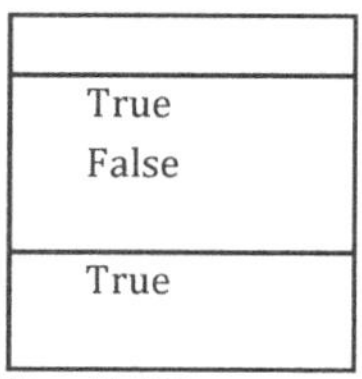

Step 7: OR

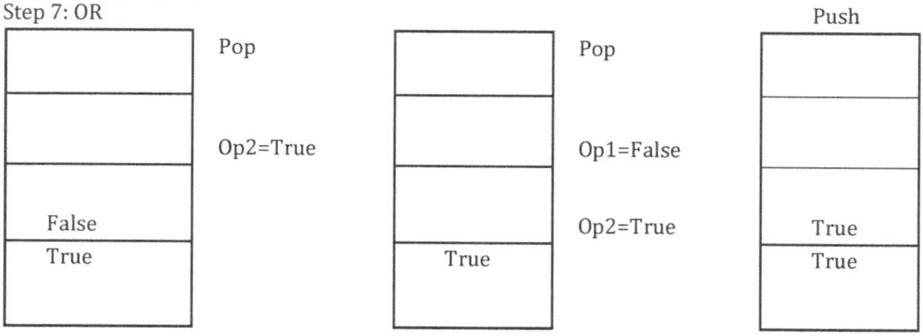

Step 8: AND Push

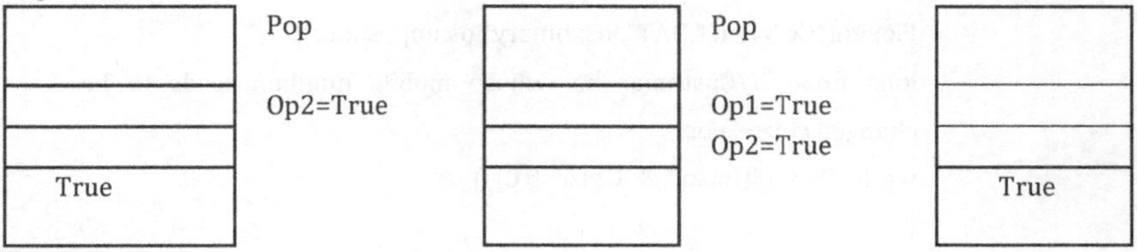

Step 9: Pop

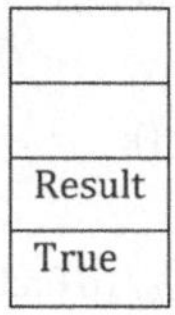

OR

Any other method for evaluating the given postfix expression showing the Stack Status.

(½ Mark for correctly evaluating expression up to each operator)

OR

(1 Mark only to be given for writing correct answer without showing the Stack Status)

4.

a) Observe the program segment given below carefully and fill the blanks mar- ked as Statement 1 and Statement 2 using tellg() and seekp() functions for performing the required task. **1**

```
#include <fstream.h>
class Customer
{
        long Cno;char Name[20],Mobile[12];
public:
        //Function to allow user to enter the Cno, Name, Mobile
void Enter();
        //Function to allow user to enter (modify) mobile number void
        Modify();
        //Function to return value of Cno
        long GetCno () {return Cno;}
};
void ChangeMobile()
{
        Customer C;
```

```
fstream F;
F.open("CONTACT.DAT",ios::binary|ios::in|ios::out);
long Cnoc; //Customer no. whose mobile number needs to be
changed cin>>Cnoc;
while (F.read((char*)& C,sizeof(C)))
{
    if (Choc==C.GetCno())
    {
        C.Modify ();
                                              //Statement 1
  int Pos=__________//To find the current
  position of file pointer
                                              //Statement 2
    ____//To move the file pointer to write the
        //modified record back onto the file
        //for the desired Cnoc
    F.write((char*)&C,sizeof(C));
    }
}
F. close( ) ;
}
```

Ans. Statement 1:

File.tellg() ;

Statement 2:

File.seekp(Pos-sizeof(C));

OR

File.seekp(-l*sizeof(C) ,ios::cur);

(½ Mark for each correct Statement)

b) Write a function in C++ to count the words "to" and "the" present in a text file "POEM.TXT". 2

[Note that the words "to" and "the" are complete words]

Ans.
```
void COUNT ()
{
    ifstream Fil;
```

```
        Fil. open          ("POEM.TXT");       OR ifstream Fil ("POEM. TXT");

        char  Word[80] ;
        int Cl = 0, C2 = 0;
        while(!Fil.eof())
        {
                Fil>>Word;
                if (strcmp (Word, "to") ==0)
                      Cl++;
                else if (strcmp (Word, "the") ==0)
                      C2++;
             }

        cout<<"Count of -to- in file:" <<Cl;

        cout«"Count  of  -the-  in  file:"«C2;

        OR cout<<"Count of -to- and -the- in file:"<<Cl+C2;

    Fil.close();  //Ignore

}

OR

void COUNT (       )

{

    ifstream      Fil("POEM.TXT");

             //    OR fstream Fil;
             //     Fil.open("POEM.TXT",ios::in); char
             STR[l0];
             int  Cl=O,  C2=0;
             while  (Fil.getline(STR,l0,''))
             {
```

```
            if (strcmp (STR, "to") ==0)
                Cl++;
            else if (strcmp(STR, "the") ==0) C2++;
        }
            cout<<"Count of -to- in file:"<<Cl;
            cout<<"Count of -the- in file:"<<C2;
    OR cout<<"Count of -to- and -the- in file:"<<Cl+C2;
            Fil.close(); //Ignore
}
OR
void COUNT()
{
        ifstream Fil;
                                                    OR ifstream
        Fill("POEM.TXT"); Fil. open ("POEM.TXT");
        char Word[BO], Chi
        int Cl =0, C2=0, 1=0;
        while(Fil.get(Ch))
        {
            if (Ch! = ' ')
                Word[1++] = Chi
            else
            {
                Word[I] = '\0';
                if (strcmp (Word, "to") ==0)
                    Cl++;
                else if (strcrap (Word, "the") ==0)
                    C2++;
                1=0;
            }
        }
        cout<<"Count of -to- in file:"<<Cl;
        cout<<"Count of -the- in file:"<<C2;
                            OR cout«"Count of -to- and -the- in
```

```
        Fil.close(); //1gnore
    }
```

OR

Any-other correct function definition

(½ Mark for opening POEM. TXT correctly)

(½ Mark for reading each word (using any method) from the file)

(½ Mark for comparing the word with 'to' and 'the')

(½ Mark for incrementing counter(s))

c) Write a function in C++ to search and display details. of all trains, whose destination is "Delhi" . from a binary file "TRAIN.DAT". Assuming the binary file is containing the objects of the following class. **3**

```
    class TRAIN
    {
        int Tno;                              // Train Number
        charFrom[20];                         // Train Starting Point
        charTo [20];                          // Train Destination
    public:
        char*    GetFrom (){return From;}
        char*    GetTo (){return To;}
        void Input () {cin>>Tno;gets(From);gets(To);}
        void Show () {cout<<Tno<<":"<<From<<":"<<To<<endl;}
    };
```

Ans.

```
    void Read ( )
    {
        TRAIN T;
        ifstream fin;
        fin. open ("TRAIN.DAT", ios::binary);
        OR ifstream fin ("TRAIN.DAT",
        ios::binary); while(fin.read((char*)&T, sizeof(T))) {
            if(strcmp(T.GetTo(),"Delhi")==0)
        T.Show() ;
         }
         fin.close(); //Ignore
     }
```

OR

Any other correct function definition

(½ Mark for opening TRAIN .DAT correctly)

(½ Mark for reading each record from TRAIN.DAT)

(½ Mark for correct loop / checking end of file)

(1 Mark for comparing value returned by GetTo() with "Delhi")

(½ Mark for displaying the matching record)

5.

a) What do you understand by Primary Key? Give a suitable example of Primary Key from a table containing some meaningful data. **2**

Ans. An attribute or set of attributes which are used to identify a tuple uniquely is known as Primary Key.

Ino	Item	Qty
I01	Pen	300
I02	Pencil	780
I04	CD	450
I09	Floppy	700

PRIMARY KEY

(1 Mark for writing correct definition/purpose of valid Primary Key)

(1 Mark for giving suitable example)

OR

(2 Marks for illustrating the purpose of Key with/without showing it as a part of a Table)

b) Consider the following tables STOCK and DEALERS and answer (b1) and (b2) parts of this question.

Table: STOCK

ItemNo	Item	Dcode	Qty	UnitPrice	StockDate
5005	Ball Pen 0.5	102	100	16	31-Mar-10
5003	Ball Pen 0.25	102	150	20	01-Jan-10
5002	Gel Pen Premium	101	125	14	14-Feb-10
5006	Gel Pen Classic	101	200	22	01-Jan-09
5001	Eraser Small	102	210	5	19-Mar-09
5004	Eraser Big	102	60	10	12-Dec-09
5009	Sharpener Classic	103	160	8	23-Jan-09

Table: DEALERS

Dcode	Dname
101	Reliable Stationers
103	Classic Plastics
102	Clear Deals

(b1). Write SQL commands for the following statements. **4**

(i) To display details of all Items in the Stock table in ascending order of StockDate.

Ans. SELECT * FROM STOCK ORDER BY StockDate;

(1 Mark for correct query)

(½ Mark for partially correct answer)

(ii) To display ItemNo and Item name of those items from Stock table whose Unit Price is more than Rupees 10.

Ans. SELECT ItemNo,Item FROM STOCK WHERE UnitPrice >10;

(1 Mark for correct query)

(½ Mark for partially correct answer)

(iii) To display the details of those items whose dealer code (Dcode) is 102 or Quantity in Stock (Qty) is more than 100 from the table Stock.

Ans. SELECT * FROM STOCK WHERE Dcode=102 OR Qty >100;

(1 Mark for correct query)

(½ Mark for partially correct answer)

(iv) To display Maximum Unit Price of items for each dealer individually as per Dcode from the table Stock.

Ans. SELECT Dcode, MAX (UnitPrice) FROM STOCK GROUP BY Dcode;

OR

Any other query that will give an equivalent output

(1 Mark for correct query)

(½ Mark for partially correct answer)

(b2). Give the output of the following SQL queries. **2**

(i) SELECT COUNT(DISTINCT Dcode) FROM Stock.

Ans. <u>Count(DISTINCT Dcode)</u>3

(½ Mark for correct output)

(ii) SELECT Qty*UnitPrice FROM Stock WHERE ItemNo=5006;

Ans. Qty*UnitPrice

4400

(½ Mark for correct output)

SELECT Item,Dname FROM Stock S, Dealers D

WHERE S.Dcode=D.Dcode AND ItemNo=5004;

Ans.

Item	Dname
Eraser Big	Clear Deals

(½ Mark for correct output)

(iv) SELECT MIN(StockDate) FROM Stock;

Ans.

MIN (StockDate)
01-Jan-09

(½ Mark for correct output)

6.(a) Verify the following algebraically : 2

X'.Y + X.Y' = (X'+Y').(X+Y)

Ans. R. H.S

(X'+y').(x+y)

= x'.(x+y)+y'.(x+y)

= x.x'+X'.y+y'.x+y'.y

= x'.y+y'.X

= x'.y+x.y'

So L.H.S=R.H.S

OR

L.H.S.

X'.Y + X.Y'

= (X'.Y+X) (X'.Y+Y')

= (X'+X).(Y+X).(X'+Y').(Y+Y')

= 1.(X+Y).(X' +Y').1

= (X+Y).(X'+Y')

= R.H.S.

(2 Marks for correct verification)

(b) Write the equivalent Boolean Expression for the following Logic Circuit. **2**

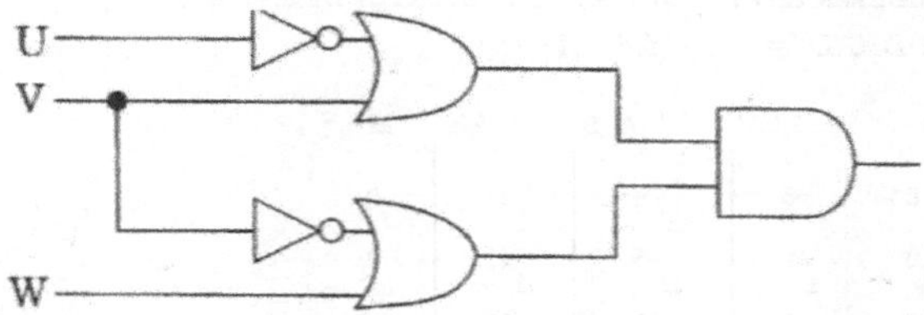

Ans. (U'+V).(V'+W)

(2 Marks for the final expre~sion (U'+V).(V'+W))

OR

(1 Mark for anv one of the correct terms out of (U'+V) or (V'+W))

(c) Write the SOP form of a Boolean function G, which is represented in a truth table as follows. **1**

P	Q	R	G
0	0	0	0
0	0	1	0
0	1	0	1
0	1	1	1
1	0	0	1
1	0	1	0
1	1	0	1
1	1	1	1

Ans. G(P,Q,R)=P'.Q.R'+P'.Q.R+P.Q'.R'+P.Q.R'+P.Q.R

OR

G(P,Q,R) = Σ (2,3,4,6,7)

(1 Mark for the correct SOP form)

Note: Deduct ½ mark if wrong variable names are used

(d) Reduce the following Boolean Expression using K-Map : 3

F (A,B,C,D) = Σ (3,4,5,6, 7,13,15)

Ans.

	A' B'	A' B	AB	AB'
C' D'	0	1 4	12	8
C' D	1	1 5	1 13	9
C D	1 3	1 7	1 13	11
C D	2	1 6	14	10

OR

	C' D'	C' D	CD	CD'
A' B'	0	1	1 3	2
A' B	1 4	1 5	1 7	1 6
A B	12	1 13	1 15	14
A B'	8	9	11	10

F(A,B,C,D) = A'B + BD + A'CD

(½ Mark for drawing K-Map with correct variable names)

(½ Mark for placing all 1s at correct positions in K-Map)

(½ Mark for each grouping)

(½ Mark for writing final expression in reduced/minimal form)

7. (a) What was the role of ARPANET in the Computer Network? 1

Ans. The first computer network was jointly designed by The Advanced Research

Ans Projects Agency (ARPA) and Department of Defence (DoD) of United States in 1969 and was called ARPANET. It was an experimental project, which connected a few computers from some of the reputed universities of USA and DoD. ARPANET allowed access to computer resource sharing projects. This ARPANET was handed over to Defence Communication Agency (DCA) for further development.

(1 Mark for mentioning that ARPANET was the first computer network)

OR

(½ Mark if only the expansion of ARPANET is mentioned)

(b) Which of the following is not a unit for data transfer rate? 1

(i) mbps

(ii) kbps

(iii) sbps

(iv) gbps

Ans. (iii) sbps

(1 Mark for the correct option/answer)

(c) What is the difference between Virus and Worms in the computers? 1

Ans. Virus: Virus is a malicious program that damages data and files and causes harm to computer system.

Worms: Worms disrupt services and create system management problems.

In some cases worms can install viruses that cause damage to system.

(1 Mark for mentioning anyone valid difference)

OR

(½ Mark for correct definition of each term)

(d) What term do we use for a software/hardware device, which is used to block unauthorized access while permitting authorized communications? This term is also used for a device or set of devices configured to permit, deny, encrypt, decrypt, or proxy all (in and out) computer traffic between different security domains based upon a set of rules and other criteria. 1

Ans. Firewall

(1 Mark for writing correct term)

"Vidya for All" is an educational NGO. It is setting up its new campus at Jaipur for its web-based activities. The campus has four buildings as shown in the diagram below.

4

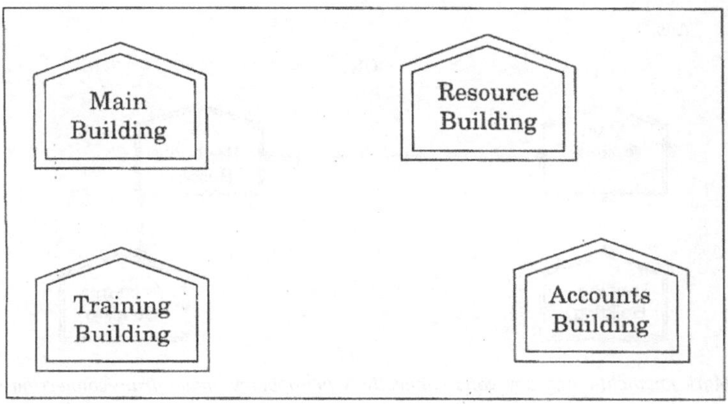

Center to center distances between various buildings as per architectural drawings (in meters) is as follows:

Main Building to Resource Building	120 m
Main Building to Training Building	40 m
Main Building to Accounts Building	135 m
Resource Building to Training Building	125 m
Resource Building to Accounts Building	45 m
Training Building to Accounts Building	110 m

Expected Number of Computers in each Building is as follows:

Main Building	15
Resource Building	25
Training Building	250
Accounts Building	10

(e1) Suggest a cable layout of connections between the buildings.

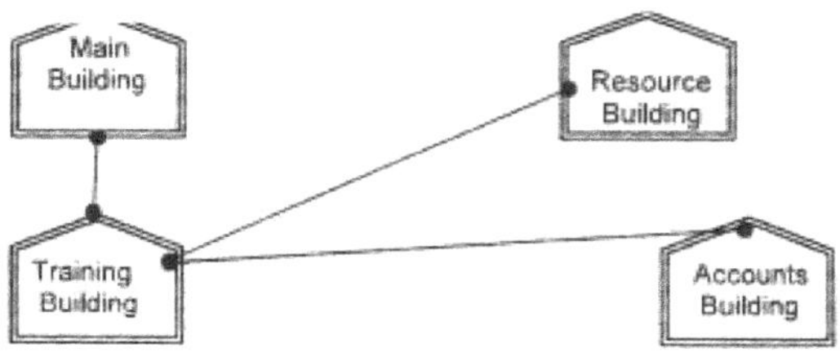

Ans.

OR

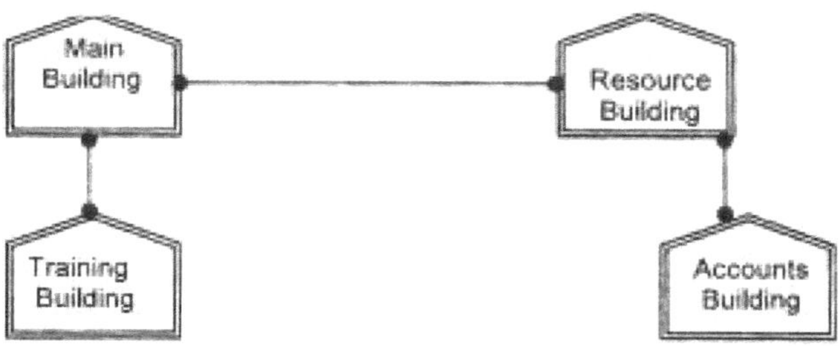

(1 Mark for mentioning any valid connectivity or topology or dia-gram connecting various buildings inside the campus)

(e2). Suggest the most suitable place (i.e. building) to house the server for this NGO. Also, provide a suitable reason for your suggestion.

Ans. Training Building as it contains maximum number of computers.

(½ Mark for mentioning the building)

(½ Mark for correct justification)

OR

(1 Mark for any other location with a valid justification)

(e3). Suggest the placement of the following devices with justification:

(i) Repeater

(ii) Hub/Switch

Ans.

(i) A Repeater should be placed when the distance between any two connecting buildings exceeds 70 m.

(ii) Every building will need one Hub / Switch, to send signals to all of the workstations connected to it.

OR

Any diagrammatic representation with valid justification

(½ Mark for correct placement of Repeater with justification)

(½ Mark for correct placement of Hub/Switch with justification)

(e4) The NGO is planning to connect its International office situated in Delhi. Which out of the following wired communication links, will you suggest for a very high speed connectivity ?

(i) Telephone Analog Line.

(ii) Optical Fiber.

(iii) Ethernet Cable.

Ans. (ii) Optical Fibre

(1 Mark for correct Option / Answer)

(f) Write the full forms of the following. **1**

(f1) FTP

(f2) FSF

Ans. (f1) FILE TRANSFER PROTOCOL

(f2) FREE SOFTWARE FOUNDATION

(½ Mark. for each full form)

(g) Name any two common Web browsers. 1

Ans. Internet explorer

Firefox

Netscape

Chrome

Opera

Safari

OR any other Web Browser

(½ Mark each for any two web browsers)

Question Paper 2015 Outside Delhi

CBSE Class 12 Computer Science

General Instructions

- SECTION A refers to programming language C++.
- SECTION B refers to programming language Python.
- SECTION C is compulsory for all Answer either SECTION A or SECTION B.
- It is compulsory to mention on the page 1 in the answer book whether you are attempting SECTION A or SECTION B.
- All Questions are Compulsory within Each Section.

Section-A

(Only for C++ Candidates)

1.

a) Find the correct identifiers out of the following, which can be used for naming Variable, Constants or Functions in a C++ program. (2)

For, while, INT, New, delete, 1stName, Add + Subtract, name1

Ans. For, INT, New, name1

(½ Mark for each correct identifier)

Note:

- Deduct ½ Mark for writing additional incorrect identifier(s).
- No marks to be awarded if all the identifiers are mentioned.

b) Observe the following program very carefully and write the name of those header file (s), which are essentially needed to compile and execute the following program successfully. (1)

```
typedef char STRING[80];
void main()
{
STRING Txt[] = "We love Peace";
int Count=0;
while (Txt[Count]!='\0')
if (isalpha(Txt[Count]))
Txt[Count++]='@' ;
else
Txt[Count++]='#' ;
```

```
puts (Txt) ;
}
```

Ans. ctype, stdio

(½ mark for each header file)

Note: Ignore any additional header file(s)

c) **Observe the following C++ code very carefully and rewrite it after removing any/all syntactical errors with each correction underlined.** **(2)**

Note: Assume all required header files are already being included in the program.

```
#Define float MaxSpeed=60.5;
void main()
{
int MySpeed
char Alert='N' ;
cin»MySpeed;
if MySpeed>MaxSpeed
Alert='Y' ;
cout<<Alert<<endline;
}
```

Ans. #definefloatMaxSpeed60.5;//Error 1,2,3

```
void main()
{
int MySpeed ;//Error 4
char Alert='N';
cin>>MySpeed;
if (MySpeed>MaxSpeed)  //Error 5
Alert='Y';
cout<<Alert<<endl;//Error 6
}
```

(½ Mark for each correction upto a maximum of 4 corrections)

OR

(1 mark for only identifying any 4 errors, without suggesting corrections)

d) Write the output of the following C++ program code. **(2)**

Note: Assume all required header files are already being included in the program.

```
void Location(int &X,int Y=4)
{
Y+=2;
X+=Y;
}
void main()
{
int PX=10,PY=2;
Location(PY) ;
cout<<PX<<" , "<<PY<<endl ;
Location(PX,PY);
cout<<PX<<" , "<<PY<<endl ;
}
```

Ans. 10, 8

20, 8

(½ Mark for each correct value)

Note:

- Deduct ½ Mark for not considering any or all endl(s) at proper place(s).
- Deduct ½ Mark for not considering any or all ',' at proper place(s).

e) Write the output of the following C++ program code. **(3)**

Note: Assume all required header files are already being included in the program.

```
class Eval
{
char Level;
int Point;
public:
Eval() {Level='E';Point=0;}
void Sink(int L)
{
Level=L;
}
void Float(int L)
```

```
{
Level += L;
Point++;
}
void Show()
{
cout<<Level<<"#"<<Point<<endl;
}
};
void main()
{
Eval E;
E.Sink(3);
E.Show();
E.Float(7);
E.Show();
E.Sink(2);
E.Show();
}
```

Ans. B#0

I#1

G#1

(1 Mark for each correct line of output)

Note:

- Deduct ½ Mark for not considering any or all endl(s) at proper place(s).
- Deduct ½ Mark for not writing any or all # symbol(s).

f) **Study the following program and select the possible output(s) from the option (i) to (iv) following it. Also, write the maximum and the minimum values that can be assigned to the variable VAL.** **(2)**

Note:

- Assume all required header files are already being included in the program.
- random(n) function generates an integer between 0 and n-1.

```
void main()
{
```

```
randomize();
int VAL;
VAL=random(3)+2;
char GUESS[]="ABCDEFGHIJK";
for (int I=l;I<=VAL;I++)
{
for(int J=VAL;J<=7;J++)
cout«GUESS[J];
cout«endl;
}
}
```

(i)	(ii)	(iii)	(iv)
BCDEFGH	CDEFGH	EFGH	FGHI
BCDEFGH	CDEFGH	EFGH	FGHI
		EFGH	FGHI

Ans (ii) and (iii)

Min Value of VAL = 2

Max Value of VAL = 4

(½ Mark for writing option (ii))

(½ Mark for writing option (iii))

Note:

Deduct ½ mark for writing each additionaloption along with both correct options.

(½ Mark for writing correct Minimum value of VAL)

(½ Mark for writing correct Maximum value of VAL)

2.

a) **What is a copy constructor? Give a suitable example in C++ to illustrate with its definition within a class and a declaration of an object with the help of it. (2)**

Ans. A copy constructor is an overloaded constructor in which an object of the same class is passed as reference parameter.

```
class Point
{
int x;
public:
Point(){x=0;}
Point(Point &p) // Copy constructor
```

```
{x = p.x;}
:
};
void main()
{
Point p1;
Point p2(p1);//Copy constructor is called here
//OR
Point p3=p1;//Copy constructor is called here
}
```

(1½ Mark to be awarded if the copy constructor is explained with an appropriate example)

OR

(1 Mark for correct explanation of copy constructor only without an example)

(½ Mark for correct declaration of an object)

b) **Observe the following C++ code and answer the questions (i) and (ii).**

```
class Passenger
{
long PNR;
char Name [20] ;
public:
Passenger() //Function 1
{ cout<<"Ready"<<endl; }
void Book(long P,char N[]) //Function 2
{ PNR = P; strcpy(Name, N); } void Print() //Function 3

{ cout«PNR << Name <<endl; }
~Passenger()     //Function 4
{ cout<<"Booking cancelled!"<<endl; } };
```

(i) Fill in the blank statements in Line 1 and Line 2 to execute Function 2 and Function 3 respectively in the following code. **(1)**

```
void main()
Passenger P;
________ //Line 1
________ //Line 2
```

}//Ends here

Ans. P.Book(1234567,"Ravi"); //Line 1

P.Print(); //Line 2

(½ Mark for writing each correct Function)

(ii) Which function will be executed at}//Ends here? What is this function referred as? (1)

Ans. Function 4

OR

~Passenger()

It is a Destructor function.

(½ Mark for writing Function 4 OR ~Passenger())

(½ Mark for referring Destructor)

c) **Write the definition of a class Photo in C++ with following description. (4)**

Private Members

Pno //Data member for Photo Number (an integer)

Category //Data member for Photo Category (a string)

Exhibit //Data member for Exhibition Gallery (a string)

FixExhibit//A member function to assign

//Exhibition Gallery as per Category

//as shown in the following table

Category	Exhibit
Antique	Zaveri
Modern J	Johnsen
Classic	Terenida

Public Members

Register()//A function to allow user to enter

//values

//Pno,Category and call FixExhibit()

//function

ViewAll()//A function to display all the data

//members 4

Ans. class Photo

{

int Pno;

```
char Category[20];
char Exhibit[20];
void FixExhibit();
public:
void Register();
void ViewAll();
};
void Photo::FixExhibit()
{
if(strcmpi(Category,"Antique")==0)
strcpy(Exhibit,"Zaveri");
else if(strcmpi(Category,"Modern")==0)
strcpy(Exhibit,"Johnsen");
else if strcmpi(Category,"Classic")==0)
strcpy(Exhibit,"Terenida");
}
void Photo::Register()
{
cin>>Pno;
gets(Category);
FixExhibit();
}
void Photo:: ViewAll()
{
cout<<Pno<<Category<<Exhibit<<endl;
}
```

(½ Mark for correct syntax for class header)

(½ Mark for correct declaration of data members)

(1 Mark for correct definition of FixExhibit())

(1 Mark for correct definition of Register() with proper invocation of Fix Exhibit() function)

(1 Mark for correct definition of ViewAll())

NOTE:

- Deduct ½ Mark if FixExhibit() is not invoked properly inside Register() function No.
- marks to be deducted for defining Member Functions inside the class.

- strcmp()/strcmpi() acceptable.

d) **Answer the questions (i) to (iv) based on the following**

```
class Interior
{
int OrderId;
char Address[20];
protected:
float Advance;
public:
Interior();
void Book(); void View();
};
class Painting:public Interior
{
int WallArea,ColorCode;
protected:
char Type;
public:
Painting();
void PBook();
void PView();
};
class Billing:public Painting
{
float Charges;
void Calculate();
public:
Billing();
void Bill();
void BillPrint();
};
```

(i) Which type of Inheritance out of the following is illustrated in the above example?

- Single Level Inheritance.
- Multi Level Inheritance.

- Multiple Inheritance.

Ans. Multi Level Inheritance

(1 Mark for mentioning correct option)

(ii) Write the names of all the data members, which are directly accessible from the member functions of class Painting.

Ans. WallArea, ColorCode, Type, Advance

(1 Mark for correct answer)

Note:

- No marks to be awarded for any partial or additional answer(s).

(iii) Write the names of all the member functions, which are directly accessible from an object of class Billing.

Ans. Bill(), BillPrint(), PBook(), PView(), Book(), View()

(1 Mark for correct answer)

Note: No marks to be awarded for any partial/additional answer(s)

- Constructors can be ignored.

(iv) What will be the order of execution of the constructors, when an object of class Billing is declared?

Ans. Interior, Painting, Billing

(1 Mark for correct answer)

Note: No marks to be awarded for any other order

3.

a) Write the definition of a function Change(int P[], int N) in C++, which should change all the multiples of 10 in the array to 10 and rest of the elements as 1. For example, if an array of 10 integers is as follows. **(2)**

P[0]	P[1]	P[2]	P[3]	P[4]	P[5]	P[6]	P[7]	P[8]	P[9]
100	43	20	56	32	91	80	40	45	21

After executing the function, the array content should be changed as follows:

P[0]	P[1]	P[2]	P[3]	P[4]	P[5]	P[6]	P[7]	P[8]	P[9]
10	1	10	1	1	1	10	10	1	1

Ans.
```
void Change(int P[ ],int N)
{
for (int i=0;i<N;i++)
if(P[i]%10==0)
P[i]=10;
else
```

P[i]=1;

}

OR

Any other correct equivalent function definition (½ Mark for correct loop)

(½ Mark for correct checking of divisibility of array elements by 10)

(½ Mark for correct use of else OR correct checking of non divisibility of array elements by 10)

(½ Mark for correct assignment of 10 and 1 for multiples and non multiples of 10 respectively)

b) A two dimensional array ARR[50][20] is stored in the memory along the row with each of its elements occupying 4 bytes. Find the address of the element ARR[30][10], if the element ARR[10] [5] is stored at the memory location 15000. **(3)**

Ans. Loc(ARR[I][J]) along the row

=BaseAddress + W [(I – LBR)*C + (J – LBC)]

(where C is the number of columns, LBR = LBC = 0 LOC(ARR[10][5])

= BaseAddress + W [I*C + J]

15000 = BaseAddress + 4[10*20 + 5]

=BaseAddress + 4[200 + 5]

=BaseAddress + 4 x 205

=BaseAddress + 820 BaseAddress = 15000820

=14180

LOC(ARR[30][10])= 14180 + 4[30 * 20 + 10]

=14180 + 4 * 610

=14180 + 2440

=16620

OR

LOC(ARR[30][10])

=LOC(ARR[10][5])+ W[(ILBR)*C + (JLBC)]

=15000 + 4[(3010)*20 + (105)]

=15000 + 4[20*20 + 5]

=15000 + 4 *405

=15000 + 1620

=16620

OR

Where C is the number of columns and LBR=LBC=1

LOC(ARR[10][5])

15000 = BaseAddress + W [(I1)*C + (J1)]

=BaseAddress + 4[9*20 + 4]

=BaseAddress + 4[180 + 4]

=BaseAddress + 4 * 184

= BaseAddress + 736 BaseAddress = 15000 736

=14264

LOC(ARR[30][10])

=14264 + 4[(301)*20 + (101)]

=14264 + 4[29*20 + 9]

=14264 + 4[580 + 9]

=14264 + 4*589

=14264 + 2356=16620

(1 Mark for writing correct formula (for row major) OR substituting formula with correct values).

(1 Mark for at least one step of intermediate calculation).

(1 Mark for final correct address).

c) Write the definition of a member function PUSH() in C++, to add a new book in a dynamic stack of BOOKS considering the following code is already included in the program: (4)

```
struct BOOKS
{
char ISBN[20], TITLE[80];
BOOKS *Link;
};
class STACK
{
BOOKS *Top;
public:
STACK()
{Top=NULL;}
void PUSH();
```

```
void POP();
~STACK();
};
```

Ans. void STACK::PUSH()

```
{
BOOKS *Temp;
Temp=new BOOKS;
gets(Temp>ISBN);
gets(Temp>TITLE);
Temp>Link=Top;
Top=Temp;
}
```

OR

Any other correct equivalent function definition

(1 Mark for creating a new node of BOOKS dynamically)

(½ Mark for entering value of ISBN)

(½ Mark for entering value of TITLE)

(1 Mark for linking the new node of BOOKS to the Top)

(1 Mark for making the new node of BOOKS as Top)

d) Write a function REVROW (int P[][5],int N, int M) in C++ to display the content of a two dimensional array, with each row content in reverse order. (3)

For example, if the content of array is as follows

15	12	56	45	51
13	91	92	87	63
11	23	61	46	81

The function should display output as:

51	45	56	12	15
63	87	92	91	13
81	46	61	23	81

Ans. void REVROW(int P[][5],int N,int M)

```
{
for(int I=0; I<N; I++)
{for(int J=M1; J>=0; J) cout<<P[I][J];
cout<<endl;
}
```

```
}
```

OR

```
void REVROW(int P[ ][5],int N,int M)
{
for(int I=0; I<N; I++)
{
for(int J=0; J<M/2; J++)
{
int T = P[I][J];
P[I][J] = P[I][MJ1];
P[I][MJ1] = T;
}
}
for(I=0; I<N; I++)
{
for(int J=0; J<M; J++)
cout<<P[I][J];
cout<<endl;
}
}
```

(1 Mark for correct nesting of loop(s))

(1½ Mark for correct logic for reversing the content of each row)

(½ Mark for correctly displaying the content)

Note: N and M can be written interchangeably for number of rows and columns

e) Convert the following infix expression to its equivalent Postfix expression, showing the stack contents for each step of conversion. (2)

U * V + R/ (ST)

U * V + R/ (ST)

=((U * V)+(R/(ST)))

Ans.

Element	Stack	Postfix
(		
(		
U		U
/*	*	
V		UV
)		UV*
+	+	
(		
R		UV*RS
/	+/	
(		
S		UV*RST
-		
T		UV*RST
)		UV*RST-
)		UV*RST-\
)		UV*RST-/+

OR

Element	Stack	Postfix
U		U
*	*	U
V	*	UV
+	+	UV*
V	+	UV*R
+	+/	UV*R
R	+/(	UV*R
/	+/(	UV*RS
R	+/(-	UV*RS
/	+/(-	UV*RST
(	+/	UV*RST-
S	+	UV*RST-\

Table missing

OR

Any other method for converting the given Infix expression to its equivalent Postfix expression showing stack contents.

(½ mark for converting expression up to each operator).

OR

(1 mark to be given for writing correct answer without showing the stack content).

4.

a) **Write function definition for TOWER() in C++ to read the content of a text file WRITEUP.TXT, count the presence of word TOWER and display the number of occurrences of this word.** **(2)**

Note:

- The word TOWER should be an independent word.
- Ignore type cases (i.e. lower/upper case).

Example:

If the content of the file WRITEUP.TXT is as follows:

Tower of hanoi is an interesting problem.

Mobile phone tower is away from here. Views from EIFFEL TOWER are amazing.

The function TOWER () should display the following:

Ans.
```
void TOWER()
{
int count=0;
ifstream f("WRITEUP.TXT");
char s[20];
while (!f.eof())
{
f>>s;
if (strcmpi(s,"TOWER")==0)
count++;
}
cout<<count;
f.close();
}
```

OR

Any other correct function definition.

(½ Mark for opening WRITEUP.TXT correctly).

(½ Mark for reading each word (using any method) from the file).

(½ Mark for comparing the word with TOWER).

(½ Mark for displaying correct count of TOWER).

NOTE:

(½ Mark to be deducted if TOWER is compared without ignoring the case).

b) Write a definition for function COSTLY() in C++ to read each record of a binary file GIFTS.DAT, find and display those items, which are priced more than 2000. Assume that the file GIFTS.DAT is created with the help of objects of class GIFTS, which is defined below. (3)

```
class GIFTS
{
int CODE;char ITEM[20]; float PRICE;
public:
void Procure()
{
cin>>CODE; gets(ITEM);cin>>PRICE;
}
void View()
{
cout<<CODE<<":"<<ITEM<<":"<<PRICE<<endl;
}
float GetPrice() {return PRICE;}
};
```

Ans. void COSTLY()

```
{
GIFTS G;
ifstream fin("GIFTS.DAT",ios::binary);
while (fin.read((char *)&G,sizeof(G)))
{
```

```
if(G.GetPrice()>2000)
G.View();
}
fin.close();
}
```

OR

Any other correct equivalent function definition.

(½ Mark for opening GIFTS.DAT correctly).

(1 Mark for reading all records from the file).

(1 Mark for checking value of PRICE > 2000).

(½ Mark for displaying the desired items).

c) **Find the output of the following C++ code considering that the binary file MEMBER.DAT exists on the hard disk with records of 100 members. (1)**

```
class MEMBER
{
int Mno; char Name[20];
public:
void In();void Out();
};
void main()
{
fstream MF;
MF.open("MEMBER.DAT",ios::binary|ios::in);
MEMBER M;
MF.read((char*)&M,sizeof(M));
MF.read((char*)&M,sizeof(M));
MF.read((char*)&M,sizeof(M));
int POSITION=MF.tellg()/sizeof(M);
cout<<"PRESENT RECORD:"<<POSITION<<endl;
MF.close();
}
```

Ans. PRESENT RECORD: 3

(1 Mark for writing PRESENT RECORD: 3)

OR

(1 Mark for writing only 3)

OR

(½ Mark for writing only PRESENT RECORD:)

Section-B

(Only for Python Candidates)

1.

a) How is _init( ) _different from _del ( )_ ? **(2)**

Ans. _init_()is the class constructor or initialization method which is automatically invoked when we create a new instance of a class.

del() is a destructor which is automatically invoked when an object (instance) goes out of

scope.

For Example:

```
class Sample:
def __init__(self):
self.data = 79
print('Data:',self.data,'created')
def __del__(self):
print('Data:',self.data,'deleted')
s = Sample()
del s
```

(2 Marks for correct differentiation).

OR

(2 Marks for differentiation through example).

OR

(1 Mark for each correct definition).

b) Name the function/method required to **(1)**

I. **check if a string contains only alphabets.**

II. **give the total length of the list.**

Ans. isalpha()

len()

(½ Mark for each correct function/ method name).

c) Rewrite the following code in python after removing all syntax error(s). Underline each correction done in the code. **(2)**

```
def Sum(Count) #Method to find sum
S=0
for I in Range(1,Count+1):
S+=I
RETURN S
print Sum[2] #Function Call
print Sum[5]
```

Ans. def Sum(Count):#Method to find sum #Error 1

```
S=0
for I in range (1,Count+1):  #Error 2
S+=I
returnS  #Error 3
print Sum(2)#Function Call #Error 4
print Sum(5)#Error 4
```

(½ Mark for each correction)

OR

(1 mark for identifying all the errors, without suggesting corrections)

d) Find and write the output of the following python code. **(2)**

```
for Name in ['John','Garima','Seema','Karan']:
print Name
if Name[0]== 'S':
break
else:
print 'Completed!'
print 'Weldone!'
```

Ans. John

Garima

Seema

Weldone!

(½ Mark for each correct line)

Note:

Deduct ½ Mark for not considering any or all line breaks at proper place(s)

e) Find and write the output of the following python code. (3)

class Emp:

def _init_(self,code,nm): #constructor self.Code=code

self.Name=nm def Manip (self) : self.Code=self.Code+10 self.Name='Karan' def Show(self,line):

print self.Code,self.Name,line

s=Emp(25,'Mamta')

s.Show(1)

s.Manip()

s.Show(2)

print s.Code+len(s.Name)

Ans. 25 Mamta 1

35 Karan 2

40

(1 Mark for each correct line)

Note:

Deduct ½ Mark for not considering any or all line break(s) at proper place(s).

f) What are the possible outcome(s) executed from the following code? Also specify the maximum and minimum values that can be assigned to variable COUNT.

TEXT="CBSEONLINE"

COUNT=random.randint(0,3)

C=9

while TEXT[C]!='L':

print TEXT[C]+TEXT[COUNT]+'*',

COUNT=COUNT+1

C=C1

(i)	(ii)	(iii)	(iv)
EC*NB*IS*	NS*IE*LO*	ES*NE*IO*	LE*NO*ON*

Ans.

(i) EC*NB*IS*

(iii) ES*NE*IO*

Minimum COUNT = 0 Maximum COUNT = 3

(½ Mark for writing option (i))

(½ Mark for writing option (iii))

Note:

- Deduct ½ mark for writing each addition aloption along with both correct options (½ Mark for writing correct Minimum value of COUNT) (½ Mark for writing correct Maximum value of COUNT).

2.

a) Illustrate the concept inheritance with the help of a python code. (2)

Ans. class Base:

```
def __init__ (self):
print "Base Constructor at work..."
def show(self):
print "Hello Base"
class Der(Base):
def __init__(self):
print "Derived Constructor at work..."
def display(self):
print "Hello from Derived"
```

(1 Mark for base class)

(1 Mark for derived class)

b) What will be the output of the following python code? Explain the try and except used in the code. (2)

```
A=0
B=6
print 'One'
try:
print 'Two'
X=B/A
Print 'Three'
except ZeroDivisionError:
```

print B*2

print 'Four'

except:

print B*3

print 'Five'

Ans. One

Two

12

Four

The code written within try triggers the exception written after except Zero Division Error: in case there is a division by zero error otherwise the default exception is executed.

OR

Any other correct explanation for usage of try and except (½ Mark for first two lines of correct output) (½ Mark for next two lines of correct output).

(½ Mark each for correct explanation of try and except).

c) Write a class PHOTO in Python with following specifications. (4)

Instance Attributes

Pno # Numeric value

Category # String value

Exhibit # Exhibition Gallery with String value

Methods:

FixExhibit() # A method to assign Exhibition

Gallery as per Category as

shown in the following table

Category	Exhibit
Antique	Zaveri
Modern	Johnsen
Classic	Terenida

Register() # A function to allow user

to enter values of Pno, Category

and call FixExhibit() method

ViewAll{} # A function to display all the data

members

Ans. class PHOTO:

```
Pno=0
Category=" "
Exhibit=" "
def FixExhibit():
if self.Category=="Antique":
self.Exhibit="Zaveri"
elif self.Category=="Modern":
self.Exhibit="Johnsen"
elif self.Category=="Classic":
self.Exhibit="Terenida"
def Register():
self.Pno=int(input("Enter Pno:"))
self.Category=input("Enter Name:")
self.FixExhibit()
def ViewAll()
print self.Pno,self.Category,self.Exhibit
```

(½ Mark for correct syntax for class header).

(½ Mark for correct declaration of instance attributes).

(1 Mark for correct definition of FixExhibit()).

(1 Mark for correct definition of Register() with proper invocation of FixExhibit() method).

(1 Mark for correct definition of ViewAll()).

NOTE:

Deduct ½ Mark if FixExhibit() is not invoked properly inside Register() method

d) What is operator overloading with methods? Illustrate with the help of an example using a python code. (2)

Ans. Operator overloading is an ability to use an operator in more than one form.

Examples:

In the following example operator + is used for finding the sum of two integers:

```
a = 7
b = 5
print(a+b) # gives the output: 12
```

Whereas in the next example, shown below the same + operator is used to add two strings:

```
a = 'Indian '
```

b = 'Government'

print(a+b) # gives the output: Indian Government

(1 Mark for correct definition of Operator overloading)

(1 Mark for correct example of Python code to illustrate Operator overloading)

e) Write a method in python to display the elements of list twice, if it is a number and display the element terminated with '*' if it is not a number. (2)

For example, if the content of list is as follows:

MyList=['RAMAN','21','YOGRAJ', '3', 'TARA']

The output should be

RAMAN*

2121

YOGRAJ*

33

TARA*

Ans. def fun(L):

for I in L:

if I.is numeric():

print(2*I) # equivalently: print(I+I)

else:

print(I+'*')

(½ Mark for correct loop)

(½ Mark for checking numeric/non numeric)

(½ Mark for displaying numeric content)

(½ Mark for displaying numeric content)

3.

a) What will be the status of the following list after fourth pass of bubble sort and fourth pass of selection sort used for arranging the following elements in descending order? (3)

34,6,12,3,45,25

Ans. Bubble Sort

34,6,12,3,45,25 (Original Content)

i. 34,12,3,45,25,6

ii. 34,12,45,25,3,6

iii. 34,45,25,12,3,6

iv. 45,34,25,12,3,6 Selection Sort

34,6,12,3,45,25 (Original Content)

i. 45,6,12,3,34,25

ii. 45,34,12,3,6,25

iii. 45,34,25,3,6,12

iv. 45,34,25,12,6,3 (Unsorted status after 4th pass).

For Bubble Sort

(1 ½ Mark if (iv) pass is correct).

OR

(½ Mark for (i) pass).

(½ Mark for (ii) pass).

(½ Mark for (iii) pass).

For Selection Sort.

(1 ½ Mark if (iv) pass is correct).

OR

(½ Mark for (i) pass).

(½ Mark for (ii) pass).

(½ Mark for (iii) pass).

b) Write a method in python to search for a value in a given list (assuming that the elements in list are in ascending order) with the help of Binary Search method. The method should return -1, if the value not present else it should return position of the value present in the list. **(2)**

Ans. def bSearch(L, key):

low = 0

high = len(L)1

found = False

while (low <= high) and (not found):

mid = (low+high)//2

if L[mid] == key:

found = True

elif L[mid] < key:

low = mid + 1

else:

high = mid 1

```
if found:
return mid+1 # may even be 'return mid'
else:
return 1
```

(½ Mark for correct Initialization of lower and upper bounds).

(½ Mark for correct loop).

(½ Mark for reassigning Mid, Low, Up bound).

(½ Mark for returning correct value).

c) Write PUSH (Names) and POP (Names) methods in python to add Names and Remove names considering them to act as Push and Pop operations of Stack. (4)

Ans.
```
def push(Name):
Stack.append(Name)
print 'Element:',Name,'inserted successfully'
def pop():
if Stack == []:
print('Stack is empty!')
else:
print('Deleted element is',Stack.pop())
```

(2 Marks for correctly pushing an element into the stack).

(1 Mark for checking empty stack in POP())

(1 Mark for popping element from stack).

d) Write a method in python to find and display the composite numbers between 2 to N. Pass N as argument to the method. (3)

Ans.
```
def composite_numbers(N):
for I in range(2, N+1):
M = I // 2
for J in range(2, M+1):
if I % J == 0:
print(I)
break
```

OR

Any other correct equivalent method definition (1 Mark for correct loops).

(1 Mark for checking composite numbers between 2 to N).

(1 Mark for displaying the numbers).

e) Evaluate the following postfix notation of expression. Show status of stack after every operation. (2)

34,23,+,4,5,*,

Ans.

Element	Stack
34	34
23	34, 23
+	57
4	57, 4
5	57, 4, 5
*	57, 20
-	37

(1 mark for evaluating till 57).

(½ mark for evaluating till 57, 20).

(½ mark for evaluating till final 37).

Note:

Only 1 mark to be awarded for evaluating final answer as 37 without showing stack contents.

4.

a) Differentiate between the following. (1)

(i) f = open ('diary. txt', 'a')

(ii) f = open ('diary. txt', 'w') 1

Ans.

(i) diary.txt is opened for writing data at the end of file.

(ii) diary.txt is opened for writing data from the beginning of file in create mode (1 mark for writing correct difference).

OR

(½ Mark for each correct explanation of (i) and (ii))

b) Write a method in python to read the content from a text file story.txt line by line and display the same on screen. (2)

Ans. def read_file():

inFile = open('story.txt', 'r')

for line in inFile:

print line

(½ Mark for opening the file)

(1 Mark for reading all lines)

(½ Mark for displaying all lines)

c) **Consider the following definition of class Student. Write method in python to write the content in a pickled file student.dat. (3)**

```
class Student:
def_init_(self,A,N} :
self.Admno=A
self.Name=N
def Show(self}:
print (self.Admno, "#" , self.Name}
```

Ans. import pickle

```
class Student:
def __init__(self, A, N):
self.Admno = A
self.Name = N
def show(self):
print(self.Admno,"#",self.Name)
def store_data(self):
piFile = open('student.dat','wb')
pickle.dump(self, piFile)
piFile.close()
```

(1 Mark for method header).

(1 Mark for opening the file student.dat in correct mode).

(1 Mark each for writing student details into the file).

Section-C (For all candidates)

5.

a) Observe the following table carefully and write the names of the most appropriate columns, which can be considered as: (2)

(i) candidate keys and (ii) primary key.

Code	Item	Qty	Price	Transaction
1001	Plastic Folder 14"	100	3400	2014-12-14
1004	Pen Stand Standard	200	4500	2015-01-31
1005	Stapler Mini	250	1200	2015-02-28
1009	Punching Machine Small	200	1400	2015-03-12
1003	Stapler Big	100	1500	2015-02-02

Ans. Candidate keys: Code, Item

Primary keys: Code

(1 Mark for writing correct Candidate keys).

(1 Mark for writing correct Primary key).

Note:

No marks to be deducted for mentioning Price and/or Transaction Date as additional candidate keys.

b) Consider the following DEPT and EMPLOYEE tables. Write SQL queries for(i)to (iv) and find outputs for SQL queries (v)to (viii). (6)

Table: DEPT

DCODE	DEPARTMENT	LOCATION
D01	INFRASTRUCTURE	DELHI
D02	MARKETING	DELHI
D03	MEDIA	MUMBAI
D04	FINANCE	KOLKATA
D05	HUMAN RESOURCE	MUMBAI

Table: EMPLOYEE

ENO	NAME	DOJ	DOB	GENDER	DCODE
1001	George K	20130902	19910901	MALE	D01
1002	Ryma Sen	20121211	19901215	FEMALE	D03
1003	Mohitesh	20130203	19870904	MALE	D05
1007	Anil Jha	20140117	19841019	MALE	D04
1004	Manila Sahai	20121209	19861114	FEMALE	D01
1005	R SAHAY	20131118	19870331	MALE	D02
1006	Jaya Priya	20140609	19850623	FEMALE	D05

Note: DOJ refers to date of joining and DOB refers to date of Birth of employees.

(i) To display Eno, Name, Gender from the table EMPLOYEE in ascending order of Eno.

Ans. SELECTEno, Name, Gender FROM Employee ORDER BY Eno;

(½ Mark for SELECT Eno, Name, Gender FROM Employee).

(½ Mark for ORDER BY Eno).

(ii) To display the Name of all the MALE employees from the table EMPLOYEE. Ans. SELECT Name FROM Employee WHERE Gender='MALE';

(½ Mark for SELECT Name FROM Employee).

(½ Mark for WHERE Gender='MALE').

(iii) To display the Eno and Name of those employees from the table EMPLOYEE who are born between '1987-01-01' and '1991-12-01'.

Ans. SELECT Eno,Name FROM Employee

WHERE DOB BETWEEN '19870101' AND '19911201'

OR

SELECT Eno,Name FROM Employee

WHERE DOB >='19870101' AND DOB <='19911201';

OR

SELECT Eno,Name FROM Employee

WHERE DOB >'19870101' AND DOB <'19911201';

(½ Mark for SELECT Eno,Name FROM Employee).

(½ Mark for WHERE DOB BETWEEN '19870101' AND '19911201' OR

WHERE DOB >='19870101' AND DOB <='19911201' OR

WHERE DOB >'19870101' AND DOB <'19911201').

(iv) To count and display FEMALE employees who have joined after '1986-01-01'.

Ans. SELECT count(*) FROM Employee

WHERE GENDER='FEMALE' AND DOJ > '19860101';

OR

SELECT * FROM Employee

WHERE GENDER='FEMALE' AND DOJ > '19860101';

(Any valid query for counting and/or displaying for female employees will be awarded 1 mark).

(v) SELECT COUNT (*),DCODE FROM EMPLOYEE GROUP BY DCODE HAVING COUNT(*)>1;

Ans. COUNTDCODE

2D01

2D05

(½ Mark for correct output)

(vi) SELECT DISTINCT DEPARTMENT FROM DEPT;

Ans. Department

INFRASTRUCTURE

MARKETING

MEDIA

FINANCE

HUMAN RESOURCE

(½ Mark for correct output)

(vii) SELECT NAME, DEPARTMENT FROM EMPLOYEE E, DEPT D WHERE E.DCODE=D.DCODE AND EN0<1003;

Ans. NAME DEPARTMENT

George K INFRASTRUCTURE

Ryma Sen MEDIA

(½ Mark for correct output)

(viii) SELECT MAX(DOJ), MIN(DOB) FROM EMPLOYEE;

Ans. MAX(DOJ) MIN(DOB)

20140609 19841019

(½ Mark for correct output)

Note: In the output queries, please ignore the order of rows.

6.

a) Verify the following using Boolean Laws. **(2)**

U'+ V= U'V'+U'.V +U.V

Ans. L.H.S

=U'+ V

=U'.(V+V')+ V.(U'+ U)

=U'.V + U'.V' + U'.V + U.V

=U'.V+U'.V'+U.V

=R.H.S

OR

R.H.S

=U'V'+U'.V +U.V

=U'.(V'+ V)+ U.V

=U'.1 + U.V

=U'+ U.V

=U'+ V

=L.H.S

(2 Marks for any valid verification using Boolean Laws)

OR

(1 Mark for partial correct verification using Boolean Laws)

b) Draw the Logic Circuit for the following Boolean Expression. **(2)**

(X'+Y).Z+W' 2

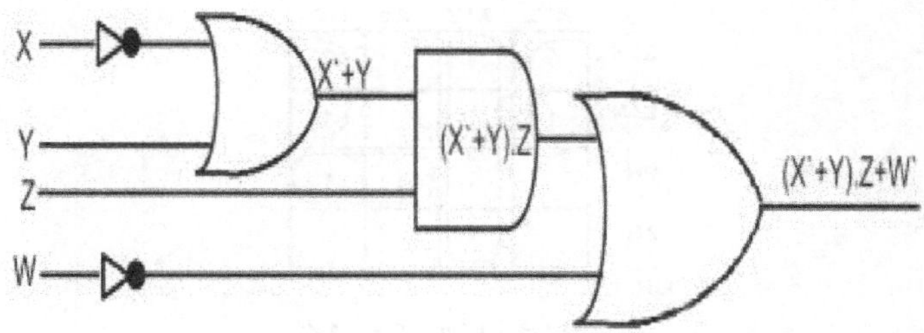

Ans.

(½ Mark for X' and W')

(½ Mark for (X'+Y))

(½ Mark for (X'+Y).Z)

(½ Mark for (X'+Y).Z+W')

c) Derive a Canonical POS expression for a Boolean function F, represented by the following truth table. **(1)**

P	Q	R	F(P, Q, R)
0	0	0	1
0	0	1	0
0	1	0	0
0	1	1	1
1	0	0	1
1	0	1	0
1	1	0	0
1	1	1	1

Ans. F(P,Q,R)= (P+Q+R')(P+Q'+R)(P'+Q+R')(P'+Q'+R)

OR

F(P,Q,R)= Π (1,2,5,6)

(1 Mark for the correct POS form)

OR

(½ Mark for writing any two term correctly)

Note: Deduct ½ mark if wrong variable names are used

d) **Reduce the following Boolean Expression to its simplest form using K-Map. (3)**

F(X,Y,Z,W) = ∑(0,1,4,5,6,7,8,9,11,15)

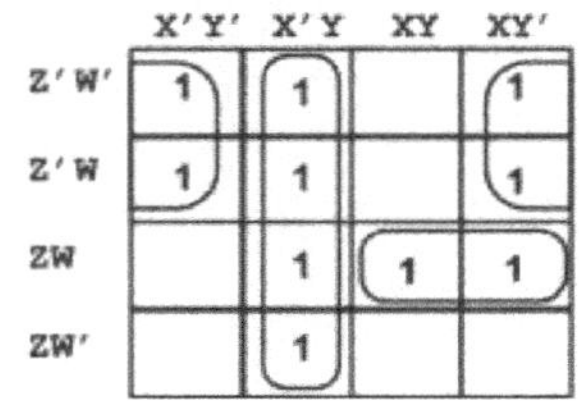

OR

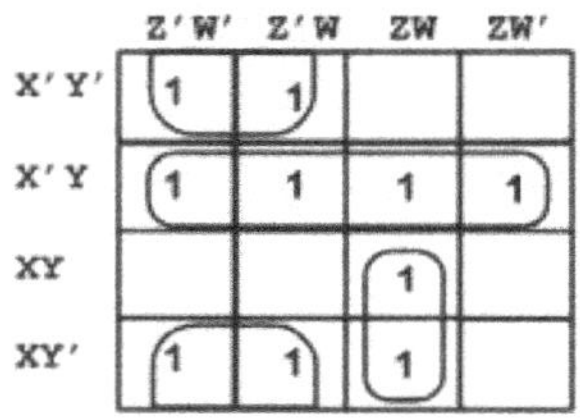

Simplified Expression: Y'Z' + X'Y + XZW

(½ Mark for drawing K-Map with correct variable names)

(½ Mark for placing all 1s at correct positions in K-Map)

(½ Mark for each of three grouping Y'Z' , X'Y , XZW)

(½ Mark for writing final expression in reduced/minimal/non redundant form as Y'Z' + X'Y + XZW)

Note: Deduct ½ mark if wrong variable names are used

7.

a) **Illustrate the layout for connecting 5 computers in a Bus and a Star topology of Networks.** **(1)**

Bus topology

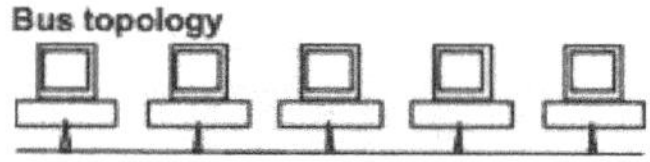

Star Topology

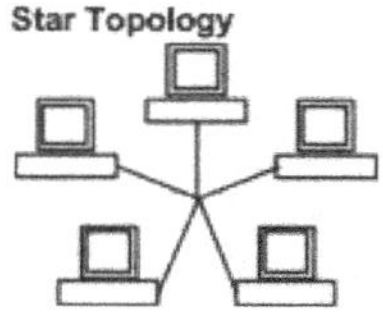

Ans.

OR any valid illustration of Bus and Star Topology.

(½ Mark for drawing each correct layout).

b) What kind of data gets stored in cookies and how is it useful? (1)

Ans. When a Website with cookie capabilities is visited, its server sends certain information about the browser, which is stored in the hard drive as a text file. It's a way for the server to remember things about the visited sites.

(1 Mark for correct kind of data stored).

c) Differentiate between packet switching over message switching? (1)

Ans. Packet Switchingfollows store and forward principle for fixed packets. Fixes an upper limit for packet size.

Message Switchingfollows store and forward principle for complete message. No limit on block size.

(1 Mark for any valid differentiation)

OR

(1 Mark for correct definition of Packet Switching only)

d) Out of the following, which is the fastest (i) wired and (ii) wireless medium of communication?

Infrared, Coaxial Cable, Ethernet Cable, Microwave, Optical Fiber (1)

Ans. (i) Wired – Optical Fiber.

(ii) Wireless - Infrared OR Microwave.

(½ Mark each for Wired and Wireless medium of communication).

e) What is Trojan Horse? (1)

Ans. A Trojan Horse is a code hidden in a program, that looks safe but has hidden side effects typically causing loss or theft of data, and possible system harm.

(1 Mark for writing correct meaning of Trojan)

f) Out of the following, which all comes under cyber crime? (1)

(i) Stealing away a brand new hard disk from a showroom.

(ii) Getting in someone's social networking account without his consent and posting on his behalf.

(iii) Secretly copying data from server of a organization and selling it to the other organization.

(iv) Looking at online activities of a friends blog.

Ans. (ii) & (iii)

(½ Mark for choosing each of the correct options)

Note:

- No marks to be given, if all options are there in the answer.
- ½ Mark to be deducted, if one extra option is given along with the correct options.

g) Xcelencia Edu Services Ltd. is an educational organization. It is planning to set up its India campus at Hyderabad with its head office at Delhi. The Hyderabad campus has 4 main buildings - ADMIN, SCIENCE, BUSINESS and MEDIA.

You as a network expert have to suggest the best network related solutions for their problems raised in (i) to (iv), keeping in mind the distances between the buildings and other given parameters.

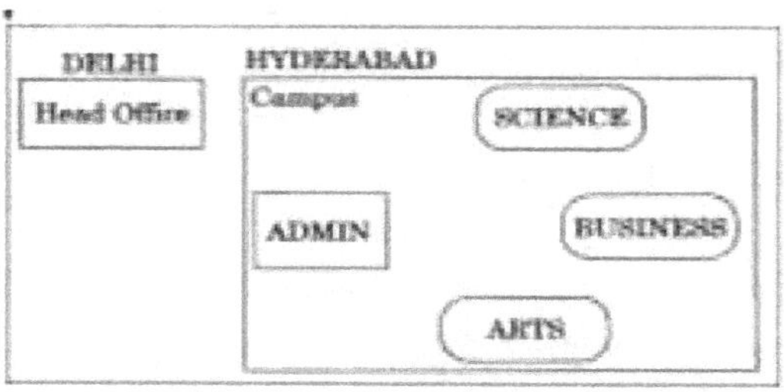

Shortest Distances between various buildings

ADMIN to SCIENCE	65M
ADMIN to BUSINESS	100M
ADMIN to ARTS	60M
SCIENCE to BUSINESS	75M
SCIENCE to ARTS	60M
BUSINESS to ARTS	50M
DELHI Head Office to HYDERABAD Campus	1600KM

Number of Computers installed at various building are as follows:

ADMIN	100
SCIENCE	85
BUSINESS	40
ARTS	12
DELHI Head Office	20

(i) Suggest the most appropriate location of the server inside the HYDERABAD campus (out of the 4 buildings), to get the best connectivity for maximum no. of computers. Justify your answer.

(1)

Ans. ADMIN (due to maximum number of computers).

OR

ARTS(due to shorter distance from the other buildings).

(1 Mark for mentioning Correct building name with reason).

OR

(½ Mark to be deducted for not giving reason).

(ii) Suggest and draw the cable layout to efficiently connect various buildings 'within the HYDERABAD campus for connecting the computers. **(1)**

Ans. Any one of the following

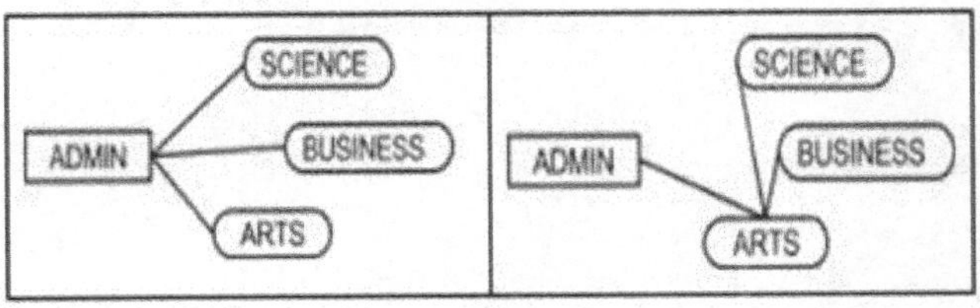

(1 Mark for drawing correct layout)

(iii) Which hardware device will you suggest to be procured by the company to be installed to protect and control the internet uses within the campus? **(1)**

Ans. Firewall OR Router

(1 Mark for correct Answer)

(iv) Which of the following will you suggest to establish the online face-to-face communication between the people in the Admin Office of HYDERABAD campus and DELHI Head Office? **(1)**

(a) E-mail (b) Text Chat (c) Video Conferencing (d) Cable TV

Ans. Video Conferencing

(1 Mark for correct Option/Answer).

CBSE Class 12 Computer Science

Section-A

(Only for Candidates, Who Opted for C++)

1.

a) Out of the following, find those identifiers, which cannot be used for naming Variable, Constants or Functions in a C++ program. (2)

Total*Tax, double, Case, My Name,

NeW, switch, Column31, _Amount

Ans. Total*Tax double My Name switch

(1/2 Mark for each correct name)

Note: Deduct 1/2 Mark for each wrong name written

b) Ronica Jose has started learning C++ and has typed the following program. When she compiled the following code written by her, she discovered that she needs to include some header files to successfully compile and execute it. Write the names of those header files, which are required to be included in the code

```
void main()
{
double X,Times,Result;
cin>>X>>Times;
Result=pow (X,Times) ;
cout<<Result<<endl;
```

Ans.

- iostream.h OR iomanip.h
- math.h

  (1/2 Mark for writing each correct header file) Note:

- Ignore any other header files, if mentioned.
- complex. h is acceptable in place of math.h

c) Rewrite the following C++ code after removing any/all syntactical errors with each correction underlined. (2)

Note: Assume all required header files are already being included in the program.

```
#define Formula(a,b) = 2*a+b
void main()
```

```
{
float X=3.2; Y=4.1;
Z=Formula(X,Y);
cout<<'Result='<<Z<<endl;
}
```

Ans. #define Formula(arb) 2*a+b

```
void main()
{
float X=3.2 , Y=4.1;
float Z=Formula(X,Y);
cout<<"Result="<<Z<<endl;
}
```

(1/2 Mark for each correction)

OR

(1 mark for identifying the errors, without suggesting corrections)

d) Find and write the output of the following C++ program code. **(2)**

Note: Assume all required header files are already included in the program,

```
typedef char TEXT[80];
void JumbleUp(TEXT T)
{
int L=strlen(T);
for (int C=0;C<L-1;C+=2)
{
char CT=T[C];
T[C]=T[C+1];
T[C+1]=CT;
}
for (C=I;C<L;C+=2)
if (T[C]>='M' && T[C]<='U')
T[C]='6';
}
void main()
{
TEXT S tr="HAEMONIOUS";
```

```
JumbleUp(Str) ;
cout<<Str<<endl;
}
```

Ans. AHM@N@OIS@

(2 Marks for correct output)

OR

(1/2 Mark for each of two correct consecutive characters not exceeding 11A marks)

e) Find and write the output of the following C++ program code. (3)

Note: Assume all required header files are already being included in the program,

```
class Share
{
long int Code;
float Rate;
int DD;
public:
Share(){Code=I0 0 0;Rate=I0 0;DD=I;}
void GetCode(long int C,float R)
{
Code=C;
Rate=R;
}
void Update(int Change,int D)
{
Rate+=Change;
DD=D;
}
void Status()
cout<<"Date:"<<DD<<endl; cout<<Code<<"#"<<Rate<<endl; };
void main()
{
Share S,T,U;
S.GetCode(1324,350) ;
T.GetCode(1435,250) ;
S.Update(50,28) ;
```

```
U.Update(-25,26);
S.Status();
T.Status();
U.Status();
}
```

Ans. Date:28

1324#400

Date:1

1435#250

Date:26

1000#75

(1/2 Mark for each correct line of output)

Note

- Deduct only 1/2 Mark for not writing any or all 'Date' OR ':' OR '#' symbol(s).
- Deduct 1/2 Mark for not considering any or all endl(s) at proper place(s).

f) **Look at the following C++ code and find the possible output(s) from the options (i) to (iv) Following it. Also, write the maximum and the minimum values that can be assigned to the variable PICKER.** **(2)**

Note: Assume all the required header files are already being included in the code. - The function random(n) generates an integer between 0 and n-1.

```
void main()
{
randomize(); int
PICKER;
PICKER=1+random(3) ;
char COLOR[] [5]={"BLUE","PINK","GREEN","RED"};
for(int I=0;I<=PICKER; 1++)
{
for(int J=0; J<=I;J++)
cout<<COLOR[J];
cout<<endl;
}
}
```

(i)	(ii)	(iii)	(iv)
PINK PINKGREEN PINKGREENRED	BLUE BLUEPINK BLUEPINKGREEN BLUEPINKGREENRED	GREEN GREENRED	BLUE BLUEPINK BLUEPINKGREEN

Ans.	
(ii)	(iv)
BLUE	BLUE
BLUEPINK	BLUEPINK
BLUEPINKGREEN	BLUEPINKGREEN
BLUEPINKGREENRED	

Minimum Value of PICKER = 1

Maximum Value of PICKER = 3

(1 Mark for mentioning both the correct options)

Note: No Mark to be awarded for writing any one additional option with (ii) and (iv).

OR

(1/2 Mark for only (iv))

(1/2 Mark each for Minimum and Maximum Value of PICKER)

2.

a) Write any four important characteristics of Object Oriented Programming? Give example of any one of the characteristics using C++. **(2)**

Ans.

- Encapsulation
- Data Hiding.
- Polymorphism.
- Inheritance.

Example of Encapsulation

```
class student
{
int rno;
char name[2 0]; Public:
void input()
{
cin>>rno;
gets(name);
```

```
}
void output()
{
cout<<rno<<" "<<name<<endl;
}
```

The data members and member functions are wrapped up together(encapsulated) into a single unit called class.

OR

Any other suitable example demonstrating a characteristic of Object Oriented Programming.

(1 Mark for correct names of 4 characteristics of OOP)

OR

(1/2 Mark for correct names of any 2 characteristics of OOP)

(1 Mark for correct example of 1 characteristic)

b) Observe the following C++ code and answer the questions (i) and (ii). Assume all necessary files are included: class BOOK.

```
{
long Code ;
char Title[20];
float Price;
public:
BOOK() //Member Function 1
{
cout<<"Bought"<<endl;
Code=IO;strcpy(Title,"NoTitle");Price=100;
}
BOOK(int C,char T[],float P) //Member Function 2 {
Code=C;
strcpy(Title,T);
Price=P;
}
void Update(float P) //Member Function 3
{
Price+=P;
```

```
}
void Display() //Member Function 4
{
cout<<Code<<":"<<Title<<":"<<Price<<endl;
}
~BOOK() //Member Function 5
{
cout<<"Book Discarded!"<<endl;
}
};
void main() //Line 1
{ //Line 2
BOOK B,C(101,"Truth",350}; //Line 3
for (int I=0;I<4;I++) //Line 4
{ //Line 5 B.Update(50);C.Update(20);
//Line 6 B.Display();C.Display(); //Line 7
} //Line8
} //Line 9
```

i. **Which specific concept of object oriented programming out of the following is illustrated by Member Function 1 and Member Function 2 combined together?** **(1)**

- Data Encapsulation.
- Polymorphism.
- Inheritance.
- Data Hiding.

Ans. Polymorphism

(1Mark for mentioning the correct concept name)

ii. **How many times the message "Book Discarded!" will be displayed after executing the above C++ code? Out of Line 1 to Line 9, which line is responsible to display the message "Book Discarded! "** **(1)**

Ans. 2 times Line 9

(1/2 Mark for writing correct number of times)

OR

(1/2 Mark for writing – "No execution due to wrong syntax in Line 3" OR any other equivalent answer conveying similar meaning)

(1/2 Mark for writing correct line number)

c) Write the definition of a class CITY in C++ with following description. (4)

Private Members

Ccode //Data member for City Code (an integer)

CName //Data member for City Name (a string)

Pop //Data member for Population (a long int)

KM //Data member for Area Coverage (a float)

Density //Data member for Population Density (a float)

DenCal() //A member function to calculate ----

//Density as Pop/KM Public Members

Record() //A function to allow user to enter values of

//Acode,Name,Pop,KM and call DenCal() function

View() //A function to display all the data members

//also display a message "Highly Populated City"

//if the Density is more than 10000 Ans. class CITY

```
{
int Ccode;
char CName[2 0];
long int Pop;
float KM;
float Density;
void DenCal();
public:
void Record();
void View(); };
void CITY::Record()
cin>>Ccode;
gets(CName); //OR cin>>CName;
cin>>Pop;
cin>>KM;
DenCal();
```

```
}
void CITY::View()
{
cout<<Ccode<<CName<<Pop<<KM<<Density; //Ignore endl
if(Density>10000)
cout<<"Highly Populated City"; //Ignore endl
}
void CITY::DenCal()
{
Density= Pop/KM;
}
```

(1/2 Mark for correct syntax for class header)

(1/2 Mark for correctly ending the class declaration with ;)

(1/2 Mark for correct declaration of data members)

(1/2 Mark for correct definition of DenCal() function)

(1 Mark for correct definition of Record() with proper invocation of DenCal() function)

(1 Mark for correct definition of View())

Note:

- Deduct 1/2 Mark if DenCal() is not invoked properly inside Record() function.
- Marks not to be deducted if any or all the member functions are defined inside the class.

d) Answer the questions (i) to (iv) based on the following. (4)

```
class ITEM
int Id;
char IName[2 0];
protected:
float Qty;
public:
ITEM() ;
void Enter(); void View();
};
class TRADER
{
int DCode;
```

```
protected:
char Manager[2 0];
public:
TRADER();
void Enter();
void View();
};
class SALEPOINT : public ITEM,private TRADER {
char Name[20],Location[20];
public :
SALEPOINT();
void EnterAll();
void ViewAll();
};
```

i. **Which type of Inheritance out of the following is illustrated in the above example?**
Single Level Inheritance.

- Multi Level Inheritance.
- Multiple Inheritance.

Ans. Multiple Inheritance

(1 Mark for writing correct option)

ii. **Write the names of all the data members, which are directly accessible from the member functions of class SALEPOINT.**

Ans.

Name, Location, Manager, Qty (1 Mark for correct answer).

Note: No marks to be awarded for any partial answer.

iii. **Write the names of all the member functions, which are directly accessible by an object of class SALEPOINT.**

Ans. EnterAll(), ViewAll(), Enter(), View()

(1 Mark for correct answer)

Note: No marks to be awarded for any partial answer

iv. **What will be the order of execution of the constructors, when an object of class SALEPOINT is declared?**

Ans.

a) ITEM()

b) TRADER()

c) SALEPOINT()

(1 Mark for writing correct order)

- No Marks to be awarded for any other combination/order.
- Names of the constructor/class without parenthesis is acceptable.

3.

a) Write the definition of a function FixSalary(float Salary[], int N) in C++, which should modify each element of the array Salary having N elements, as per the following rules. **(2)**

Existing Salary Values	Required Modification in Value
If less than 100000	Add 35% in the existing value
If >=100000 and <20000	Add 30% in the existing value
If >=200000	Add 20% in the existing value

Ans.
```
void FixSalary(float Salary[ ], int N)
{
for (int i=0;i<N;i++)
if(Salary[i]<100000)
Salary[i]+= 0.35 *Salary[i];
else if (Salary[i]>=100000 && Salary[i]<20000)
Salary[i]+= 0.3 * Salary[i];
else if(Salary[i]>=200000)
Salary[i]+= 0.20 * Salary[i];
}
```

OR

Any other correct equivalent function definition

(1/2 Mark for correctly writing the loop).

(1/2 Mark for correctly checking all conditions).

(1 Mark for correct increment of Salary for all conditions).

OR

(1/2 Mark for checking only one of the conditions correctly)

(1/2 Mark for incrementing only one of the Salary correctly)

Note:

- Marks not to be deducted for writing second condition check for the range as >=100000 && <200000 instead of >=100000 && <20000.
- Marks not to be deducted for incrementing Salary as Salary[i]+=Salary[i]*20/100; OR Salary[i]+=20/100*Salary[i]; and likewise for all increments.

b) R[10][50] is a two dimensional array, which is stored in the memory along the row with each of its element occupying 8 bytes, find the address of the element R[5][15], if the element R[8][10] is stored at the memory location 45000. (3)

Ans.

Loc(R[I][J])

=BaseAddress + W [(I - LBR)*C + (J - LBC)]

(where

W=size of each element = 8 bytes,

R=Niunber of Rows=10, C=Niunber of Columns=50)

Assuming LBR = LBC = 0

LOC(R[8][10])

45000 = BaseAddress + W[I*C + J]

45000 = BaseAddress + 8[8*50 + 10]

45000 = BaseAddress + 8[400 + 10]

45000 = BaseAddress + 8 x 410

BaseAddress = 45000 - 3280

= 41720

LOC(R[5][15])= BaseAddress + W[I*C + J]

41720 + 8 [5*50 + 15]

41720 + 8 [250 + 15]

41720 + 8 x 265

41720 + 2120

43840

Loc(R[I][J])

=Reference Address + W [(I - LR)*C + (J - LC)]

(where

W=size of each element = 8 bytes,

R=Number of Rows=10, C=Number of Columns=50)

Reference Address= Address of given cell R[8][10]=45000

LR = Row value of given cell = 8

LC = Column value of given cell = 10

LOC(R[5][15])= LOC(T[8][10]) + 8[(5 - 8)*50 + (15 - 10)]

LOC(R[15][5]) = 45000 + 8[-3*50 + 5]

45000 + 8 [-150 + 5]

45000 + 8 x (-145)

45000 - 1160

43840

(1 Mark for writing correct formula (for Row major) OR substituting formula with correct values).

(1Mark for correct calculation).

(1 Mark for final correct address).

c) **Write the definition of a member function DELETE() for a class QUEUE in C++, to remove a product from a dynamically allocated Queue of products considering the following code is already written as a part of the program. (4)**

```
struct PRODUCT
{
int PID; char PNAME[20];
PRODUCT *Next;
};
class QUEUE
{
PRODUCT *R,*F; public:
QUEUE(){R=NULL;F=NULL;
}
void INSERT();
void DELETE();
~QUEUE();
};
```

Ans. void QUEUE::DELETE()

```
{
if( F!=NULL)
```

```
{
PRODUCT *T = F;
cout<<T->PID<<T->PNAME;
F=F->Next;
delete T;
if (F==NULL)
{
R=NULL;
}
}
else
cout<<"Queue Empty";
}
```

(1/2 Mark for checking empty queue)

(1/2 Mark for assigning front to temporary pointer)

(1 Mark for reassigning front)

(1 Mark for deleting previous front using temporary pointer)

(1/2 Mark for checking emptied queue after deletion)

(1/2 Mark for assigning rear to NULL if queue was emptied after deletion)

d) Write definition elements of mid R number of row For example, if for a function DISPMID(int A[][5],int R,int C) in C++ to display the elements of middle row and middle column from a two dimensional array A having s and C number of columns. For examples, if the content of array is as follows. (3)

215	912	516	401	515
103	901	921	802	601
285	209	609	360	172

The function should display the following as output 103 901 921 802 601 516 921 609

Ans. void DISPMID(int A[] [5] ,int R,int C)

```
{
for (int J=0;J<C;J++)
```

```
cout<<A [R/2 ] [J]« " ";
cout<<endl;
for (int I=0;I<R;I++)
cout<<A[I][C/2]<< " ";
}
void DISPMID(int A[][5],int R,int C)
if(R%2!=0)
{
for (int J=0;J<C;J++)
cout<<A [R/2 ] [J]« " " ;
}
else
cout<<"No Middle Row";cout<<endl;
if(C%2!=0)
{
for (int I=0;I<R;I++)
cout<<A[I][C/2]<< " ";
}
else
cout<<"No Middle Column";
}
```

OR

Any other correct equivalent function definition

(1/2 Mark for correct loop for displaying middle row elements)

(1 Mark for correct statement to display middle row elements)

(1/2 Mark for correct loop for displaying middle column elements)

(1 Mark for correct statement to display middle column elements)

e) Convert the following Infix expression to its equivalent Postfix expression, showing the stack contents for each step of conversion. (2)

p/(Q-R)*S+T

Ans. P/ (Q-R) *S+T =

(P / (Q-R) * S + T)

Element	Stack of Operators	Postfix Expression
(	(	
P	(	P
/	(/	P
(	(/(	P
Q	(/(	PQ
-	(/(-	PQ
R	(/(-	PQR
)	(/	PQR-
*	(*	PQR-/
S	(*	PQR-/S
+	(+	PQR-/S*
T	(+	PQR-/S*T
)		PQR-/S*T+

= PQR-/S*T+

OR

P/(Q-R)*S+T = (((P / (Q-R)) * S) + T)

Element	Stack of operators	Postfix Expression
(		
(		
(		
P		P
/	/	
(		
Q		PQ
-	/-	
R		PQR
)	/	PQR-
)		PQR-/
*	*	
S		PQR-/S
(		PQR-/S*
+	+	
T		PQR-/S*T
)		PQR-/S*T+
= PQR-/S*T+		

OR

Any other method for converting the given infix expression to its equivalent postfix expression showing stack contents.

(1/2 Mark for correctly converting till each operator)

OR

(1 Mark to be given for writing correct answer without showing the stack content on each step).

4.

a) **Write function definition for DISP3CHAR() in C++ to read the content of a text file KIDINME.TXT, and display all those words, which have three characters in it. Example: If the content of the file KIDINME.TXT is as follows.** **(2)**

When I was a small child, I used to play in the garden with my grand mom. Those days were amazingly funful and I remember all the moments of that time

When I was a small child, I used to play in the garden with my grand mom. Those days were amazingly funful and I remember all the moments of that time.

The function DISP3CHAR() should display the following:

was the mom and all the

Ans.

```
void DISP3CHAR()
{
ifstream Fil;
Fil.open("KIDINME.TXT");
char W[20] ;
Fil>>W;
while(!Fil.eof()) // OR while(Fil)
{
if (strlen(W)) == 3)
cout<<W<< " ";
Fil>>W;
}
Fil.close(); //Ignore
```

}

OR

Any other correct function definition

(1/2 Mark for opening KIDINME. TXT correctly)

(1/2 Mark for reading each word (using any method) from the file)

(1/2 Mark for checking length of the extracted word to be of 3 letters)

(1/2 Mark for displaying the 3 letter extracted word correctly)

Note: No marks to be deducted if words with length 4 and including a '.' is also checked

b) Write a definition for function ONOFFER( ) in C++ to read each object of a binary file TOYS.DAT, find and display details of those toys, which has status as "ON OFFER". Assume that the file TOYS.DAT is created with the help of objects of class TOYS, which is defined below. (3)

```
class TOYS
{
int TID;char Toy[20],Status[20]; float MRP;
public:
void Getinstock()
cin>>TID;gets(Toy);gets(Status);cin>>MRP;
}
void View()
{
cout<<TID<<" : "«Toy«" : "<<MRP<<"" : "<<Status<<endl;
}
char *SeeOffer(){return Status;}.
};
```

Ans. void ONOFFER()

```
{
TOYS T;
ifstream fin;
fin.open("TOYS.DAT", ios::binary);
while(fin.read((char*)&T, sizeof(T)))
{
if(strcmp(T.SeeOffer(),"ON OFFER")==0)
T.View() ;
```

```
}
fin.close(); //Ignore
}
```

OR

Any other correct function definition

(1 Mark for opening TOYS .DAT correctly)

(1/2 Mark for reading records from TOYS.DAT)

(1/2 Mark for comparing Remarks with ON OFFER (ignore case sensitive checking))

(1 Mark for displaying record)

c) Find the output of the following C++ code considering that the binary file CLIENT.DAT exists on the hard disk with a data of 1000 clients. (1)

```
class CLIENT
{
int Ccode;char CName[2 0];
public:
void Register();void Display();
};
void main()
{
fstream CFile;
CFile.open("CLIENT.DAT",ios::binary|ios::in);
CLIENT C;
CFile.read((char*)&C, sizeof (C)) ;
cout<<"Rec:"<<CFile.tellg()/sizeof(C)<<endl;
CFile.read((char*)&C, sizeof (C)) ;
CFile.read((char*)&C, sizeof (C)) ;
cout<<"Rec:"<<CFile.tellg()/sizeof(C)<<endl;
CFile.close();
}
```

Ans. Rec: 1 Rec: 3

(1/2 Mark for each correct value of CFile.tellg()/sizeof(C) as 1 and 3 respectively).

Section-B

(Only for Candidates, Who Opted for Python)

1.

a) **Out of the following, find those identifiers, which cannot be used for naming Variable or Functions in a Python program** **(2)**

Total*Tax, While, class, switch,

3rdRow, finally, Column31, _Total

Ans. Total*Tax, class, 3rdRow, finally

(1/2 Mark for each correct name)

Note: Deduct 1/2 Mark for each wrong name written

b) **Name the Python Library modules which need to be imported to invoke the following functions.** **(1)**

(i) sqrt()

(ii) dump()

Ans.

1. math
2. pickle

(1/2 Mark for writing each correct Library modules) Note: Ignore any other Library modules, if mentioned.

c) **Rewrite the following code in python after removing all syntax error(s). Underline each correction done in the code (2) for Name in**

[Ramesh, Suraj, Priya]

IF Name [0] ='S': print(Name)

Ans. for Name in ["Ramesh", "Suraj", "Priya"] : // ' ' can be used

if Name[0] == 'S' :

print(Name)

(1/2 Mark for each correction)

OR

(1 mark for identifying the errors, without suggesting corrections)

d) Find and write the output of the following python code (2)

Values=[10,20,30,40]

for Val in Values:

for I in range(l, Val%9):

```
print(I,"*",end="")
print ()
```

Ans.

```
                  ()        ()
                  (1, *)    (1 *)
1*                ()        (1 * 2 * 3)
1*                (1, *)    (1 * 2 * 3 *)
2*                (2, *)
1*                ()        1*
2*                (1, *)    1*2*
3*                (2, *)    1*2*3*
                  (3, *)
                  ()
```

(2 marks for correct output)

OR

(1/2 mark for each correct value with '*' not exceeding 2 Marks)

OR

(2 mark for mentioning the syntax error in line print (i,"*",end="") ;

e) Find and write the output of the following python code. **(3)**

```
class Book:
def init (self,N=100,S="Python"): #constructor
self.Bno=N
self.BName=S
def Assign(self, N,S):
self.Bno= self.Bno + N
self.BName= S + self.BName
def ShowVal(self) :
print(self.Bno,"#",self.BName)
s=Book()
t=Book(200)
u=Book(300,"Made Easy")
s.ShowVal()
t.ShowVal()
u.ShowVal()
s.Assign(5, "Made ")
```

```
t.Assign(15,"Easy ")
u.Assign(25,"Made Easy")
s.ShowVal()
t.ShowVal()
u.ShowVal ()
```

Ans.

Python 2.7 output	Other Versions output
100 # Python	(100, '#', 'Python')
200 # Python	(200, '#', 'Python')
300 # Made Easy	(300, '#', 'Made Easy')
105#Made Python	(105, '#', 'Made Python')
215 # Easy Python	(215, '#', 'Easy Python')
325 # Made EasyMade Easy	(325, '#', 'Made EasyMade Easy')

(1/2 Mark for each correct line of output)

Note: • Deduct Vi Mark for not writing any or all '#' symbol(s)

• Deduct Vi Mark for not considering any or all line breaks at proper place(s)

f) What are the possible outcome(s) executed from the following code? Also specify the maximum and minimum values that can be assigned to variable PICKER. (2)

```
import random
PICKER=random.randint(0,3)
COLOR=["BLUE","PINK","GREEN","RED"];
for I in COLOR:
for J in range(l,PICKER):
print(I,end="")
print ()
```

(i)	(ii)	(iii)	(iv)
PINK	BLUEPINK	PINK	PINKPINK
GREEN	BLUEPINKGREEN	PINKGREEN	GREENGREEN
RED	BLUEPINKGREENRED	GREENRED	REDRED

Ans. Option (i) and (iv) are possible

OR

Option (i) only

PICKER maxval=3 minval=0

(1 Mark for mentioning correct option(s))

Note: No marks to be awarded for writing any other option.

(1/2 Mark each for Minimum and Maximum Value of PICKER)

2.

a) What is the difference between Multilevel and Multiple inheritance? Give suitable examples to illustrate both. (2)

Ans.

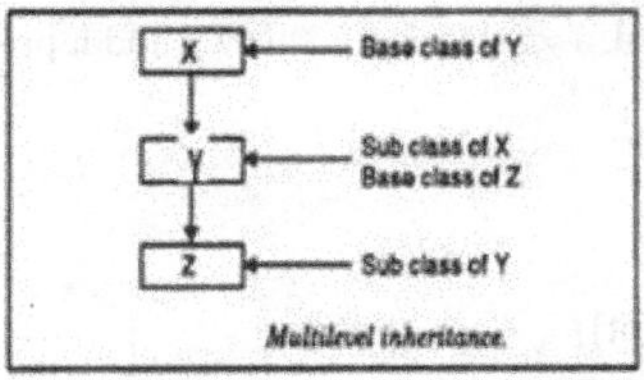

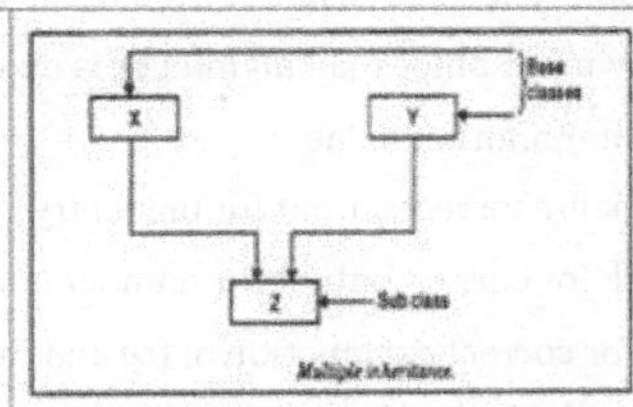

X is the parent class of Y and Y is the parent class of Z

The Child class Z has parents X and Y

(1 mark for correct difference)

(1 mark for correct example)

b) What will be the output of the following python code considering the following set of inputs? (2)

AMAR

THREE

A123

1200

Also, explain the try and except used in the code.

```
Start=0
while True: try:
Number=int(raw_input("Enter Number"))
break
except ValueError:
Start=Start+2
print("Re-enter an integer")
print(Start)
```

Ans. Output:

Enter Number AMAR

Re-enter an integer

Enter Number THREE

Re-enter an integer

Enter Number Al23

Re-enter an integer

Enter Number 1200

Explanation: The code inside try makes sure that the valid number is entered by the user. When any input other than an integer is entered, a value error is thrown and it prompts the user to enter another value.

(1/2 mark for correct output for text entry)

(1/2 mark for correct output for number entry)

(1 mark for correct explanation of try and except)

c) Write a class CITY in Python with following specifications. **(4)**

Instance Attributes

- Ccode # Numeric value
- CName # String value
- Pop # Numeric value for Population
- KM # Numeric value
- Density # Numeric value for Population Density

Methods

- DenCal() # Method to calculate Density as Pop/KM
- Record() # Method to allow user to enter values Ccode,CName,Pop,KM and call DenCal() method
- View() # Method to display all the members also display a message "Highly Populated City" if the Density is more than 10000.

Ans. class CITY:

def init (self) :

self.Ccode = 0

self.CName = ""

self.Pop = 0

self.KM =0

self.Density=0

def DenCal(self):

self.Density = self.Pop / self.KM

def Record(self):

self.Ccode = input("Enter CCode")

self.CName = raw_input("Enter CName")

self.Pop = input("Enter population")

self.KM = input("Enter KM")

DenCal(self) // or self.DenCal() def View(self):

print CCode,CName,Pop, KM, Density

if self.Density > 10000:

print("Highly populated city")

OR print("Highly populated city")

(1/2 Mark for correct syntax for class header)

(1 Mark for correct declaration of instance attributes)

(1/2 Mark for correct definition of DenCal() function)

(1 Mark for correct definition of Record() with proper invocation of DenCal() function)

(1 Mark for correct definition of View())

NOTE: Deduct 1/2 Mark if DenCal() is not invoked properly inside Record() function.

d) How do we implement abstract method in python? Give an example for the same **(2)**

Ans. Abstract method: An unimplemented method is called an abstract method. When an abstract method is declared in a base class, the derived class has to either define the method or raise "NotImplementedError"

OR

Abstract Method can be used to enable parent class method execution.

class Shape(object):

def findArea(self):

pass

class Square(Shape):

def init (self,side) :

self.side = side

def findArea(self):

return self.side * self.side

(1 mark for correct explanation)

(1 mark for any correct example)

e) What is the significance of super() method? Give an example for the same. (2)

Ans. super() function is used to call base class methods which has been extended in derived class.

```
class GradStudent(Student):
def init (self) :
super(GradStudent, self). init ()
self.subject = ""
self.working = ""
def readGrad (self):
# Call readStudent method of parent class
super(GradStudent, self).readStudent()
```

(1 mark for correct explanation)

(1 mark for correct example)

3.

a) What will be the status of the following list after the First, Second and Third pass of the selection sort method used for arranging the following elements in descending order? (3)

Note: Show the status of all the elements after each pass very clearly underlining the changes.

12, 14, -54, 64, 90, 24

Ans.

	12	14	-54	64	**90**	24
Pass 1	90	14	-54	**64**	12	24
Pass 2	90	64	-54	14	12	**24**
Pass 3	90	64	24	**14**	12	-54

(1 mark for each correct pass)

b) For a given list of values in descending order, write a method in python to search for a value with the help of Binary Search method. The method should return position of the value and should return -1 if the value not present in the list. (2)

Ans.
```
def binarysrch(nums,x):
high = len(nums)
low =0
while low < high:
mid = (low + high)//2
```

```
midval = nums[mid]
if midval > x:
low = mid + 1
elif midval < x:
high = mid
else:
return mid
return -1
```

(1/2 mark for assignment of high/ub and low/lb)

(1/2 mark for appropriate looping condition)

(1/2 mark for calculation of Mid)

(1/2 mark for changing high/ub and low/lb)

c) Write Insert(City) and Delete(City) methods in python to add City and Remove City considering them to act as Insert and Delete operations of the data structure Queue. **(4)**

Ans.

```
class queue:
city = [ ] def Insert(self):
a= raw_input("Enter city") queue.city.append(a)
def Delete(self):
if (queue.city == [ ] ): print "Queue empty" else:
print "Deleted element is", queue.city[0] queue.city.delete()
```

OR

```
class queue:
city = [ ]
def Insert(self):
a     = raw_input("Enter city") queue.a.append(a)
def Delete(self):
if (queue.city == [ ] ): print("Queue empty") else:
print("Deleted element is", queue.city[0]) queue.city.delete()
```

(1/2 mark insert header)

(1/2 mark for accepting a value from user)

(1/2 mark for adding value in list)

(1/2 mark for delete header)

(1/2 mark for checking empty list condition)

(1/2 mark for displaying "Empty Message")

(1/2 mark for displaying the value to be deleted)

(1/2 mark for deleting value from list)

d) Write a method in python to find and display the prime numbers between 2 to N. Pass N as argument to the method. (3)

Ans.
```
def prime (N) :
for a in range(2,N):
Prime=1
for I in range(2,a):
if a%i ==0:
Prime=0
if Prime==1:
print a
```

OR

```
def prime (N) :
for a in range(2,N):
for I in range(2,a):
if a%i ==0:
break
else:
print a
```

OR

Any other correct code performing the same

(1/2 mark function header)

(1/2 mark for outer loop)

(1/2 mark for inner loop)

(1 mark for divisibility check)

(1/2 mark for displaying prime number)

e) Evaluate the following postfix notation of expression. Show status of stack after every operation. (2)

12, 2, /, 34, 20, -, +, 5, +

Ans.

Element	Stack
12	12
2	12, 2
/	6
34	6, 34
20	6, 34, 20
-	6, 14
+	20
5	20, 5
+	25
Final Result = 25	
(1/2 Mark for evaluation till each operator)	

OR

(1 Mark for only writing the Final answer without showing stack status)

4.

a) Write a statement in Python to perform the following operations. (1)

- To open a text file "MYPET.TXT" in write mode.
- To open a text file "MYPET.TXT" in read mode.

Ans.

fl = open("MYPET.TXT",'w')

f2 = open("MYPET.TXT", 'r')

(1/2 Mark for each correct statement)

b) Write a method in python to write multiple line of text contents into a text file daynote.txt line. (2)

Ans. def writel():f = open("daynote.txt",'w')

while True:

line = raw_input("Enter line")

f.write(line)

choice = raw_input("Are there more lines")

if choice == 'N':

break

f.close ()

Note: Using writelines() is also correct

(1/2 Mark for opening file in appropriate mode)

(1/2 Mark for end of file check and loop)

(1/2 Mark for taking input from user)

(1/2 Mark for writing the line into the file)

c) **Consider the following definition of class Employee, write a method in python to search and display the content in a pickled file emp.dat, where Empno is matching with 'A0005'.**

(3)

class Employee: def init (self,E,NM) : self.Empno=E self. EName=NM def Display(self): print(self.Empno,"-" , self. EName) Ans.

def search():

f = open("emp.dat", 'rb') try:

while True:

e = pickle.load(f)

if e.Empno == 'A0005': e. display()

except EOFError: pass

f.close ()

(1/2 Mark for correct function header)

(1/2 Mark for opening the file emp.dat correctly)

(V2 Mark for correct file check and loop)

(1/2 Mark for correct load())

(1/2 Mark for correct checking of Empno)

(1/2 Mark for displaying the record)

Section-C

(For all the Candidates)

5.

a) Observe the following PARTICIPANTS and EVENTS tables carefully and write the name of the RDBMS operation which will be used to produce the output as shown in RESULT? Also, find the Degree and Cardinality of the result. (2)

Participants

PNO	NAME
1	Aruanabha Tariban
2	John Fedricks
3	Kanti Desai

Events

EVENTCODE	EVENTNAME
1001	IT Quiz
1002	Group Debate

Results

PNO	NAME	EVENTCODE	EVENTNAME
1	Aruanabha Tariban	1001	IT Quiz
1	Aruanabha Tariban	1002	Group Debate
2	John Fedricks	1001	IT Quiz
2	John Fedricks	1002	Group Debate
3	Kanti Desai	1001	IT Quiz
3	Kanti Desai	1002	Group Debate

Ans. Cartesian Product

Degree = 4 Cardinality = 6

(1 Mark for writing the correct name of RDBMS operation)

(1/2 Mark for writing correct degree)

(1/2 Mark for writing correct cardinality)

b) Write SQL queries for (i) to (iv) and find outputs for SQL queries (v) to (viii), which are based on the tables. (6)

Table: Vehicle

VCODE	VEHICLE TYPE	PER/KM
V01	VOLVO BUS	150
V02	AC DELUXE BUS	125
V03	ORDINARY BUS	80
V05	SUV	30
V04	CAR	18

Note: PERKM is Freight Charges per kilometer

Table: Travel

CNO	CNAME	TRAVELDATE	KM	VCODE	NOP
101	K. Niwal	2015-12-13	200	V01	32
103	Fredrick Sym	2016-03-21	120	V03	45
105	Hitesh Jain	2016-04-23	450	V02	42
102	Ravi Anish	2016-01-13	80	V02	40
107	John Malina	2015-02-10	65	V04	2
104	Sahanubhuti	2016-01-28	90	V05	4
106	Ramesh Jaya	2016-04-06	100	V01	25

Note:

- Km is Kilometers travelled.
- NOP is number of passengers travelled in vehicle.

i. **To display CNO, CNAME, TRAVELDATE from the table TRAVEL in descending order of CNO.**

Ans. SELECT CNO, CNAME, TRAVELDATE FROM TRAVEL ORDER BY CNO DESC; (1/2 Mark for SELECT CNO, CNAME, TRAVELDATE FROM TRAVEL) (1/2 Mark for ORDER BY CNO DESC)

ii. **To display the CNAME of all the customers from the table TRAVEL who are traveling by vehicle with code V01 or V02.**

Ans. SELECT CNAME FROM TRAVEL WHERE VCODE='V0l' OR VCODE='V02'; SELECT CNAME FROM TRAVEL WHERE VCODE IN ('V01' , 'V02') ; (1/2 Mark for correct SELECT) (1/2 Mark for correct WHERE clause)

iii. **To display the CNO and CNAME of those customers from the table TRAVEL who travelled between '2015-12-31' and '2015-05-01'.**

Ans. SELECT CNO, CNAME from TRAVEL WHERE TRAVELDATE >= '2015-05-01' AND TRAVELDATE <= '2015-12-31';

OR

SELECT CNO, CNAME from TRAVEL

WHERE TRAVELDATE BETWEEN '2015-05-01' AND '2015-12-31';

OR

SELECT CNO, CNAME from TRAVEL

WHERE TRAVELDATE <= '2015-12-31'

AND TRAVELDATE >= '2015-05-01';

OR

SELECT CNO, CNAME from TRAVEL

WHERE TRAVELDATE BETWEEN '2015-12-**31'** AND '2015-05-01'; (1/2 Mark for correct SELECT)

(1/2 Mark for correct WHERE clause)

iv. **To display all the details from table TRAVEL for the customers, who have travel distance more than 120 KM in ascending order of NOP.**

Ans. SELECT * FROM TRAVEL WHERE KM > 120 ORDER BY NOP; (1/2 Mark for correct ? SELECT)

(1/2 Mark for correct ? WHERE clause)

v. **SELECT COUNT(*),VCODE FROM TRAVEL GROUP BY VCODE HAVING COUNT(*)>1;**

Ans.

<u>COUNT(*)</u> VCODE

2 V01

2 V01

(1/2 Mark for correct output)

vi. **SELECT DISTINCT VCODE FROM TRAVEL;**

Ans.

<u>DISTINCT VCDOE</u>

V01

V02

V03

V04

V05

(1/2 Mark for correct output)

vii. **SELECT A.VCODE, CNAME, VEHICLETYPE**

FROM TRAVEL A, VEHICLE B

WHERE A. VCODE = B.VCODE AND KM<90

Ans.

VCODE	CNAME	VEHICLETYPE
V02	Ravi Anish	AC DELUXE BUS
V04	John Malina	CAR
(1/2 Mark of correct output)		

SELECT CNAME, KM*PERKM

FROM TRAVEL A, VEHICLE B

WHERE A. VCODE=B. VCODE AND A. VCODE='V05'

Ans.

CNAME	KM*PERKM
Sahanubhuti	2700

(1/2 Mark for correct output)

6.

a) Verify the following using Boolean Laws. **(2)**

X'+ Y'Z = X'.Y'.Z'+ X'.Y.Z'+ X'Y.Z+ X'.Y'.Z+ X.Y'.Z

Ans.

LHS

X' + Y'.Z

= X'.(Y + Y') . (Z + Z') + (X + X') . Y'.Z

= X'.Y.Z + X'.Y.Z' + X'.Y'.Z + X'.Y'.Z' + X.Y'.Z + X'.Y'.Z

= X'.Y.Z + X'.Y.Z' + X'.Y'.Z + X'.Y'.Z' + X.Y'.Z

= X'.Y'.Z' + X'.Y.Z' + X'.Y.Z + X'.Y'.Z + X.Y'.Z

= RHS

OR

RHS

X'.Y'.Z' + X'.Y.Z' + X'.Y.Z + X'.Y'.Z + X.Y'.Z

X'.Y'.Z + X'.Y'.Z' + X'.Y.Z + X'.Y.Z' + X.Y'.Z

X'.Y'.(Z+Z') + X'.Y.(Z+Z') + X.Y'.Z

X' .Y' + X' .Y + X.Y' .Z

X' . (Y' +Y) +X.Y' . Z

X' + X.Y'.Z

(X' + X) . (X' + Y' . Z)

X' + Y' . Z

LHS

(2 Marks for correct Verification)

OR

(1 Mark for expanding LHS up to 1 correct step)

OR

(1 Mark for reducing RHS up to 1 correct step)

b) Write the Boolean Expression for the result of the Logic Circuit as shown below.

(2)

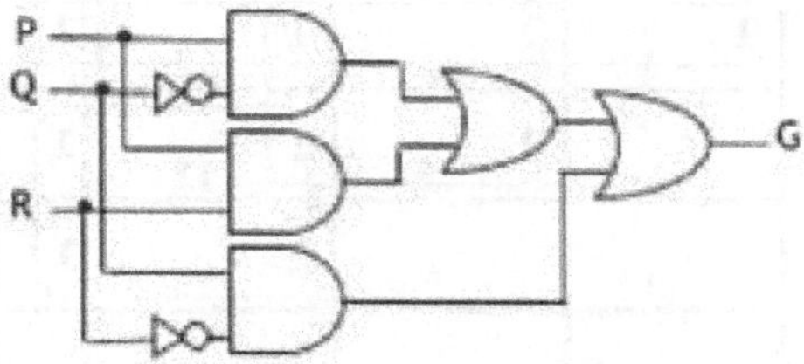

Ans. P.Q' + P.R + Q.R'

(2 Marks for correctly writing the full expression)

OR

(1/2 Mark each for correctly writing any one term)

c) Derive a Canonical SOP expression for a Boolean function G, represented by the following truth table **(1)**

A	B	C	G(A, B, C)
0	0	0	1
0	0	1	0
0	1	0	1
0	1	1	0
1	0	0	0
1	0	1	0
1	1	0	1
1	1	1	1

Ans. G(A,B,C) = A'.B'.C' + A'.B.C' + A.B.C' + A.B.C

OR

G(A,B,C) = $\Sigma(0,2,6,7)$

(1 Mark for correctly writing the SOP form)

Note: Deduct 1A mark if wrong variable names **are** written in the expression

d) Reduce the following Boolean Expression to its simplest form using K-Map. (3)

F (P,Q,R,S)= L (0,4,5,8,9,10,11,12,13,15)

F(P,Q,R,S) = R'S'+ PQ' + QR'+ PS

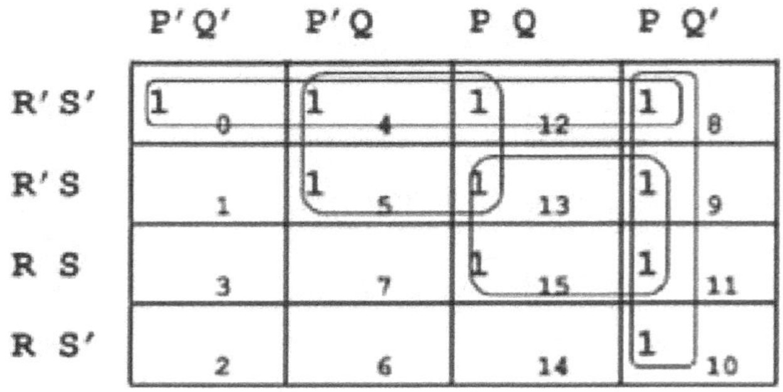

OR

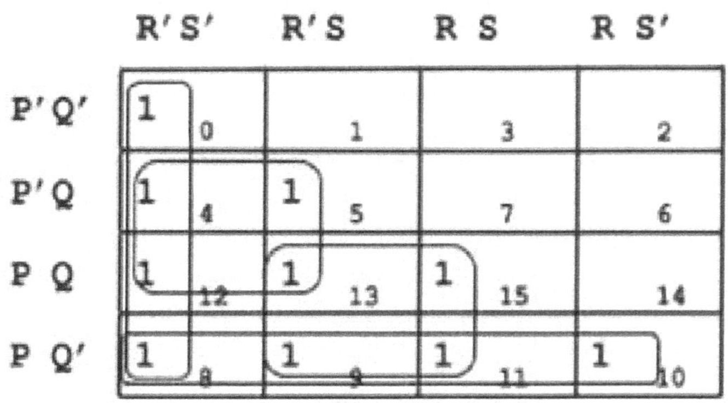

(1/2 Mark for drawing K-Map with correct variable names)

(1/2 Mark each for 4 groupings)

(1/2 Mark for writing final expression in reduced/minimal form)

Note: Deduct Vi mark if wrong variable names are used

7.

a) Differentiate between PAN and LAN types of networks. **(1)**

Ans.

PAN - Personal Area Network	LAN - Local Area Network
A personal area network - PAN - is a computer network organized around an individual person.	LAN interconnects a high number of access or node points or stations within a confined physical area upto a kilometer.

(1 mark for one correct point of difference)

OR

(1 mark for Any other correct difference for PAN and LAN)

b) Which protocol helps us to transfer files to and from a remote computer?

Ans. FTP OR Telnet OR TCP

(1 Mark for any one correct protocol name)

c) Write two advantages of 3G over 2G Mobile Telecommunication Technologies in terms of speed and services? (1)

Ans. Speed

- Faster web browsing
- Faster file transfer Service
- Better video clarity
- Better security

OR

(Any other correct advantage can be considered)

(1/2 Mark for each of any one point for Speed/Service)

d) Write two characteristics of Web 2.0. (1)

Ans. • Makes web more interactive through online social medias

- Supports easy online information exchange
- Interoperability on the internet
- Video sharing possible in the websites

OR

Any two of the above or any other two correct characteristics of Web 2.0 (1/2 Mark each for any two correct answers)

e) What is the basic difference between Computer Worm and Trojan Horse? (1)

Ans.

Trojan Horse	**Computer Worm**
It is a "Malware" computer program presented as useful or harmless in order to induce the user to install and run them.	It is a self-replicating computer program. which uses a network to send copies of itself to other computers on the network and it may do so without any user intervention

Any other correct difference between Trojan Horse and Computer Worm

(1 Mark for writing correct difference between Trojan Horse and Computer Worm)

OR

(1/2 Mark each for writing correct explanation of Trojan Horse / Computer Worm)

f) **Categories the following under Client side and Server Side script category? (1)**

(i) Java Script

(ii) ASP

(iii) VBSript

(iv) JSP

Ans.

Client Side Scripts	Server Side Scripts
VB Script	ASP
Java Script	JSP
(1 Mark for correct answer)	

OR

(1/2 Mark for any two correct client/server side script names)

g) **Intelligent Hub India is a knowledge community aimed to uplift the standard of skills and knowledge in the society. It is planning to setup its training centers in multiple towns and villages pan India with its head offices in the nearest cities. They have created a model of their network with a city, a town and 3 villages as follows. As a network consultant, you have to suggest the best network related solutions for their issues/problems raised in (i) to (iv), keeping in mind the distances between various locations and other given parameters.**

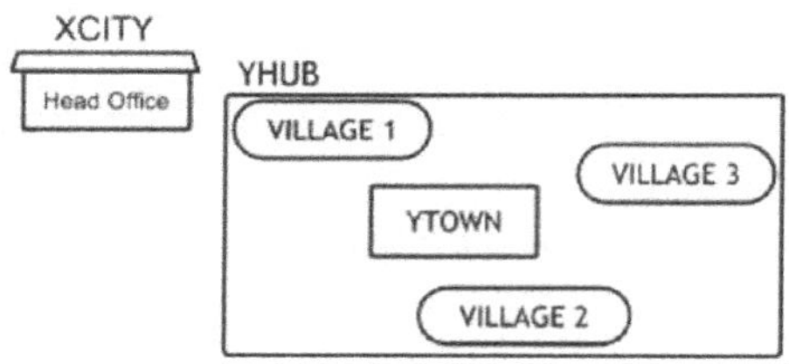

Shortest distances between various locations:

VILLAGE 1 to YTOWN	2 KM
VILLAGE 2 to YTOWN	1.5 KM
VILLAGE 3 to YTOWN	3 KM
VILLAGE 1 to YTOWN 2	3.5 KM
VILLAGE 1 to YTOWN 3	4.5 KM
VILLAGE 1 to YTOWN 3	3.5 KM
CITY Head Office to YHUB	30 KM

Number of Computers installed at various locations are as follows:

YTOWN	100
VILLAGE 1	10
VILLAGE 2	15
VILLAGE 3	15
CITY OFFICE	5

Note:

In Villages, there are community centers, in which one room has been given as training center to this organization to install computers.

The organization has got financial support from the government and top IT companies.

h) Suggest the most appropriate location of the SERVER in the YHUB (out of the 4 locations), to get the best and effective connectivity. Justify your answer. (1)

Ans. YTOWN

Justification

- Since it has the maximum number of computers.
- It is closest to all other locations.

(1/2 Mark for correct answer)

(1/2 Mark for any one correct justification)

i) Suggest the best wired medium and draw the cable layout (location to location) to efficiently connect various locations within the YHUB. (1)

Ans. Optical Fiber

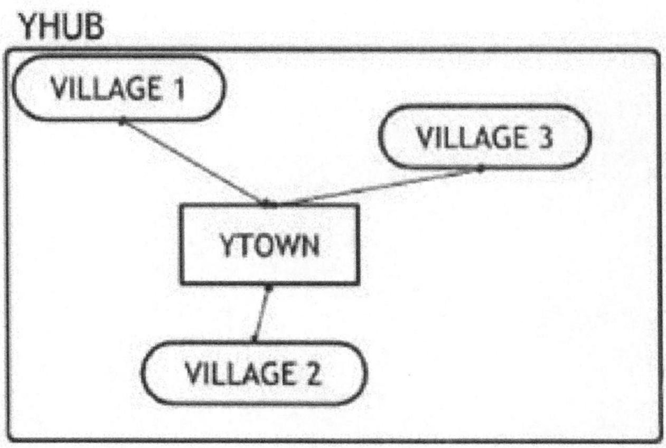

(1/2 Mark for correct wired medium)

(1/2 mark for correct topology)

j) **Which hardware device will you suggest to connect all the computers within each location of YHUB? (1)**

Ans. Switch OR Hub

(1 Mark for correct answer)

k) **Which service/protocol will be most helpful to conduct live interactions of Experts from Head Office and people at YHUB locations? (1)**

Ans. Videoconferencing OR VoIP OR any other correct service/protocol (1 Mark for writing any one of the above answers).

CBSE AISSCE 2016-2017 Marking Scheme for Computer Science

(Sub Code: 083 Paper Code 91 Outside Delhi)

General Instructions

- The answers given in the marking scheme are SUGGESTIVE. Examiners are requested to award marks for all alternative correct Solutions/Answers conveying the similar meaning
- All programming questions have to be answered with respect to C++ Language/ Python only.
- In C++/Python, ignore case sensitivity for identifiers (Variable/Functions/Structures /Class Names).
- In Python indentation is mandatory, however, number of spaces used for indenting may vary
- In SQL related questions–both ways of text/character entries should be acceptable for Example: "AMAR" and 'amar' both are acceptable.
- In SQL related questions – all date entries should be acceptable for Example: 'YYYY-MM-DD', 'YY-MM-DD', 'DD-Mon-YY', "DD/MM/YY", 'DD/MM/YY', "MM/DD/YY", 'MM/DD/YY' and {MM/DD/YY} are correct.
- In SQL related questions–semicolon should be ignored for terminating the SQL statements.
- In SQL related questions, ignore case sensitivity.

Section A

(Only for candidates, who opted for C++)

1 (a) Write the type of C++ tokens (keywords and user defined identifiers) from the following: 2

(i) new

(ii) While

(iii) case

(iv) Num_2

(i) new - Keyword

Ans (ii) While - User defined Identifier

(iii) case - Keyword

(iv) Num_2 - User defined Identifier

(½ Mark for writing each correct keywords)

(½ Mark for writing each correct user defined identifiers)

(b) Anil typed the following C++ code and during compilation he found three errors as follows: 1

(i) Function strlen should have prototype

(ii) Undefined symbol cout

(iii) Undefined symbol endl

On asking, his teacher told him to include necessary header files in the code. Write the names of the header files, which Anil needs to include, for successful compilation and execution of the following code

```
void main()
{
    char Txt[] = "Welcome";
    for(int C= 0; C<strlen(Txt); C++)
     Txt[C] = Txt[C]+1;
    cout<<Txt<<endl;
}
```

Ans string.h

iostream.h OR fstream.h OR iomanip.h

(½ Mark each for writing correct header files)

NOTE:

Ignore additional header file(s)

(c) Rewrite the following C++ code after removing any/all syntactical errors with each correction underlined. 2

Note: Assume all required header files are already being included in the program.

```
void main()
{
  cout<<"Enter an Alphabet:";
  cin>>CH;
  switch(CH)
        case 'A' cout<<"Ant";    Break;
        case 'B' cout<<"Bear" ; Break;
}
```

Ans

```
void main()
{
  cout<<"Enter an Alphabet:";
  char CH;                                    // Error 1
  cin>>CH;
  switch(CH)
  {                                           // Error 2(i)
      case 'A' :                              // Error 3(i)
                 cout<<"Ant";  break;         // Error 4(i)
      case 'B' :                              // Error 3(ii)
                 cout<<"Bear"; break;         // Error 4(ii)
  }                                           // Error 2(ii)
}
```

(½ Mark for correcting Error 1)

(½ Mark for correcting Error 2(i) and Error 2(ii))

(½ Mark for correcting Error 3(i) and Error 3(ii))

(½ Mark for correcting Error 4(i) and Error 4(ii))

OR

(1 Mark for identifying all the errors without corrections)

(d) Find and write the output of the following C++ program code: Note: Assume all required header files are already included in the program. 2

```
#define Diff(N1,N2) ((N1>N2)?N1-N2:N2-N1)
void main()
{
    int A,B,NUM[] = {10,23,14,54,32};
    for(int CNT =4; CNT>0; CNT--)
    {

    A=NUM[CNT];
    B=NUM[CNT-1];
    cout<<Diff(A,B)<<'#';
  }
}
```

Ans 22#40#9#13#

(½ Mark for writing each correct value)

OR

(1 Mark to be awarded if the output written in reverse order as 13#9#40#22#)

Note: Deduct ½ Mark for not considering any/all # as separator and/or writing the values in different lines

(e) Find and write the output of the following C++ program code: Note: Assume all required header files are already being included in the program. 3

```
void main()
{
  int *Point, Score[]={100,95,150,75,65,120};
  Point = Score;
  for(int L = 0; L<6; L++)
  {
     if((*Point)%10==0)
        *Point /= 2;
     else
        *Point -= 2;
     if((*Point)%5==0)
        *Point /= 5;
     Point++;
  }
  for(int L = 5; L>=0; L--)
    cout<<Score[L]<<"*";
}
```

Ans 12*63*73*15*93*10*

(½ Mark for writing each correct value)

Note:

- *Deduct ½ Mark for not considering any/all * as separator and or writing the values in different lines*
- *Deduct ½ Mark if the output written in reverse order as 10*93*15*73*63*12**
- *Full 3 Marks to be awarded if "Multiple declaration/syntax error for L" is mentioned*

(f) Look at the following C++ code and find the possible output(s) from the options (i) to (iv) following it. Also, write the maximum values that can be assigned to each of the variables N and M. 2

Note:

- Assume all the required header files are already being included in the code.
- The function random(n) generates an integer between 0 and n-1

```
void main()
{
    randomize();
    int N=random(3),M=random(4);
    int DOCK[3][3] = {{1,2,3},{2,3,4},{3,4,5}};
    for(int R=0; R<N; R++)
    {
        for(int C=0; C<M; C++)
            cout<<DOCK[R][C]<<"  ";
        cout<<endl;
    }
}
```

(i)	(ii)
1 2 3	1 2 3
2 3 4	2 3 4
3 4 5	

(iii)	(iv)
1 2	1 2
2 3	2 3
	3 4

Ans

Correct Options : (ii) and (iii)

Maximum value of N = 2

Maximum value M = 3

(1 Mark for writing the correct options)

NOTE:

No marks to be awarded for writing any other option or any other combination

(½ Mark for writing correct Maximum value of N)

(½ Mark for writing correct Maximum value of M)

2. (a) Differentiate between protected and private members of a class in context of Object Oriented Programming. Also give a suitable example illustrating accessibility/non-accessibility of each using a class and an object in C++. 2

Ans

private	protected
Implicit Visibility Mode	Explicit Visibility Mode
Not accessible to member functions of derived class	Accessible to member functions of derived class

Example:

```
class A
{
      int X;

protected:
     int Y;
public:
     void Z();
};
```

OR

Any other correct example demonstrating difference between private and protected members of a class

(Full 2 Marks for any one correct difference between private and protected members in a class using a suitable code in C++)

OR

(1 Mark for writing any one correct difference between private and protected members in a class without any example)

(b) Observe the following C++ code and answer the questions (i) and (ii). Note: Assume all necessary files are included.

class TEST

```
{
  long TCode;
  char TTitle[20];
  float Score;
public:
  TEST()                          //Member Function 1
  {
     TCode=100;strcpy(TTitle,"FIRST Test");Score=0;
  }
  TEST(TEST &T)                   //Member Function 2
  {
     TCode=E.TCode+1;
     strcpy(TTitle,T.TTitle);
     Score=T.Score;
  }
};
void main()
{
  ____________________            //Statement 1
  ____________________            //Statement 2
}
```

(i) Which Object Oriented Programming feature is illustrated by the Member Function 1 and Member Function 2 together in the class TEST? 1

Ans Polymorphism OR Constructor overloading OR Function Overloading

(1Mark for mentioning the correct concept name)

(ii) Write Statement 1 and Statement 2 to execute Member Function 1 and Member Function 2 respectively. 1

Ans

```
TEST T1;          //Statement 1
TEST T2(T1);      //Statement 2
```

OR

```
TEST T2=T1;       //Statement 2
```

(½ Mark for writing statement 1 correctly)

(½ Mark for writing statement 2 correctly OR ½ Mark for mentioning E not declared)

(c) Write the definition of a class BOX in C++ with following description: Private Members 4

- BoxNumber // data member of integer type
- Side // data member of float type
- Area // data member of float type
- ExecArea() // Member function to calculate and assign // Area as Side * Side

Public Members

- GetBox() // A function to allow user to enter values of // BoxNumber and Side. Also, this // function should call ExecArea() to calculate Area
- ShowBox()// A function to display BoxNumber, Side // and Area

Ans

```
class BOX
{
    int BoxNumber;
    float Side ; float Area ;
    void ExecArea(){Area=Side*Side;}
public:
    void GetBox();
    void ShowBox();
};
void BOX::GetBox()
{
    cin>>BoxNumber>>Side;
    ExecArea(); }
```

(½ Mark for declaring class header correctly)

(½ Mark for declaring data members correctly)

(1 Mark for defining ExecArea() correctly)

(½ Mark for taking inputs of BoxNumber and Side in GetBox())

(½ Mark for invoking ExecArea() inside GetBox())

(½ Mark for defining ShowBox() correctly)

(½ Mark for correctly closing class declaration with a semicolon)

NOTE: Marks to be awarded for defining the member functions inside or outside the class

(d) Answer the questions (i) to (iv) based on the following: 4

```
class First
{ int X1;
protected:
 float X2;
public:
First();
void Enter1(); void Display1(); };
class Second : private First
{
int Y1;
protected:
float Y2;
public:
Second();
void Enter2();
void Display();
};
class Third : public Second
{
 int Z1;
public:
Third();
void Enter3();
void Display();
};
void main()
{ Third T;      //Statement 1
________;//Statement 2 }
```

(i) Which type of Inheritance out of the following is illustrated in the above example? Single Level Inheritance, Multilevel Inheritance, Multiple Inheritance,

Ans Multilevel Inheritance

(1 Mark for writing correct option)

(ii) Write the names of all the member functions, which are directly accessible by the object T of class Third as declared in main() function.

Ans Enter2(), Display() of class Second

Enter3(), Display() of class Third

OR

Enter2()

Second::Display()

Enter3()

Display() OR Third::Display()

(1 Mark for writing all correct function names)

NOTE:

- *Marks not to be awarded for partially correct answer*
- *Ignore the mention of Constructors*

(iii) Write Statement 2 to call function Display() of class Second from the object T of class Third.

Ans T.Second::Display();

(1 Mark for writing Statement 2 correctly)

(iv) What will be the order of execution of the constructors, when the object T of class Third is declared inside main()?

Ans

First, Second, Third

(1 Mark for writing correct order)

- *No Marks to be awarded for any other combination/order.*
- *Names of the constructor/class without parenthesis is acceptable*

3 (a) Write the definition of a function AddUp(int Arr[], int N) in C++, in which all even positions (i.e. 0,2,4,...) of the array should be added with the content of the element in the next position and odd positions (i.e. 1,3,5,...) elements should be incremented by 10. 3

Example: if the array Arr contains

23 30 45 10 15 25

Then the array should become

53 40 55 20 40 35

NOTE:

- The function should only alter the content in the same array.
- The function should not copy the altered content in another array.
- The function should not display the altered content of the array.
- Assuming, the Number of elements in the array are Even.

Ans

```
void AddUp(int Arr[], int N)
{
   for(int i=0; i<N; i++)
  {
    if(i%2==0)
        Arr[i]=Arr[i]+Arr[i+1];
    else
        Arr[i]=Arr[i]+10;
  }
}
```

OR

Any other correct C++ code for the required function definition.

(1 Mark for correctly writing the loop)

(1 Mark for correctly checking condition for even/odd locations)

(½ Mark for adding the element in the next position to the even positioned elements)

(b) Write a definition for a function SUMMIDCOL(int MATRIX[][10],int N,int M) in C++, which finds the sum of the middle column's elements of the MATRIX (Assuming N represents number of rows and M represents number of columns, which is an odd integer). 2

Example: if the content of array MATRIX having N as 5 and M as 3 is as follows:

1	2	1
2	1	4
3	4	5
4	5	3
5	3	2

The function should calculate the sum and display the following: Sum of Middle Column: 15

Ans

```
void SUMMIDCOL(int MATRIX[][10],int N,int M)
{
   int mid=M/2;
   int sum=0;
   for(int i=0; i<N; i++)
{
    sum=sum+MATRIX[i][mid];
}
  cout<<" Sum of Middle Column"<<sum;
}
```

OR

Any other correct C++ code for the required function definition

(½ Mark for correctly writing the loop)

(1 Mark for adding middle column elements)

(½ Mark for displaying the sum of middle column elements)

(c) ARR[15][20] is a two-dimensional array, which is stored in the memory along the row with each of its elements occupying 4 bytes. Find the address of the element ARR[5][15], if the element ARR[10][5] is stored at the memory location 35000. 3

Ans ROW MAJOR:

Loc(ARR[I][J]) =Base Address + W [(I – LBR)*C + (J – LBC)]

(where W=size of each element = 4 bytes, R=Number of Rows=15, C=Number of Columns=20)

Assuming LBR = LBC = 0

LOC(ARR[10][5])

35000 = BaseAddress + W(I*C + J)

35000 = BaseAddress + 4(10*20 + 5)

35000 = BaseAddress + 4(205)

35000 = BaseAddress + 820

BaseAddress = 35000 - 820

= 34180

LOC(ARR[5][15])= BaseAddress + W(I*C + J)

= 34180 + 4(5*20 + 15)

= 34180 + 4(100 + 15)

= 34180 + 4 x 115

= 34180 + 460

= 34640

OR

Loc(ARR[I][J]) = Ref. Address + W ((I – LR)*C + (J – LC))

(where

W=size of each element = 4 bytes,

R=Number of Rows =15, C=Number of Columns=20

Reference Address= Address of given cell ARR[10][5]=35000

LR = Row value of given cell = 10

LC = Column value of given cell = 5

LOC(ARR[5][15]) = LOC(ARR[10][5]) + 4((5-10)*20 + (15-5))

LOC(ARR[5][15]) = 35000 + 4(-100 + 10)

= 35000 + 4[-90]

= 35000 -360

= 34640

(1 Mark for writing correct formula (for Row major) OR substituting formula with correct values)

(1Mark for correct calculation)

(1 Mark for final correct address)

d) Write the definition of a member function PUSHGIFT() for a class STACK in C++, to add a GIFT in a dynamically allocated stack of GIFTs considering the following code is already written as a part of the program: 4

```
strut GIFT
{
    int GCODE;            //Gift Code
    char GDESC[20];       //Gift Description
    GIFT *Link;
};
class STACK
{
  Gift *TOP;
public:
  STACK(){TOP=NULL;}
  void PUSHGIFT();
  void POPGIFT();
  ~STACK();
};
```

ANS

```
void STACK::PUSHGIFT()
{
    GIFT *T = new GIFT;
    cin>>T->GCODE;
    gets(T->GDESC);
    T->Link = TOP;
    TOP = T;
}
```

(1 Mark for creating a new Node)

(1 Mark for fetching values of GCODE and GDESC)

(1 Mark for assigning TOP to the Link of the new Node)

(1 Mark for assigning TOP to the new Node)

NOTE: GIFT/Gift - Both acceptable

(e) Convert the following Infix expression to its equivalent Postfix expression, showing the stack contents for each step of conversion: 2

X - (Y + Z) / U * V

Ans

ELEMENT	Stack	POSTFIX
X		X
-	-	X
(	-(	X
Y	-(	XY
+	-(+	XY
Z	-(+	XYZ
)	-	XYZ+
/	-/	XYZ+
U	-/	XYZ+U
*	-*	XYZ+U/
V	-*	XYZ+U/V
		XYZ+U/V*-

or

ELEMENT	Stack	POSTFIX
(		
X		X
-	-	
(		
(		
(		
Y		XY
+	- +	
Z		XYZ
)	-	XYZ+
/	-/	
U		XYZ+U
)	-	XYZ+U/
*	-*	
V		XYZ+U/V
)		XYZ+U/V*
)		XYZ+U/V*-

`Postfix= XYZ+U/V*-`

OR

Any other method for converting the given infix expression to its equivalent postfix expression showing stack contents.

(½ Mark for correctly converting till each operator)

OR

(1 Mark to be given for writing correct answer without showing the stack content on each step)

4. (a) Polina Raj has used a text editing software to type some text in an article. 3

After saving the article as MYNOTES.TXT, she realised that she has wrongly typed alphabet K in place of alphabet C everywhere in the article.

Write a function definition for PURETEXT() in C++ that would display the corrected version of the entire article of the file MYNOTES.TXT with all the alphabets "K" to be displayed as an alphabet "C" on screen.

Note: Assuming that MYNOTES.TXT does not contain any C alphabet otherwise.

Example:

If Polina has stored the following content in the file MYNOTES.TXT:

I OWN A KUTE LITTLE KAR.

I KARE FOR IT AS MY KHILD.

The function PURETEXT() should display the following content:

I OWN A CUTE LITTLE CAR.

I CARE FOR IT AS MY CHILD.

Ans void PURETEXT()

```
{
   char ch;
   ifstream F("MYNOTES.TXT" );
   while(F.get(ch))
{
   if(ch=='K')
      ch='C';
   cout<<ch; }
   F.close(); //IGNORE
}
```

```
OR
fstream F;
F.open("MYNOTES.TXT", ios::in);
OR
fstream F("MYNOTES.TXT", ios::in);
```

OR

Any other correct function definition

(1 Mark for opening MYNOTES.TXT correctly)

(1 Mark for reading each character (using any method) from the file)

(1 Mark for displaying 'C' in place of 'K')

(b) Write a definition for function COUNTPICS ( ) in C++ to read each object of a binary file PHOTOS.DAT, find and display the total number of PHOTOS of type PORTRAIT. Assume that the file PHOTOS.DAT is created with the help of objects of class PHOTOS, which is defined below: 2

```
class PHOTOS
{
    int PCODE;
    char PTYPE[20];//Photo Type as "PORTRAIT","NATURE"
public:
    void ENTER()
    { cin>>PCODE;gets(PTYPE);  }
    void SHOWCASE()
    { cout<<PCODE<<":"<<PTYPE<<endl;
    }
    char *GETPTYPE(){return PTYPE;}
};
```

Ans

```
void COUNTPICS()
{
  ifstream F;
  F.open("PHOTOS.DAT",
                    ios::binary);
  int count=0; PHOTOS obj;
  while(F.read((char*)&obj,
                    sizeof(obj)))
  {
    if(strcmp(obj.GETPTYPE(),"PORTRAIT")==0)
        count++;
  }
  cout<<"Number of PORTRAIT photos :"<<count;
  F.close(); //IGNORE
}
```

```
OR
fstream F;
F.open("PHOTOS.DAT",
          ios::binary|ios::in);
```

OR

Any other correct function definition

(½ Mark for opening PHOTOS.DAT correctly)

(½ Mark for reading records from PHOTOS.DAT)

(½ Mark for comparing PHOTOS of type PORTRAIT(ignore case sensitive checking) with strcmp or strcmpi)

(½ Mark for displaying counter for matching records)

(c) Find the output of the following C++ code considering that the binary file CLIENTS.DAT exists on the hard disk with a data of 200 clients. 1

```
class CLIENTS
{
     int CCode;char CName[20];
     void REGISTER();void DISPLAY();
  };
  void main()
  {  fstream File; File.open("CLIENTS.DAT",ios::binary|ios::in);
     CLIENTS C;
     File.seekg(6*sizeof(C));
     File.read((char*)&C,sizeof(C));
     cout<<"Client Number:"<<File.tellg()/sizeof(C)+ 1;
     File.seekg(0,ios::end);
     cout<<" of "<<File.tellg()/sizeof(C)<<endl;
     File.close(); }
```

Ans Client Number 8 of 200

(½ Mark for displaying correct value of File.tellg()/sizeof(C) + 1)

(½ Mark for displaying correct value of File.tellg()/sizeof(C))

Section B

(Only for candidates, who opted for Python)

1 (a) Which of the following can be used as valid variable identifier(s) in Python? 2

(i) 4thSum

(ii) Total

(iii) Number#

(iv) _Data

Ans ii) Total iv) _Data

(1 mark for each correct option)

NOTE: Deduct ½ Mark for each wrong name written

(b) Name the Python Library modules which need to be imported to invoke the following functions 1

(i) floor()

(ii) randint()

Ans math

rndom

(½ Mark for writing each correct Library modules)

NOTE:

Ignore any other Library modules, if mentioned.

(c) Rewrite the following code in python after removing all syntax error(s). Underline each correction done in the code. 2

```
STRING=""WELCOME
NOTE""
for S in range[0,8]:
    print STRING(S)
print S+STRING
```

Ans STRING="WELCOME"

NOTE=""

for S in range(0,8):

    print STRING[S]

print S,STRING

Also range(0,8) will give a runtime error as the index is out of range. It should be range(0,7)

(½ Mark for each for any four corrections)

OR

(1 mark for identifying the errors, without suggesting corrections)

(d) Find and write the output of the following python code: 2

```
TXT   = ["20","50","30","40"]
CNT   = 3
TOTAL = 0
for C in [7,5,4,6]:
T = TXT[CNT]
TOTAL = float (T) + C
print TOTAL
CNT-=1
```

Ans 47.0

35.0

54.0

26.0

(½ mark for each correct line of output)

NOTE:

Deduct ½ Mark for writing the answer in same line

Deduct ½ Mark for writing numbers without decimal point

(e) Find and write the output of the following python code: 3

```
class INVENTORY:
    def __init__(self,C=101,N="Pad",Q=100):#constructor
        self.Code=C
        self.IName=N
        self.Qty=int(Q);
    def Procure(self,Q):
        self.Qty = self.Qty + Q
    def Issue(self,Q):
        self.Qty -= Q
    def Status(self):
        print self.Code,":",self.IName,"#",self.Qty
I1=INVENTORY()
I2=INVENTORY(105,"ThumbPin",50)
I3=INVENTORY(102,"UClip")
I1.Procure(25)
I2.Issue(15)
I3.Procure(50)
I1.Status()
I3.Status()
I2.Status()
```

Ans Output

101 : Pad # 125

102 : U Clip # 150

105 : Thumb Pin # 35

(1 mark for each correct line of output)

NOTE:

- *Deduct ½ Mark for not writing any or all ':' / '#' symbol(s)*
- *Deduct ½ Mark for not considering any or all line breaks at proper place(s)*

(f) What are the possible outcome(s) executed from the following code? Also specify the maximum and minimum values that can be assigned to variable N. import random 2

```
NAV  = ["LEFT","FRONT","RIGHT","BACK"];
NUM  = random.randint(1,3)
NAVG = ""
for C in range(NUM,1,-1):
NAVG = NAVG+NAV[I]
print NAVG
```

(i) BACKRIGHT

(ii) BACKRIGHTFRONT

(iii) BACK

(iv) LEFTFRONTRIGHT

Ans (i) BACKRIGHT

Max value 3 and minimum value 1 for variable NUM

OR

I or N not defined

OR

; wrongly placed in line 2

(1 mark for mentioning the first option)

NOTE: No marks to be awarded for writing any other option or any other combination

(½ mark each for max and min values of NUM)

OR

(Full 2 Marks for mentioning the specific error(s))

2 (a) List four characteristics of Object Oriented programming. 2

Ans
- Encapsulation
- Data Hiding
- Abstraction
- Inheritance
- Polymorphism

(½ mark for naming each characteristic - upto 4 characteristics)

(b) class Exam: 2

```
Regno=1
Marks=75
def __init__(self,r,m):          #function 1
      self.Regno=r
      self.Marks=m
def Assign(self,r,m):            #function 2
      Regno = r
      Marks = m
def Check(self):                 #function 3
print self.Regno, self.Marks
print Regno, Marks
```

(i) In the above class definition, both the functions - function 1 as well as function 2 have similar definition. How are they different in execution?

Ans (i) Function 1 is the constructor which gets executed automatically as soon as the object of the class is created. Function 2 is a member function which has to be called to assign the values to Regno and Marks.

(ii) Function 1 E1=Exam(1,95) # Any values in the parameter

Function 2 E1.Assign(1,95) # Any values in the parameter

(1 mark for correct difference)

(c) Define a class BOX in Python with following specifications 4

Instance Attributes

- BoxID # Numeric value with a default value 101
- Side # Numeric value with a default value 10
- Area # Numeric value with a default value 0

Methods:

- ExecArea() # Method to calculate Area as
  # Side * Side
- NewBox() # Method to allow user to enter values of
  # BoxID and Side. It should also
  # Call ExecArea Method
- ViewBox() # Method to display all the Attributes

Ans class BOX: # can also be given as class BOX( ):

```
class BOX: # can also be given as   class BOX( ):
                # or class BOX(Object):
    def __init__(self):
      self.BoxID=101
      self.Side=10
      self.Area=0
    def ExecArea(self):
        self.Area=self.Side*self.Side
    def NewBox(self):
            self.BoxID=input("Enter BoxID")
            self.Side=input("Enter side")
            self.ExecArea()  # OR   ExecArea(self)
    def ViewBox(self):
          print self.BoxID
          print self.Side
          print self.Area
```

```
def __init__(self,B,S,A):
#Any variable instead of B, S, A may be used
        self.BoxID=B
        self.Side=S
        self.Area=A
```

(½ Mark for correct syntax for class header)

(½ Mark for correct declaration of instance attributes)

(1 Mark for correct definition of ExecArea( ) method)

(1 Mark for correct definition of NewBox( ) with proper invocation of ExecArea( ))

(1 Mark for correct definition of ViewBox( ))

NOTE: Deduct ½ Mark if ExecArea( ) is not invoked properly inside NewBox( ) method

(d) Differentiate between static and dynamic binding in Python? Give suitable examples of each. 2

Ans Static Binding: It allows linking of function call to the function definition during compilation of the program.

Dynamic Binding: It allows linking of a function during run time. That means the code of the function that is to be linked with function call is unknown until it is executed. Dynamic binding of functions makes the programs more flexible.

(1 mark for each correct explanation of static and dynamic binding)

OR

(1 for each correct example of static and dynamic binding)

(e) Write two methods in python using concept of Function Overloading (Polymorphism) to perform the following operations: 2

(i) A function having one argument as Radius, to calculate Area of Circle as 3.14#Radius#Radius

(ii) A function having two arguments as Base and Height, to calculate Area of right angled triangle as 0.5#Base#Height.

Ans

```
def Area(R):
        print 3.14*R*R
def Area(B,H):
        print 0.5*B*H
```

Note:

Python does not support function overloading "as illustrated in the example shown above". If you run the code, the second Area(B,H) definition will overide the first one.

(1 mark for each function definition)

OR

(Full 2 Marks for mentioning Python does not support function overloading)

3. (a) What will be the status of the following list after the First, Second and Third pass of the bubble sort method used for arranging the following elements in ascending order? 3

Note: Show the status of all the elements after each pass very clearly underlining the changes.

52, 42, -10, 60, 90, 20

Ans I Pass

52	42	-10	60	90	20
42	**52**	**-10**	60	90	20
42	-10	**52**	**60**	90	20
42	-10	52	**60**	**90**	20
42	-10	52	60	**90**	**20**
42	-10	52	60	**20**	**90**

II Pass

42	-10	52	60	20	90
-10	42	52	60	20	90
-10	42	52	60	20	90
-10	42	52	60	20	90
-10	42	52	20	60	90

III Pass

-10	42	52	20	60	90
-10	42	52	20	60	90
-10	42	52	20	60	90
-10	42	20	52	60	90

(1 mark for last set of values of each correct pass)

(b) Write definition of a method EvenSum(NUMBERS) to add those values in the list of NUMBERS, which are odd. 3

Ans

```
def EvenSum(NUMBERS):
    n=len(NUMBERS)
    s=0
    for i in range(n):
        if (i%2!=0):
            s=s+NUMBERS[i]
    print(s)
```

(½ mark for finding length of the list)

(½ mark for initializing s (sum) with 0)

(½ mark for reading each element of the list using a loop)

(½ mark for checking odd location)

(½ mark for adding it to the sum)

(½ mark for printing or returning the value)

(c) Write Addnew(Member) and Remove(Member) methods in python to Add a new Member and Remove a Member from a List of Members, considering them to act as INSERT and DELETE operations of the data structure Queue. 4

Ans

```
class queue:
    Member=[]
    def Addnew(self):
        a=input("enter member name: ")
        queue.Member.append(a)
def Remove(self):
        if (queue.Member==[]):
           print "Queue empty"
         else:
           print "deleted element is: ",queue.Member[0]
                  del queue.Member[0] # queue.Member.delete()
```

(½ mark for Addnew header)

(½ mark for accepting a value from user)

(½ mark for adding value in list)

(½ mark for Remove header)

(½ mark for checking empty list condition)

(½ mark for displaying removed Member)

(½ mark for displaying the value to be deleted)

(½ mark for deleting value from list)

NOTE: Marks not to be deducted for methods written without using a class

(d) Write definition of a Method MSEARCH(STATES) to display all the state names from a list of STATES, which are starting with alphabet M. 2

For example:

If the list STATES contains

["MP","UP","WB","TN","MH","MZ","DL","BH","RJ","HR"]

The following should get displayed

MP

MH

MZ

Ans

```
def MSEARCH(STATES):
    for i in STATES:
        if i[0]=='M':
            print i
```

(½ mark method header)

(½ mark for loop)

(½ mark for checking condition of first letter M)

(½ mark for displaying value)

(e) Evaluate the following Postfix notation of expression: 2

4.2.*.22.5.6.+./.-

Ans

Element	Stack Contents
4	4
2	4, 2
*	8
22	8,22
5	8, 22, 5
6	8, 22, 5, 6
+	8, 22, 11
/	8, 2
-	6

Answer: 6

(½ Mark for evaluation till each operator)

OR

(1 Mark for only writing the Final answer without showing stack status)

4 (a) Differentiate between file modes r+ and rb+ with respect to Python. 1

Ans r+ Opens a file for both reading and writing. The file pointer placed at the beginning of the file.

rb+ Opens a file for both reading and writing in binary format. The file pointer placed at the beginning of the file.

(1 mark for correct difference)

OR

(½ Mark for each correct use of r+ and rb+)

(b) Write a method in python to read lines from a text file MYNOTES.TXT, and display those lines, which are starting with an alphabet 'K'. 2

Ans

```
def display():
file=open('MYNOTES.TXT','r')
line=file.readline()
while line:
    if line[0]=='K':
        print line
    line=file.readline()
file.close()  #IGNORE
```

(½ Mark for opening the file)

(½ Mark for reading all lines)

(½ Mark for checking condition for line starting with K)

(½ Mark for displaying line)

(c) Considering the following definition of class FACTORY, write a method in Python to search and display the content in a pickled file FACTORY.DAT, where FCTID is matching with the value '105'. 3

```
class Factory:
    def __init__(self,FID,FNAM):
        self.FCTID = FID          # FCTID   Factory ID
        self.FCTNM = FNAM         # FCTNM   Factory Name
        self.PROD  = 1000         # PROD    Production
    def Display(self):
        print self.FCTID,":",self.FCTNM,":",self.PROD
```

Ans

```
import pickle
def ques4c( ):
    f=Factory( )
    file=open('FACTORY.DAT','rb')
    try:
      while True:
          f=pickle.load(file)
          if f.FCTID==105:
                  f.Display()
    except EOF Error:
          pass
    file.close()   #IGNORE
```

(½ Mark for correct method header)

(½ Mark for opening the file FACTORY.DAT correctly)

(½ Mark for correct loop)

(½ Mark for correct load( ))

(½ Mark for correct checking of FCTID)

(½ Mark for displaying the record)

Section C
(For all the candidates)

5 (a) Observe the following table MEMBER carefully and write the name of the RDBMS operation out of (i) SELECTION (ii) PROJECTION (iii) UNION (iv) CARTESIAN PRODUCT, which has been used to produce the output as shown in RESULT. Also, find the Degree and Cardinality of the RESULT. 2

MEMBER

NO	MNAME	STREAM
M001	JAYA	SCIENCE
M002	ADIYTA	HUMANITIES
M003	HANSRAJ	SCIENCE
M004	SHIVAK	COMMERCE

RESULT

NO	MNAME	STREAM
M002	ADITYA	HUMANITIES

(i) SELECTION

Ans Degree=3

Cardinality=1

(1 Mark for writing the correct name of RDBMS operation)

(½ Mark for writing correct degree)

(½ Mark for writing correct cardinality)

(b) Write SQL queries for (i) to (iv) and find outputs for SQL queries (v) to (viii), which are based on the tables 6

DVD

DCODE	DTITLE	DTYPE
F101	Henry Martin	Folk
C102	Dhrupad	Classical
C101	The Planets	Classical
F102	Universal Soldier	Folk
R102	A day in life	Rock

MEMBER

MID	NAME	DCODE	ISSUEDATE
101	AGAM SINGH	R102	2017-11-30
103	ARTH JOSEPH	F102	2016-12-13
102	NISHA HANS	C101	2017-07-24

(i) To display all details from the table MEMBER in descending order of ISSUEDATE.

Ans SELECT * FROM MEMBER ORDER BY ISSUEDATE DESC;

(½ Mark for correct SELECT statement)

(½ Mark for correct ORDER BY clause)

(ii) To display the DCODE and DTITLE of all Folk Type DVDs from the table DVD

Ans SELECT DCODE,DTITLE FROM DVD WHERE DTYPE='Folk';

(½ Mark for correct SELECT statement)

(½ Mark for correct WHERE clause)

(iii) To display the DTYPE and number of DVDs in each DTYPE from the table DVD

Ans SELECT COUNT(*),DTYPE FROM DVD GROUP BY DTYPE;

(½ Mark for correct SELECT statement)

(½ Mark for correct GROUP BY clause)

(iv) To display all NAME and ISSUEDATE of those members from the table MEMBER who have DVDs issued (i.e ISSUEDATE) in the year 2017

Ans SELECT NAME, ISSUEDATE FROM MEMBER WHERE ISSUEDATE>='2017-01-01'AND ISSUEDATE<='2017-12-31';

OR

SELECT NAME, ISSUEDATE FROM MEMBER WHERE ISSUEDATE BETWEEN '2017-01-01' AND '2017-12-31';

OR

SELECT NAME, ISSUEDATE FROM MEMBER WHERE ISSUEDATE LIKE '2017%';

(½ Mark for correct SELECT statement)

(½ Mark for correct WHERE clause)

(v) SELECT MIN(ISSUEDATE) FROM MEMBER;

<u>MIN(ISSUEDATE)</u>

Ans 2016-12-13

(½ Mark for correct output)

(vi) SELECT DISTINCT DTYPE FROM DVD;

<u>DISTINCT DTYPE</u>

Ans Folk

Classical

Rock

(½ Mark for correct output)

NOTE: Values may be written in any order

(vii) SELECT D.DCODE,NAME,DTITLE

FROM DVD D, MEMBER M WHERE D.DCODE=M.DCODE;

Ans

DCODE	NAME	DTITLE
R102	AGAM SINGH	A day in life
F102	ARTH JOSEPH	Universal Soldier
C101	NISHA HANS	The Planets

(½ Mark for correct output)

(viii) SELECT DTITLE FROM DVD

WHERE DTYPE NOT IN ("Folk". "Classical"):

DTITLE

Ans A day in life

(½ Mark for correct output)

NOTE:

No marks to be awarded for any other output

6 a. State DeMorgan's Laws of Boolean Algebra and verify them using truth table. 2

(i) (A.B)'=A'+B'

Ans (ii) (A+B)'=A'.B'

Truth Table Verification: (i)

A	B	A.B	(A.B)'	A'	B'	A'+B'
0	0	0	1	1	1	1
0	1	0	1	1	0	1
1	0	0	1	0	1	1
1	1	1	0	0	0	0

(ii)

A	B	A+B	(A+B)'	A'	B'	A'.B'
0	0	0	1	1	1	1
0	1	1	0	1	0	0
1	0	1	0	0	1	0
1	1	1	0	0	0	0

(1 Mark for stating any one De Morgan's Theorems correctly)

(1 Mark for correctly verifying any one De Morgan's Theorems using Truth Table)

b. Draw the Logic Circuit of the following Boolean Expression using only NOR Gates: (A+B).(C+D) 2

Ans

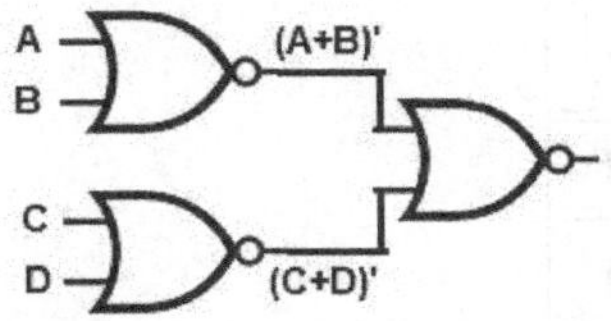

(Full 2 Marks for drawing the Logic Circuit for the expression correctly)

OR

(½ Mark for drawing Logic circuit for (A NOR B) correctly)

(½ Mark for drawing Logic circuit for (C NOR D) correctly)

c. Derive a Canonical POS expression for a Boolean function G, represented by the following truth table: 1

X	Y	Z	G(X,Y,Z)
0	0	0	0
0	0	1	0
0	1	0	1
0	1	1	0
1	0	0	1
1	0	1	1
1	1	0	0
1	1	1	1

Ans

G(X,Y,Z)= (X+Y+Z).(X+Y+Z').(X+Y'+Z').(X'+Y'+Z)

OR

G(X,Y,Z)= ∏(0,1,3,6)

(1 Mark for correctly writing the POS form)

OR

(½ Mark for any two correct terms)

Note: Deduct ½ mark if wrong variable names are written in the expression

d. Reduce the following Boolean expression to its simplest form using K-Map: 3

E(U,V,Z,W)=Σ (2,3,6,8,9,10,11,12,13)

Ans

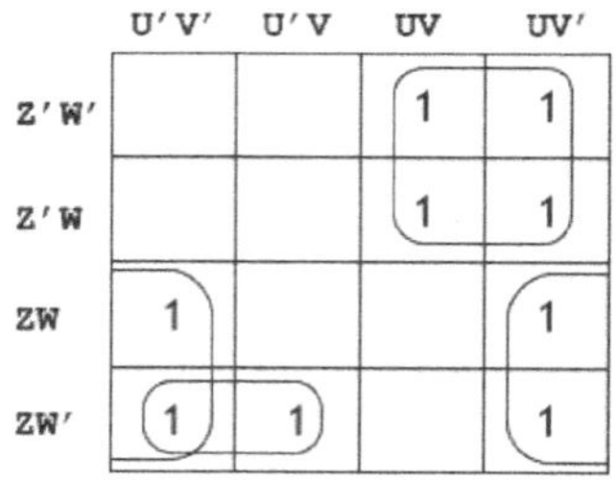

OR

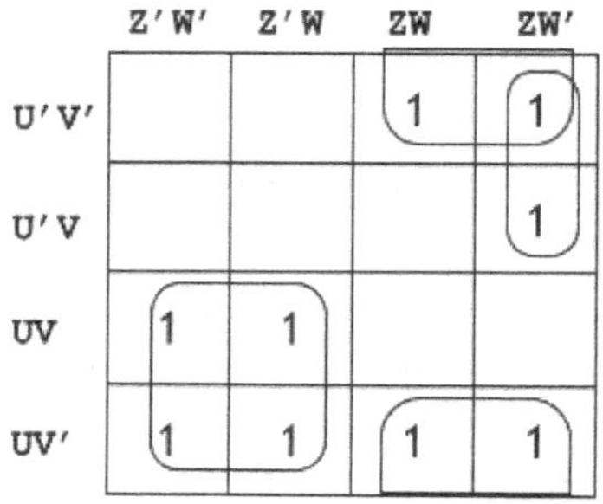

E(U,V,Z,W)=UZ'+V'Z+U'ZW'

(½ Mark for drawing K-Map with correct variable names)

(½ Mark for correctly plotting 1s in the given cells)

(½ Mark each for 3 groupings)

(½ Mark for writing final expression in reduced/minimal form)

NOTE

- *Deduct ½ mark if wrong variable names are used*
- *Deduct ½ mark for any redundant group appearing in final expression*

7 (a) Differentiate between communication using Optical Fiber and Ethernet Cable in context of wired medium of communication technologies. 2

Ans Optical Fibre

- Very Fast
- Expensive
- Immune to electromagnetic interference

Ethernet Cable

- Slower as compared to Optical Fiber
- Less Expensive as compared to Optical Fiber
- prone to electromagnetic interference

Full 2 marks for any one correct difference between Optical Fibre and Ethernet Cable

OR

1 Mark for writing correct features of any one wired medium out of Optical Fibre or Ethernet Cable

(b) Janish Khanna used a pen drive to copy files from his friend's laptop to his office computer. Soon his office computer started abnormal functioning. Sometimes it would restart by itself and sometimes it would stop different applications running on it. 2

Which of the following options out of (i) to (iv), would have caused the malfunctioning of the computer? Justify the reason for your chosen option:

(i) Computer Virus

(ii) Spam Mail

(iii) Computer Bacteria

(iv) Trojan Horse

Ans (i) Computer Virus

OR

(iv) Trojan Horse

Justification:

- Pen drive containing Computer Virus/Trojan Horse was used before the abnormal functioning started, which might have corrupted the system files.
- Computer Virus/Trojan Horse affects the system files and start abnormal functioning in the computer

(1 Mark for writing any of the options (i) OR (iv))

(1 Mark for writing any one correct justification)

(c) Ms. Raveena Sen is an IT expert and a freelancer. She recently used her skills to access the Admin password for the network server of Super Dooper Technology Ltd. and provided confidential data of the organization to its CEO, informing him about the vulnerability of their network security. Out of the following options (i) to (iv), which one most appropriately defines Ms.Sen? Justify the reason for your chosen option: 2

(i) Hacker

(ii) Cracker

(iii) Operator

(iv) Network Admin

Ans (i) Hacker: A Hacker is a person who breaks into the network of an organization without any malicious intent.

(1 Mark for writing correct option)

(1 Mark for writing correct justification)

(d) Hi Standard Tech Training Ltd is a Mumbai based organization which is expanding its office set-up to Chennai. At Chennai office compound, they are planning to have 3 different blocks for Admin, Training and Accounts related activities. Each block has a number of computers, which are required to be connected in a network for communication, data and resource sharing.

As a network consultant, you have to suggest the best network related solutions for them for issues/problems raised by them in (i) to (iv), as per the distances between various blocks/locations and other given parameters.

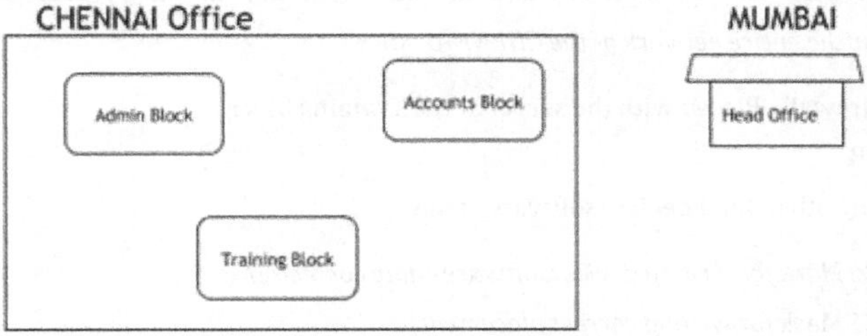

Shortest distances between various blocks/locations:

Admin Block to Account Block	300 Metres
Accounts Block to Training Block	150 Metres
Admin Block to Training Block	200 Metres
MUMBAI Head Office to CHENNAI Office	1300 KM

Number of computers installed at various blocks are as follows:

Training Block	150
Accounts Block	30
Admin Block	40

(i) Suggest the most appropriate block/location to house the SERVER in the CHENNAI Office (out of the 3 blocks) to get the best and effective connectivity. Justify your answer. 1

Ans Training Block - Because it has maximum number of computers.

(½ Mark for correct Block/location)

(½ Mark for valid justification)

(ii) Suggest the best wired medium and draw the cable layout (Block to Block) to efficiently connect various blocks within the CHENNAI office compound. 1

Ans Best wired medium: Optical Fibre OR CAT5 OR CAT6 OR CAT7 OR CAT8 OR Ethernet Cable

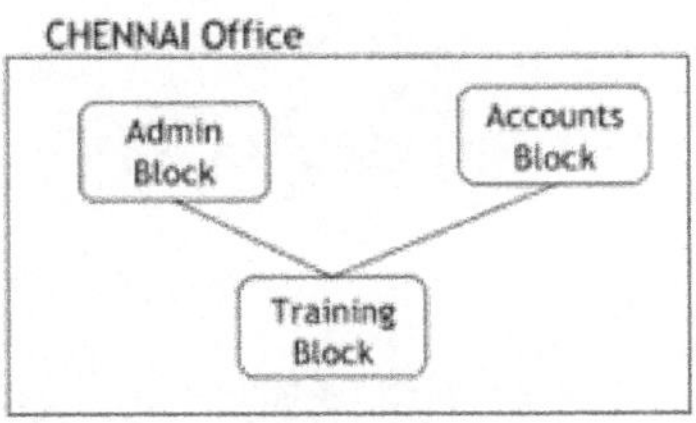

(½ Mark for writing best wired medium)

(½ Mark for drawing the layout correctly)

(iii) *Suggest a device/software and its placement that would provide data security for the entire network of the CHENNAI office.* 1

Ans Firewall - Placed with the server at the Training Block

OR

Any other valid device/software name

(½ Mark for writing device/software name correctly)

(½ Mark for writing correct placement)

(iv) Suggest a device and the protocol that shall be needed to provide wireless Internet access to all smartphone/laptop users in the CHENNAI office 1

Ans Device Name: WiFi Router OR WiMax OR RF Router OR Wireless Modem OR RF Transmitter

Protocol : *WAP OR 802.16 OR TCP/IP OR VOIP OR MACP OR 802.11*

(Full 1 Mark for either writing correct writing device name OR writing correct protocol)